What others are ~~saying about Dr. James Dobson's~~ obson's

~~Bringing Up Boys~~ 1

"STRONG, STABLE, GODLY ... ...e. Married or single, if you have a son, you will want to have this book as a ready reference. It's a comprehensive study by a godly man who knows his subject."

KAY ARTHUR
nationally syndicated broadcaster and Bible teacher

"I CAN'T THNK OF a more important subject. Thankfully America's premier expert is speaking. All people, Christian and non-Christian alike, should read this and take it to heart. It just could save America."

CHUCK COLSON
founder and chairman, Prison Fellowship Ministries

"CLEAR, COMPASSIONATE, and a 'must' for every boy who aspires to godly manhood."

ELISABETH ELLIOT
author and international speaker

"I ONLY WISH Dr. Dobson's book would have been available when I was raising my two boys. He touches every essential area about boys, and I'm excited about the enrichment and encouragement this book will bring to families."

GARY SMALLEY
founder, The Smalley Relationship Center;
author and national speaker

"OVER THE YEARS, Dr. James Dobson has written books that have become THE definitive works to their audience. *Bringing Up Boys* is filled with hard data to give it credibility and authority, stories to make its message clear and plain, and the author's whole heart to fill it with passion. If you have a son, this book is must reading. This book is a classic . . . the definitive work on raising sons."

ROBERT D. WOLGEMUTH
author and general editor for *The Dad's Devotional Bible*

"JIM DOBSON has done it again! Not only does he have his fingers on the pulse of one of the greatest needs in America, but he has the heart and answers that are needed. This book will revolutionize your view of how to raise sons. Read it and apply it—for the sake of the next generation of men!"

DENNIS RAINEY
executive director, Family Life

"I HAVE BEEN a psychologist for 35 years, and I only wish I had owned James Dobson's *Bringing Up Boys* through those years. This book takes a huge leap in advancing our understanding of one of the most complex and provocative topics of our age. Dobson deals with the detailed questions relating to why boys and girls are different and why boys have had such difficulty relating effectively to their challenges. This is a must-read book for every person in our culture."

NEIL CLARK WARREN
psychologist, author, and speaker

"WITH HUMILITY AND HONESTY Dr. Dobson tells us how to connect with a God who is enough! Enough to help, encourage, forgive, and empower us! Wisdom gained here will make our sons' and grandsons' lives replete with grace that goes on, and grows on, to godly young manhood."

JILL BRISCOE
international speaker and author;
Briscoe Ministries, Inc.

OTHER BOOKS BY DR. JAMES DOBSON

Hide or Seek
The New Dare to Discipline
Love Must Be Tough
The Strong-Willed Child
Parenting Isn't for Cowards
Emotions: Can You Trust Them?
Complete Marriage and Family Home Reference Guide
When God Doesn't Make Sense
Straight Talk to Men and Their Wives
Children at Risk (with Gary L. Bauer)
Preparing for Adolescence
Love for a Lifetime
What Wives Wish Their Husbands Knew about Women

bringing up
BOYS

DR. JAMES DOBSON

Tyndale House Publishers, Inc.
Wheaton, Illinois

Visit Tyndale's exciting Web site at www.tyndale.com

Cover photographs by Brian MacDonald

Photo of Dr. Dobson and his son, Ryan, by Ron Van Tongeren

Photo of Dr. Dobson and kids by Tom Kimmell

Edited by Lisa A. Jackson

Designed by Julie Chen

ISBN 0-8423-6929-5

Printed in the United States of America

07   06   05   04   03   02   01
7   6   5   4   3   2   1

*This book is affectionately dedicated to
my son, Ryan (pictured on the back cover),
who has brought such joy and happiness to his mother and me.*

*Of all the titles I have been granted, including
psychologist, author, professor, and president,
the one that I cherish most is simply "Dad."*

*Being a father to Ryan and his sister, Danae,
has been the highlight of my life.*

TABLE OF CONTENTS

ACKNOWLEDGMENTS

APPRECIATION IS EXPRESSED to several key assistants and coworkers who have contributed significantly to the writing of this book. Chief among them is Craig Osten, who tirelessly searched the professional literature and popular press on my behalf for relevant studies and material. His skill as a researcher was inspiring to watch. For example, I asked him one day to look for an obscure quote that I remembered vaguely from the writings of Russian philosopher Alexander Solzhenitsyn. I couldn't recall the actual wording, but it conveyed the idea that Solzhenitsyn's generation didn't know why it had meaning. I didn't remember the name of the book containing this thought, the year it was written, or any other details that would help identify its source. Nevertheless, Craig went after it characteristically like a bloodhound tracking a convict. The next morning, he brought the word-for-word statement to me and said that the author was not Solzhenitsyn but Dr. Francis Schaeffer and that it was included in a dusty 1972 text entitled *He Is There and He Is Not Silent*. The actual quotation now appears in the final chapter of *Bringing Up Boys* and reads as follows: "The dilemma of modern man is simple: he does not know why man has any meaning. . . . This is the damnation of our generation, the heart of modern man's problem."*

Thank you, Craig, for your diligence and competence throughout

*Francis A. Schaeffer, *He Is There and He Is Not Silent* (Carol Stream, Ill.: Tyndale House Publishers, 1972).

the arduous task of writing this book. The final manuscript would have been very different, and much less complete, without your contribution.

I also want to thank my personal assistant, Patty Watkins, and her three associates, Sherry Hoover, Joy Thompson, and Mary Jo Steinke, for their consistent help. This team, along with Bill Berger and Ron Reno, is composed of "get it done" people who never give up. I am also grateful to Herb and Dona Fisher and Elsa Prince Broekhuizen, who provided comfortable "hiding places" where I could go to write in solitude. I must also acknowledge the contributions of Drs. Walt Larimore and Brad Beck, who reviewed and tweaked the chapter dealing with the physiology and neurology of masculinity, and neurologist Randall Bjork, M.D., who provided additional consultation. I also benefited significantly from the suggestions made by psychologist Dr. Tim Irwin and from the letters included in this manuscript written by Rev. Ren Broekhuizen, Dr. C. H. McGowen, and Karen Cotting. To each of you and so many others, thanks so much for your kindness and involvement.

Finally, I want to express my deepest love and appreciation to the very special lady in my life. After nearly forty-one years of marriage and more than twenty books, Shirley knows what it means to have a husband who becomes "lost" for days in a manuscript that seems to go on forever. In this case, some thirty months of our lives were invested in the writing of *Bringing Up Boys*, all while we continued to lead a large and fast-moving organization. It was Shirley who encouraged me to address the subject of boys in the first place, and she stood by me when the task seemed overwhelming. That is not surprising. She has been my inspiration, my support, and my passion for more than four decades. And the best is yet to come.

THE WONDERFUL WORLD OF BOYS

CHAPTER 1

GREETINGS TO ALL the men and women out there who are blessed to be called parents. There is no greater privilege in living than bringing a tiny new human being into the world and then trying to raise him or her properly during the next eighteen years. Doing that job right requires all the intelligence, wisdom, and determination you will be able to muster from day to day. And for parents whose family includes one or more boys, the greatest challenge may be just keeping them alive through childhood and adolescence.

We have a delightful four-year-old youngster in our family named Jeffrey who is "all boy." One day last week, his parents and grandparents were talking in the family room when they realized that the child hadn't been seen in the past few minutes. They quickly searched from room to room, but he was nowhere to be found. Four adults scurried throughout the neighborhood calling, "Jeffrey? Jeffrey!" No answer. The kid had simply disappeared. Panic gripped the family as terrible possibilities loomed before them. Had he been kidnapped? Did he wander away? Was he in mortal danger? Everyone muttered a prayer while running from place to place. After about fifteen minutes of sheer terror, someone suggested they call 911. As they reentered the house, the boy jumped out and said, "Hey!" to his grandfather. Little Jeffrey, bless his heart, had been hiding under the bed while chaos swirled around him. It was his idea of a joke. He honestly

1

thought everyone else would think it was funny too. He was shocked to learn that four big people were very angry at him.

Jeffrey is not a bad or rebellious kid. He is just a boy. And in case you haven't noticed, boys are different from girls. That fact was never in question for previous generations. They knew intuitively that each sex was a breed apart and that boys were typically the more unpredictable of the two. Haven't you heard your parents and grandparents say with a smile, "Girls are made out of sugar and spice and everything nice, but boys are made of snakes and snails and puppy-dog tails"? It was said tongue-in-cheek, but people of all ages thought it was based on fact. "Boys will be boys," they said knowingly. They were right.

Boys are usually (but not always) tougher to raise than their sisters are. Girls can be difficult to handle too, but there is something especially challenging about boys. Although individual temperaments vary, boys are designed to be more assertive, audacious, and excitable than girls are. Psychologist John Rosemond calls them "little aggressive machines."[1] One father referred to his son as "all afterburner and no rudder." These are some of the reasons why Maurice Chevalier never sang, "Thank Heaven for Little Boys." They just don't inspire great sentimentality.

In an article entitled, "What Are Boys Made Of?" reporter Paula Gray Hunker quoted a mother named Meg MacKenzie who said raising her two sons is like living with a tornado. "From the moment that they come home from school, they'll be running around the house, climbing trees outside and making a commotion inside that sounds as if a herd of elephants has moved in upstairs. I'll try to calm them down, but my husband will say, 'This is what boys do. Get used to it.'"

Hunker continued, "Mrs. MacKenzie, the lone female in a household of males, says this tendency [of boys] to leap—and then listen—drives her crazy. 'I can't just tell my boys, "Clean up." If I do, they'll put one or two toys away and assume that the task is done. I've learned that I have to be very, very specific.' She has found that boys do not respond to subtle hints but need requests clearly outlined. 'I'll put a basket of clean laundry on the stairs, and the boys will pass it by twenty times and not once will it occur to them to stop and carry it upstairs,' she says."[2]

Does that sound familiar? If you host a birthday party for five-year-olds, the boys will probably behave very differently from the girls. One or more of them is likely to throw cake, put his hands in the punch bowl, or mess up the games for the girls. Why are they like this? Some would say their mischievous nature has been learned from the culture. Really? Then why are boys more aggressive in every society around the globe? And why

2

did the Greek philosopher Plato write more than 2,300 years ago, "Of all the animals, the boy is the most unmanageable"?[3]

One of my favorite little books is entitled *Up to No Good: The Rascally Things Boys Do,* edited by Kitty Harmon. It is a compilation of stories told "by perfectly decent grown men" recalling their childhood years. Here are several examples that made me smile:

> In seventh grade, the biology teacher had us dissect fetal pigs. My friends and I pocketed the snout of the pig and stuck it on the water fountain so that the water shot straight up out of the pig's nostrils. No one really noticed it until they were bent over just about to drink. The problem is that we wanted to stick around and see the results, but then we started laughing so hard that we got caught. We all got the paddle for that.
>
> MARK, OHIO, B. 1960

> A friend and I found a coffee can of gasoline in the garage and decided to pour some down a manhole, light it, and see what would happen. We popped the manhole open, poured some gas in, and replaced the cover so that it was ajar. We kept throwing matches down but nothing happened, so we poured all the gas in. Finally, there was a noise like a jet engine starting up, and then a big *BOOM!* The manhole cover flew up and a flame shot up about fifteen feet in the air. The ground was rumbling like an earthquake, and the manhole cover crashed about twelve feet away in the neighbor's driveway. What happened was the gas ran down the sewer lines for a block or so and vaporized with all the methane in there, and blew up all our neighbors' toilets. I'm a plumber now; that's how I know exactly what happened.
>
> DAVE, WASHINGTON, B. 1952

> I am blind, and as a kid sometimes I played with other blind kids. And we always found just as many, or more, ways to get into trouble as sighted boys. Like the time I was over at a blind friend's house, and he took me into the garage to show me his older brother's motorcycle. We decided to take it out for a spin. Why not? We rode down the street feeling for the curb, and at each intersection we'd stop, turn off the engine and listen, and then cross. We rode all the way to the high school track, where we could really let loose. First we piled up some dirt at the turns of the track so we'd feel the bump and know

we were still on the track. Then we took off, going faster and faster and having a blast. What we didn't know was that people showed up to run on the track and were trying to wave us off. We couldn't hear them over the roar of the motocycle engine and nearly ran them over. They called the police, who showed up and tried to wave us over too, but we kept going. Finally they got their sirens and bullhorns going and we stopped. They were furious and wouldn't believe us when we explained that we hadn't seen them. We proved we were blind by showing them our braille watches, and they escorted us home.   MIKE, CALIFORNIA, B. 1953[4]

As these stories illustrate, one of the scariest aspects of raising boys is their tendency to risk life and limb for no good reason. It begins very early. If a toddler can climb on it, he will jump off it. He careens out of control toward tables, tubs, pools, steps, trees, and streets. He will eat anything but food and loves to play in the toilet. He makes "guns" out of cucumbers or toothbrushes and likes digging around in drawers, pill bottles, and Mom's purse. And just hope he doesn't get his grubby little hands on a tube of lipstick. A boy harasses grumpy dogs and picks up kitties by their ears. His mom has to watch him every minute to keep him from killing himself. He loves to throw rocks, play with fire, and shatter glass. He also gets great pleasure out of irritating his brothers and sisters, his mother, his teachers, and other children. As he gets older, he is drawn to everything dangerous—skateboards, rock climbing, hang gliding, motorcycles, and mountain bikes. At about sixteen, he and his buddies begin driving around town like kamikaze pilots on sake. It's a wonder any of them survive. Not every boy is like this, of course, but the majority of them are.

Canadian psychologist Barbara Morrongiello studied the different ways boys and girls think about risky behavior. Females, she said, tend to think hard about whether or not they could get hurt, and they are less likely to plunge ahead if there is any potential for injury. Boys, however, will take a chance if they think the danger is worth the risk. Impressing their friends (and eventually girls) is usually considered worth the risk. Morrongiello shared a story about a mother whose son climbed on the garage roof to retrieve a ball. When she asked him if he realized he could fall, he said, "Well, I might not."[5]

A related study by Licette Peterson confirmed that girls are more fearful than boys are. For example, they brake sooner when riding their bikes. They react more negatively to pain and try not to make the same mistake twice. Boys, on the other hand, are slower to learn from calamities. They tend to think that their injuries were caused by "bad luck."[6] Maybe their luck will be better next time. Besides, scars are cool.

Our son, Ryan, encountered one dangerous situation after another as a boy. By the time he was six, he was personally acquainted with many of the local emergency room attendants and doctors. And why not? He had been their patient repeatedly. One day when he was about four, he was running through the backyard with his eyes closed and fell into a decorative metal "plant." One of the steel rods stuck him in the right eyebrow and exposed the bone underneath. He came staggering through the back door bathed in blood, a memory that still gives Shirley nightmares. Off they went to the trauma center—again. It could have been much worse, of course. If the trajectory of Ryan's fall had been different by as much as a half inch, the rod would have hit him in the eye and gone straight to his brain. We have thanked God many times for the near misses.

I was also one of those kids who lived on the edge of disaster. When I was about ten, I was very impressed by the way Tarzan could swing through the trees from vine to vine. No one ever told me, "Don't try this at home." I climbed high into a pear tree one day and tied a rope to a small limb. Then I positioned myself for a journey to the next tree. Unfortunately, I made a small but highly significant miscalculation. The rope was longer than the distance from the limb to the ground. I kept thinking all the way down that something didn't seem right. I was still gripping the rope when I landed flat on my back twelve feet below and knocked all the air out of the state of Oklahoma. I couldn't breathe for what seemed like an hour (it must have been about ten seconds) and was sure I was dying. Two teeth were broken and a loud gonging sound echoed in my head. But later that afternoon, I was up and running again. No big deal.

The next year, I was given a chemistry set for Christmas. It contained no explosives or toxic materials, but in my hands, anything could be hazardous. I mixed some bright blue chemicals in a test tube and corked it tightly. Then I began heating the substance with a Bunsen burner. Very soon, the entire thing exploded. My parents had just finished painting the ceiling of my room a stark white. It was soon decorated with the most beautiful blue stuff, which remained splattered there for years. Such was life in the Dobson household.

It must be a genetic thing. I'm told my father was also a terror in his time. When he was a small boy, a friend dared him to crawl through a block-long drainpipe. He could only see a pinpoint of light at the other end, but he began inching his way into the darkness. Inevitably, I suppose, he became stuck somewhere in the middle. Claustrophobia swept over him as he struggled vainly to move. There he was, utterly alone and stranded in the pitch black pipe. Even if adults had known about his predicament, they couldn't have reached him. Rescue workers would have had to dig up the entire pipe to locate and get him out. The boy who was to become my dad finally made it to the other end of the drain and survived, thankfully, to live another day.

Two more illustrations: My father and all of his four brothers were high-risk kids. The two eldest were twins. When they were only three years old, my grandmother was shelling beans for the night meal. As my grandfather left for work, he said within hearing distance of the children, "Don't let the kids put those beans up their noses." Bad advice! As soon as their mom's back was turned, they stuffed their nasal passages with beans. It was impossible for my grandmother to get them out, so she just left them there. A few days later, the beans began to sprout. Little green shoots were actually growing out their nostrils. A family doctor worked diligently to dig out the tiny plants one piece at a time.

And years later, the five boys stood looking at an impressive steeple on a church. One of them dared the others to climb the outer side and see if they could touch the very highest point. All four of them headed up the structure like monkeys. My father told me that it was nothing but the grace of God that prevented them from tumbling from the heights. It was just a normal day in the life of five rambunctious little boys.

What makes young males act like that? What inner force compels them to teeter on the edge of disaster? What is it about the masculine temperament that drives boys to tempt the laws of gravity and ignore the gentle voice of common sense—the one that says, "Don't do it, Son"? Boys are like this because of the way they are wired neurologically and because of the influence of hormones that stimulate certain aggressive behavior. We will explore those complex and powerful masculine characteristics in the next chapter. You can't understand males of any age, including yourself or the one to whom you might be married, without knowing something about the forces that operate within.

We want to help parents raise "good" boys in this postmodern age. The culture is at war with the family, especially its youngest and most vulnerable members. Harmful and enticing messages are shouted at them from movies and television, from the rock-music industry, from the advocates of so-called safe-sex ideology, from homosexual activists, and from the readily available obscenity on the Internet. The question confronting parents is, "How can we steer our boys *and* girls past the many negative influences that confront them on every side?" It is an issue with eternal implications.

Our purpose in this regard will be to assist mothers and fathers as they "play defense" on behalf of their sons—that is, as they protect their boys from immoral and dangerous enticements. But that is not enough. Parents also need to "play offense"—to capitalize on the impressionable years of childhood by instilling in their sons the antecedents of character. Their assignment during two brief decades will be to transform their boys from immature and flighty youngsters into honest, caring men who will be respectful of women, loyal and faithful in marriage, keepers of commitments, strong and decisive leaders, good workers, and secure in their masculinity. And of course, the ultimate goal for people of faith is to give each child an understanding of Scripture and a lifelong passion for Jesus Christ. This is, I believe, *the* most important responsibility for those of us who have been entrusted with the care and nurturance of children.

Parents a century ago had a much better "fix" on these long-term objectives and how to achieve them. Some of their ideas are still workable today, and I will share them presently. I'll also provide a review of the latest research on child development and parent-child relationships. My prayer is that the findings and recommendations gleaned from that body of information, combined with my own professional experience spanning more than thirty years, will offer encouragement and practical advice to those who pass this way.

So buckle your seat belts. We have a lot of interesting ground to cover. But first, here's a little poem to get us started. It is taken from the lyrics to a song I love, sent to me by my friend Robert Wolgemuth. When Robert was a youngster, his mother, Grace Wolgemuth, sang "That Little Boy of Mine" to him and his siblings. I first heard it when Robert and his wife, Bobbie, sang it to my mother in a nursing home in 1983. It made all of us cry.

That Little Boy of Mine:

Two eyes that shine so bright,
Two lips that kiss goodnite,
Two arms that hold me tight,
That little boy of mine.

No one could ever know how much your coming has
meant.
Because I love you so, you're something heaven
has sent.

You're all the world to me.
You climb upon my knee.
To me you'll always be,
That little boy of mine.[7]

Vive la Différence

CHAPTER 2

ONE OF THE most enjoyable aspects of my responsibility at Focus on the Family is to review the letters, telephone calls, and e-mails that flood into our offices. I don't see them all, since they number more than 250,000 per month. I do, however, receive regular summaries consisting of actual paragraphs and comments that our staff selects for me to read. Included among them are wonderful messages from parents and children that brighten (and sometimes sadden) my days. One of the most treasured came from a nine-year-old girl named Elizabeth Christine Hays, who sent me her picture and a list she had composed about girls and boys. She and her mother subsequently gave me permission to share her delightful letter, as follows.

> *Dear James Dopson,*
>
> *I hope you like my list of girls are better than boys. You are a good guy. I am a Christian. I love Jesus.*
>
> *Love,*
> *Elizabeth Christine Hays*
>
> *P.S. Please don't throw my list away.*

GIRLS ARE MORE BETTER THAN BOYS

1. girls chew with their mouths closed.
2. girls have better hand writing.

3. girls sing better.
4. girls are more talented.
5. girls can do their hair better.
6. girls cover their mouths when they sneeze.
7. girls don't pick their nose.
8. girls go to the bathroom politely.
9. girls learn faster.
10. girls are more kinder to animals.
11. girls don't smell as bad.
12. girls are more smarter.
13. girls get more things what they want.
14. girls don't let stinkers as much.
15. girls are more quieter.
16. girls don't get as durty.
17. girls are cleaner.
18. girls are more attractive.
19. girls don't each as much.
20. girls walk more politely.
21. girls aren't as strict.
22. girls sit more politely.
23. girls are more creative.
24. girls look better than boys.
25. girls comb their hair better.
26. girls shave more.
27. girls put on deodorant on more often.
28. girls don't have as much bodyodor.
29. girls don't want their hair messed up.
30. girls like to get more tan.
31. girls have more manners.

I was so amused by Elizabeth Christine's creativity that I included her list in my next monthly letter and mailed it to approximately 2.3 million people. The response from both boys and girls was fascinating—and funny. Not everyone was pleased, however, including a rather irritated mother who thought we had insulted her son. She wrote, "Would you consider publishing a similar letter entitled 'Boys Are More Better Than Girls'?" Then she commented, "I doubt it; it would not be politically correct." Well, that was the first time I've ever been accused of being PC! With a challenge like that I simply had to balance the scales. In my next monthly letter, I invited boys to send me their written opinions of girls. Here are selected items from the many lists that I received in the next couple of weeks.

WHY BOYS ARE MORE BETTER THAN GIRLS

1. Boys can sit in front of a scary movie and not close their eyes once.
2. Boys don't have to sit down every time they go.
3. Boys don't get embarrassed easily.
4. Boys can go to the bathroom in the woods.
5. Boys can climb trees better.
6. Boys can hang on to their stomachs on fast rides.
7. Boys don't worry about "diet-this" and "diet-that."
8. Boys are better tractor drivers than girls.
9. Boys rite better than girls.
10. Boys can build better forts than girls.
11. Boys can take pain better than girls.
12. Boys are way more cooler.
13. Boys have less fits.
14. Boys don't waste their life at the mall.
15. Boys aren't afraid of reptiels.
16. Boys shave more than girls.
17. Boys don't do all those wiggaly movmets when they walk.
18. Boys don't scratch.
19. Boys don't brade another's hair.
20. Boys aren't smart alickes.
21. Boys don't cry and feel sorry when they kill a fly.
22. Boys don't use as mutch deoderent.
23. Boys were created first.
24. Boys learn to make funny noises with their armpits faster.
25. Boys can tie better knots—specially girls pony tails.
26. Boys get to blow up more stuff.
27. Without boys there would be no babies. [Now there's a new thought!]
28. Boys eat with a lot of heart.
29. Boys don't WINE.
30. Boys hum best.
31. Boys are proud of their odor.
32. Boys don't cry over a broken nail.
33. Boys don't need to ask for directions.
34. Boys can spell Dr. Dobson's name correctly.
35. Boys aren't clichish.
36. Boys don't hog the phone.
37. Boys aren't shopacholics.

38. Boys bait their own hook when they fish.
39. Boys don't hang panty hose all over the bathroom.
40. Boys don't wake up with bad hair.
41. Boys aren't stinker. [what?]
42. Boys don't take two million years to get ready.
43. Boys couldn't care less about Barby.
44. Boys don't have to have 21 pairs of shoes (three for every day of the week!!!).
45. Boys don't put a tub of makeup on all the time.
46. Boys don't care if their noses aren't perfect.
47. Boys respect everything and everyone including GIRLS!

In addition to receiving many of these "more better" lists, I was sent some delightful notes from children written in their own handwriting. Obviously, the debate about boys and girls had sparked some animated discussions in families all across North America. Here are a few examples from our mail:

> I really like the page about "girls are more better than boys."
> I fond it because I was walking by the table and the word "girl" caught my eye. I believe every word on that piece of paper. I have been trying to convince my friend, Lenny, that girls are better than boys, now I have proof. NO OFENSE! Thank you for not throwing it away and for publishing it. I am eight, almost nine years old.   FAITH, AGE 8

> Most boys really don't care about the list Elizabeth made. Boys care more about sports, having fun, and not caring about the way they look (unless they are going somewhere nice). I was made to write this letter. Most boys do not like to write.   MICHAEL, AGE 12

> Elizabeth hasn't got a clue.   ANTHONY, AGE 8

> We got your letter today with the list that was called, "Girls Are More Better Than Boys." I didn't think it was all true. I just thought some of it was true because my brother does his hair better than mine.   STEPHANIE, AGE 9

> I really enjoyed reading Elizabeth Christine Hays' letter to you. I especially enjoyed her 31 reasons why girls are better than boys. My parents had me read these reasons to my brothers. The two oldest boys laughed through the whole thing. It was

plain they didn't agree. But when I was done, my four-year-old brother said, "So girls *are* better than boys." SARAH, AGE 15

I am eight years old. I read the letter that Elizabeth Hays wrote about girls being better than boys. I don't think anything on that list is true. I have two brothers that are just as special as I am. There is a verse in the Bible that says, "For the Lord does not see as man sees; for man looks at the outward appearance, but the Lord looks at the heart" (1 Samuel 16:7, NKJV). We should all try to look at other people the way the Lord looks at us. ELISHA, AGE 8

I was reading throu [your letter] and I saw the list of thirty-one reasons girls are better than boys. Know what I did with it? I stomped on it! your friend, Peyton. [no age given] P.S. you have permission to print this.

Don't you love the spontaneity and creativity of children? Boys and girls have such a fresh take on almost everything, and as we have seen, they view life from opposite ends of the universe. Even a child can see that boys and girls are different. Unfortunately, what is obvious to most children and adults became the object of heated controversy in the 1970s, when a goofy new idea took root. A small but noisy band of feminists began insisting that the sexes were identical except for their reproductive apparatus, and that any uniqueness in temperament or behavior resulted from patriarchal cultural biases.[1] It was a radical concept that lacked any scientific support, except that which was flawed and politically motivated. Nevertheless, the campaign penetrated the entire culture. Suddenly, professors and professionals who should have known better began nodding in agreement. No doubt about it. Males and females were redundant. Parents had been wrong about their kids for at least five thousand years. The media ran with the notion and the word *unisex* found its way into the language of the enlightened. Anyone who challenged the new dogma, as I did in a 1975 book titled *What Wives Wish Their Husbands Knew about Women,* was branded as sexist or something worse.

The feminist movement then took a new and dangerous turn. Its leaders began trying to redesign the way children were being raised (which is why the issue is of concern to us today, all these years later). Television talk-show host Phil Donahue and dozens of wanna-bes told parents day after day that their daughters were victims of terrible sexist bias and that their sons should be raised more like girls. There was great urgency to their message. Things *had* to change immediately! they said. Donahue's feminist girlfriend and later wife, Marlo Thomas, coauthored a best-selling book at about the same time titled *Free to Be You and Me,* which the publishers described as "the first real guide to nonsexist child rearing." It urged boys to play with dolls and tea sets and told them they could be anything they wanted to be, including (no kidding!) "grandmas and mommies." It featured dozens of poems and stories about role reversals, such as a mother nailing shingles on the roof, building new shelves in the family room, and working with cement. Meanwhile, Father was in the kitchen making breakfast. Every effort was made to teach kids that fathers made great moms and mothers were pretty tough dudes.[2] The book sold several million copies. And the movement had only just begun.

Germaine Greer, author of *The Female Eunuch,* was even more extreme. She said the traditional family had "castrated women." She believed mothers should be less nurturing of their daughters because to treat them gently and kindly would reinforce sexual stereotypes and make them more "dependent" and feminine. Greer also insisted that children are better off being raised by institutions rather than parents.[3] It is difficult to believe today that her book offering those and similarly outrageous views also soared to the top of all the best-seller lists. That illustrates just how culturally dominant radical feminism was at that time.

Perhaps the most influential of the early feminists was Gloria Steinem, founder of the National Organization for Women and editor of *Ms.* magazine. Here is a sampling of her perspective on marriage and child rearing:

> We've had a lot of people in this country who have had the courage to raise their daughters more like their sons. Which is great because it means they're more equal. . . . But there are many fewer people who have had the courage to raise their sons more like their daughters. And that's what needs to be done.[4]

> We need to stop raising boys to think that they need to prove their masculinity by being controlling or by not showing emotion or by not being little girls. You can ask [boys] . . . "What if you were a little girl?" They get very upset at the very idea they might be this inferior thing. They've already got this idea that in order to be boys they have to be superior to girls and that's the problem.[5]

> [Marriage is] not an equal partnership. I mean, you lose your name, your credit rating, your legal residence, and socially, you're treated as if his identity were yours. I can't imagine

being married. If everybody has to get married, then clearly it is a prison, not a choice.[6] (Steinem married in 2000.)

All women are supposed to want children. But I could never drum up any feelings of regret.[7]

Think for a moment about the above quotes from Steinem, Greer, and the other early feminists. Most of them were never married, didn't like children, and deeply resented men, yet they advised millions of women about how to raise their children and, especially, how to produce healthy boys. There is no evidence that Steinem or Greer ever had any significant experience with children of either sex. Isn't it interesting that the media (to my knowledge) never homed in on that incongruity? And isn't it sad that these women were allowed to twist and warp the attitudes of a generation of kids?

Of major concern to the feminists was what they considered to be the "sexism" in children's toys. As with so many issues during that era, it was Germaine Greer who was most vocal. She said, "So where does the difference [between the sexes] come from? If it's all bred into us by people like toy makers, who steer boys toward these trucks, girls to the dolls, and by teachers, parents, employers—all the wicked influences of a sexist society—then maybe this is a social problem that needs to be fixed."[8]

Great pressure was exerted on companies to "fix" the problem. I remember being contacted during that time by an attorney who asked for my help in defending the Sav-On drugstore chain. The corporation had been sued by a feminist attorney, Gloria Allred, representing the parents of seven little girls who, they insisted, had been emotionally damaged by their lack of access to certain toys in one of the stores. Allred said with a straight face that great harm was being inflicted on these children by the presence of two signs, Boys' Toys and Girls' Toys, placed eight feet above the aisle.[9] A psychiatrist then testified (and was handsomely rewarded for it, I'm sure) that the youngsters had been deeply and irreparably wounded by Sav-On's "discrimination." No one asked why the parents of the children didn't simply take them to another store. Still, Sav-On caved in and agreed to remove the "gender-related" signs in their stores.[10]

Retailers of toys were thereafter put on notice that segregation of merchandise by sex was not to be tolerated. They got the message. For more than two decades, Toys "R" Us implemented a "gender-neutral" approach to marketing as demanded by feminists. It was not successful. Finally, the company administered more than ten thousand customer surveys to learn more about the preferences of children. It turned out that boys and girls were interested in different things. What a surprise! Armed with that information, executives at Toys "R" Us decided it was politically safe, at last, to display the toys in separate sections called Boys World and Girls World. This return to a traditional approach brought a storm of protest from the Women's Reproductive Health Initiative and the Feminist Karate Union.[11] The company stood firm and other toy retailers followed suit. It made no sense to do anything else.

Christina Hoff Sommers addressed the flap over toys in her outstanding book, *The War against Boys.* She reported that Hasbro Toys tried to accommodate feminists by producing a new dollhouse designed to interest both boys and girls. That way they could sell twice as many units. There was, however, a slight miscalculation in the way children would respond. Girls tended to "play house," using the plastic structure in the traditional way. Their dolls got married, arranged toy furniture, had babies, and did the things they had seen their mothers doing. The boys played with the dollhouse too, but not as anticipated. They catapulted the baby carriage off the roof and generally messed up the game for the girls.[12] Back to the drawing board.

Well, the unisex movement prevailed until the late 1980s when it fell victim, at last, to medical technology. The development of noninvasive techniques, such as magnetic resonance imaging and PET scans, allowed physicians and physiologists to examine the functioning of the human brain in much greater detail. What they found totally destroyed the assertions of feminists. Men and women's brains looked very distinct when examined in a laboratory. Under proper stimulation, they "lit up" in different areas, revealing unique neurological processes.[13] It turns out that male and female brains are "hardwired" differently, which, along with hormonal factors, accounts for behavioral and attitudinal characteristics associated traditionally with masculinity and femininity. It was these sexual benchmarks that feminists attempted to suppress or discredit, but they failed. Still, you have to admire their ambition. They tried to redesign half of the human family in a single generation.

Unfortunately, the ideas that were spawned in the seventies and perpetuated in a different form today are deeply ingrained in the culture, even though they have never made sense. Child-rearing practices have been forever changed. Many parents, for example, are reluctant or ill equipped to teach their boys how they are different from girls or what their masculinity really means. There is also a new source of confusion emanating from the powerful gay and lesbian agenda. Its propagandists are teaching a revolutionary view of sexuality called "gender feminism," which insists that sex assignment is irrelevant. Genetics can be simply overridden. What matters is the "gender" selected for us by parents when we are babies, or the sex role we choose for ourselves later in life. Mary Brown Parlee articulated this perspective in *Psychology Today*. "The sex 'assigned' to a baby at birth is as much a *social decision* as a recognition of biological fact."[14]

Another feminist writer expressed it like this: "Although many people think that men and women are the natural expression of a genetic blueprint, gender is a product of human thought and culture, a social construction that creates the 'true nature' of all individuals."[15] Therefore, if we protect children from social and religious conditioning, people will be free to move into and out of existing gender roles according to their preferences. Taking that concept to its illogical conclusion, the feminists and homosexual activists want to dissolve the traditional roles of mothers and fathers and, in time, eliminate such terms as *wife, husband, son, daughter, sister, brother, manhood, womanhood, boy, girl, masculine,* and *feminine.* These references to sexual identity are being replaced with gender-neutral terms, such as *significant other, spouse, parent, child,* and *sibling.*

Clearly, there are serious implications here for mothers and fathers. I urge you to protect your boys from those who are espousing these postmodern views. Shield both your sons and daughters from gender feminism and from those who would seek to confuse their sexuality. Protect the masculinity of your boys, who will be under increasing political pressure in years to come. Buffer them from the perception that most adult males are sexual predators who are violent and disrespectful to women.

It is also important for us as adults to understand our own sexual identities. If we don't know who we are, our kids will be doubly confused about who they are. Any uncertainty, any ambiguity in that assignment must be seen as damaging not only to our sons and daughters but also to the long-term stability of society itself.

Finally, I urge you to base your teachings about sexuality on the Scriptures, which tell us, "God created man in his own image, in the image of God he created him; male and female he created them" (Genesis 1:27). Jesus, who was the first Jewish leader to give dignity and status to women, said, "Haven't you read . . . that at the beginning the Creator 'made them male and female,'" and, "For this reason a man will leave his father and mother and be united to his wife, and the two will become one flesh" (Matthew 19:4-5). That is the divine plan. It leaves no doubt that the Creator made not one sex but two, each beautifully crafted to "fit with" and meet the needs of the other. Any effort to teach children differently is certain to produce turmoil in the soul of a child.

We have seen what sexual identity is not. Now let's take a brief look at what makes males unique and how that understanding helps us raise healthy boys.

QUESTIONS AND ANSWERS

We have a nine-year-old boy who is not the way you described at all. He is quiet, careful, thoughtful, and very, very shy. Does that mean he is not "all boy"? Should we be trying to change him, to make him more assertive and aggressive?

The wonderful thing about the way human beings are designed is their marvelous variability and complexity. We are all different and unique. My description of aggressive, risk-taking boys represents an effort to characterize young males, showing what is typical and how they are different from their sisters. However, they also differ from one another on a thousand traits. I remember taking my ten-year-old son and his friend on a skiing trip one day. As we rode the gondola to the top of the mountain, I prepared to take a picture of the two boys with the beautiful landscape visible behind them. Ryan, my son, was smiling and clowning for the camera, while Ricky was just sitting quietly. Ryan then asked Ricky to wave and goof off like he was doing. Ricky replied solemnly, "I'm not that kind of person." It was true. The two boys were at opposite ends of the continuum in their personalities. I still have that picture of the two kids—one going crazy and the other appearing bored half to death. Each of them "all boy."

Your son is certainly not alone in his characteristic shyness. According to the New York Longitudinal Study, approximately 15 percent of babies are somewhat quiet and passive in the nursery.[16] That feature of their temperaments tends to be persistent throughout childhood and beyond. They may be very spontaneous or funny when they are comfortable at home. When they are with strangers, however, their tongues are thrust into their cheeks and they don't know what to say. Some kids are like this because they have been hurt or rejected in the past. The more likely explanation is that they were born that way. Some parents are embarrassed by the introversion of their children and try to change them. It is a fool's errand. No amount of goading or pushing by their parents will make them outgoing, flamboyant, and confident.

My advice to you is to go with the flow. Accept your child just the way he is made. Then look for those special qualities that give your boy individuality and potential. Nurture him. Cultivate him. And then give him time to develop into his own unique personality like no other human being on earth.

So What *Is* the Difference?

CHAPTER 3

LET ME RETURN now to the questions posed in the first chapter. They are: "What makes young males act as they do?" "What inner force compels them to teeter on the edge of disaster?" and "What is it about the masculine temperament that drives boys to tempt the laws of gravity and ignore the gentle voice of common sense—the one that says, 'Don't do it, Son'?" We might also ask why boys tend to be competitive, aggressive, assertive, and lovers of cars, trucks, guns, and balls. The answers to each of these questions can be found in three physical features and processes that operate from within, as described below. Stay with me now, because the technical information provided below may not thrill your heart, but it is very important to our understanding of boys.

The first factor to be considered is the hormone testosterone, which is largely responsible for maleness (even though smaller amounts of it occur in the bodies of girls and women). It shows up at six or seven weeks after conception, when all embryos are technically "female."[1] That is when a dramatic spiking of testosterone occurs for those who have inherited a "Y" (or male) chromosome. It begins masculinizing their tiny bodies and transforming them into boys. In a real sense, this "hormonal bath," as it is sometimes called, actually damages the walnut-shaped brain and alters its structure in many ways. Even its color changes. The corpus callosum, which is the rope of nerve fibers that connects the two hemispheres, is made less efficient. That limits the number of electrical transmissions that can

19

flow from one side of the brain to the other, which will have lifelong implications. Later, a man will have to think longer about what he believes—especially about something with an emotional component. He may never fully comprehend it. A woman, on the other hand, will typically be able to access her prior experience from both hemispheres and discern almost instantly how she feels about it.[2]

Another consequence of this flood of testosterone in the prenatal period is the localization of language development. For a right-handed man, it is isolated largely in the left hemisphere of his brain. For a woman, it is better distributed on both sides. For this reason, she will probably be more articulate than he from early childhood. I learned that fact the hard way. I had a stroke in 1998 that resulted from a very tiny blood clot that stuck in the left temporal lobe above my ear. It totally interfered with my ability to talk, write, or even ask for water. The neurologist said I lost what is called "the eloquence cortex," or the area of the brain responsible for complex creative thought. Thanks to prayer, some marvelous physicians, and a miracle drug called TPA, I recovered almost entirely within twenty-four hours. If the stroke had occurred before TPA had been developed a few years earlier, I probably would have been sentenced to a world of silence—at least until I had undergone extensive speech therapy. My point is that my ability to speak is obviously localized entirely in that small section of my brain on the left side. A woman suffering the same disorder, however, might have retained some verbal proficiency. Because of their more diffuse brain functions, women retain understanding of speech better after a stroke than men do, and it may be shown in the near future that women will preserve motor speech capability better after a stroke for the same reason.[3] Life just isn't fair.

The impact of testosterone will have many other profound influences on a boy's developing mind and body. In fact, it will affect his every thought and deed for the rest of his life. Another flood of testosterone will occur at the beginning of puberty, which will transform him from a boy to a man. (After puberty, testosterone in males is fifteen times that in females, and estrogen in females is eight to ten times that in males.)[4] It is this second hormonal burst that is primarily responsible for the sudden appearance of facial and pubic hair, squeaky voices, pimply faces, larger muscles, sexual awakening, and, eventually, other characteristics of adult masculinity.

These powerful substances, referring not only to testosterone but also to the female hormone estrogen, account for at least some of the strange behavior that drives parents crazy. They explain why a happy, cooperative twelve-year-old boy or girl can suddenly turn into a sullen, depressed adolescent at thirteen. Human chemistry appears to go haywire for a time. There's a tendency for parents to despair during this period because everything they've tried to teach seems to have misfired. Self-discipline, cleanliness, respect for authority, the work ethic, and even common courtesy may look like lost causes for several years. But better days are coming. The mechanisms that set kids aflame will eventually cool down. That's why I recommend that you not look too quickly for the person your child will become. It is also why I believe parents should seek to "just get them through it" rather than try to fix everything that bugs them as parents.

The spiking of hormones during the prenatal period and again at the beginning of adolescence may not be new concepts to you. What is less generally understood is that the masculine engine and, to a lesser degree, female physiology, continue to be fueled by testosterone throughout life. Here is the way it was described in a fascinating article written by Andrew Sullivan and published in *The New York Times*.

The He Hormone

Testosterone [T] is clearly correlated in both men and women with psychological dominance, confident physicality and high self-esteem. In most combative, competitive environments, especially physical ones, the person with the most wins. Put any two men in a room together and the one with more testosterone will tend to dominate the interaction. Working women have higher levels of testosterone than women who stay at home, and the daughters of working women have higher levels of testosterone than the daughters of housewives. A 1996 study found that in lesbian couples in which one partner assumes the male, or "butch," role and another assumes the female, or "femme," role, the "butch" woman has higher levels of testosterone than the "femme" woman. In naval medical tests, midshipmen have been shown to have higher average levels of testosterone than plebes. Actors tend to have more testosterone than ministers, according to a 1990 study. Among 700 male prison inmates in a 1995 study, those with the highest T levels tended to be those most likely to be in trouble with the prison authorities and to engage in unprovoked violence. This is true among women as well as among men, according to a 1997 study of 87 female inmates in a maximum-security prison.

Although high testosterone levels often correlate with dominance in interpersonal relationships, it does not guarantee more social power. Testosterone levels are higher among blue-collar workers, for example, than among white-collar workers, according to a study of more than 4,000 former military personnel conducted in 1992. A 1998 study found that trial lawyers—with their habituation to combat, conflict and swagger—have higher levels of T than other lawyers. It is even possible to tell who has won a tennis match not by watching the game, but by monitoring testosterone-filled saliva samples throughout. Testosterone levels rise for both players before the match. The winner of any single game sees his T production rise; the loser sees it fall. The ultimate winner experiences a post-game testosterone surge, while the loser sees a collapse. This is true even for people watching sports matches. A 1998 study found that fans backing the winning side in a college basketball game and a World Cup soccer match saw their testosterone levels rise; fans rooting for the losing teams in both games saw their own T levels fall. There is, it seems, such a thing as vicarious testosterone.

This, then, is what it comes down to: testosterone is a facilitator of risk—physical, criminal, personal. Without the influence of testosterone, the cost of these risks might seem to far outweigh the benefits. But with testosterone charging through the brain, caution is thrown to the wind. The influence of testosterone may not always lead to raw physical confrontation. In men with many options it may influence the decision to invest money in a dubious enterprise, jump into an ill-advised sexual affair or tell an egregiously big whopper. At the time, all these decisions may make some sort of testosteroned sense. The White House, anyone?[5]

These conclusions were drawn from numerous scientific studies, although some of them must be considered preliminary. There is still much to be learned about brain chemistry. No doubt exists, however, that there is a link between hormones and human behavior. Testosterone in particular drives the masculine interest in car racing, professional football, hockey, basketball, wrestling, hunting, fishing, sailing, mountain climbing, military history, guns, prize fighting, karate, etc. Many women enjoy these activities too, but far fewer are preoccupied, or obsessed, with them. Testosterone almost certainly plays a role in the fact that the vast majority of crimes of violence are committed by men, and that the prison population is occupied by a vastly disproportionate number of males.

Even in ancient times, it was understood that certain "undesirable" behavior in men was somehow related to the testicles. Male slaves and prisoners of war were made eunuchs (by castration). This was done so they would lose sexual interest in the royal women and so they would be less likely to do violence in the king's court. It worked. We do the same thing today to stallions, bulls, rams, and other male domestic animals. Their aggressive behavior lessens when the flow of testosterone is interrupted. When levels are high, as they are during mating time, males often engage in vicious and sometimes mortal conflict. One researcher said this explains why you probably shouldn't mess with a bull moose during rutting season.[6]

Testosterone is responsible in humans, at least in part, for what might be called "social dominance." Gregg Johnson wrote, "Of two hundred and fifty cultures studied [by anthropologists], males dominate in almost all. Males are almost always the rule makers, hunters, builders, fashioners of weapons, workers in metal, wood, or stone. Women are primary care givers and most involved in child rearing. Their activities center on maintenance and care of home and family. They are more often involved in making pottery, baskets, clothes, and blankets. They gather wood, preserve and prepare food, obtain and carry firewood and water. They collect and grind grain. The data point to biological pre-determinants of gender-related behavior."[7]

Is this biological "predetermination" still operative in sophisticated, modern nations today? The evidence indicates that it is. After thirty years of feminist influence and affirmative-action programs, there are currently only seven female chief executive officers among the Fortune 500 corporations in the United States. That's right, 493 are males.[8] Of the one hundred U.S. senators, only eleven are women.[9] There have been forty-three presidents of the United States, all of them males. The National Organization for Women has pointed to these discrepancies to "prove" that patriarchy and discrimination prevail in the culture. The more likely explanation, however, is biochemical and anatomical. Men, in whose bodies surge ten to twenty times as much testosterone as in women, are more likely to reach for wealth, power, fame, and status because they are urged in that direction from within. Women, on the other hand, elect to bear children, which takes them out of the competitive hunt for a while. There are exceptions, of course, but the obvious tendencies are difficult to deny.

Hormonal influences not only motivate the drive for power in humans, they also impact the way we relate to one another. When several men visit a skeet-shooting range, they tend to concentrate on blasting the next target. They tease and talk together, but winning is on their minds. Women, by contrast, tend to laugh and applaud each others' "hits" excitedly. They are more interested in relationships than in coming out on top. That difference is seen in countless settings. Consider the greatest rivalry in women's professional tennis during the 1980s, which on eighty occasions pitted Chris Evert against Martina Navratilova. Here's how Martina described their friendship at that time: "We always were very respectful of the other one's victories, and sadness. After a match, I would come over and console her, sometimes she came over and consoled me. Or she'd leave me a note, or I'd leave her a note. Just, you know, 'Sorry,' or whatever. 'I'm sure you'll get me next time.' We'd leave it in each other's bag in the locker room. Once in a while we'd send champagne to each other. It was all very civilized."[10]

Compare that civility with how Jimmy Connors and John McEnroe related during their years in the sun. John wrote about his courtside tirades in his book *Playing with Pure Passion:*

> Eventually I was so into [my displays of temper] that I really believed I was doing the right thing. And later it just was like a bad habit, like not being able to stop smoking. I think people related to me. I'm an honest guy, not some phony. When you're out on the court, and it's 100 degrees out there and some guy is sending balls at you at 100 miles an hour, in the heat of the moment you do say different things than when you can sit back later. In my first big Wimbledon, when I got to the semis and played Jimmy [Connors], I was worried about just being in the same locker room and having him blow me off. If looks could kill, I'd have been lying on the floor. I realized there was a whole other game before you get on the court. Talking to the press was sometimes harder than playing the match. That time Jimmy intimidated me. But later, when I won my first big match, I realized that either the players were a whole lot worse than I thought or I was a whole lot better.[11]

Can you imagine John leaving a note in Jimmy's bag telling him, "I'm sorry you lost," or "I'm sure you'll get me next time"? No way, José. Competition for them was not just a tennis match. It was a clash of titans on a field of battle. Not all male athletes are as volatile as Connors and McEnroe, and some females can be pretty nasty on the court too. But the competitive drive in male athletes is more likely to be expressed in confrontational ways. I used to play basketball with a former All American who is one of the nicest guys I've ever known. He will literally give you the shirt off his back. But when he walked on the court, he became mean. He would humiliate you if he could—and usually, he could. I used to tease him about the "thin veneer of civilization" that disappeared when he was in the heat of the contest. There had to be huge quantities of testosterone and adrenaline surging through his masculine veins.

Now what about boys? If the "he hormone" can have this kind of influence on grown men, how does it affect the behavior of young males? In very much the same way. Most experts believe boys' tendency to take risks, to be more assertive, to fight and compete, to argue, to boast, and to excel at certain skills, such as problem solving, math, and science, is directly linked to the way the brain is hardwired and to the presence of testosterone. This may explain why boys have "ants in their pants" when they are in the classroom and why teachers call them little "wiggly worms." The problem is that boys are often taught at such a tempo that it becomes difficult for them to adjust. Testosterone also accounts for boys' early desire to be the strongest, bravest, toughest, rootin-shootin hombré on the range. It's just the way God made them.

SEROTONIN

Let's turn briefly to another hormone that affects human behavior. It is called serotonin, and it carries information from one nerve cell to another. Thus, it is called a "neurotransmitter." Serotonin's purpose is to pacify or soothe the emotions and to help an individual control his or her impulsive behavior. It also facilitates good judgment. Studies of monkeys in the wild revealed that those with low serotonin levels were more likely to take dangerous leaps from branch to branch. (Sounds rather like me in the pear tree, doesn't it?) Rats with inadequate serotonin tended to be more aggressive and violent. Studies of the spinal fluid of murderers indicated that many of them have very low levels of this hormone, as do arsonists and those with hair-trigger tempers. Depression and suicidal tendencies are related to insufficient serotonin.[12]

If testosterone is the gasoline that powers the brain, serotonin slows the speed and helps one steer. And . . . you guessed it. Females typically have more of it than males.

THE AMYGDALA

The third aspect of neurobiology that helps us understand the differences between males and females concerns a portion of the brain known as the amygdala. It is a structure about the size of an almond that functions as a small but powerful "emotional computer." When a physical or emotional threat is perceived by the senses, the amygdala instantly orders the adrenal glands and other defensive organs to swing into action. This is accomplished by regulating the release of various hormones that maximize the chances for survival during times of imminent danger. There is also evidence that the amygdala never forgets a fearful moment, which is why traumatized people often find it so difficult to get over their hair-raising experiences.[13]

What makes the amygdala of interest to us is its role in regulating aggression. It sits smack-dab in the middle of the hypothalamus at the base of the brain, which is the seat of the emotions. When the amygdala perceives a threat or challenge, it fires electrical impulses by way of neural connections into the hypothalamus that put it in a nasty mood. Add testosterone to that situation and you have the potential for a fiery response. Let me emphasize this final point: the amygdala can respond only to what is in its memory bank. It does not think or reason. It emits an "irrational" chemical and electrical response that may save your life in an emergency—but it can also precipitate violence and make matters much worse.[14]

Well, here we go again. The amygdala is larger in males than in females, which helps explain why boys are more likely than girls to be volatile and to engage in what psychotherapist Michael Gurian called "morally-at-risk behavior."[15]

To recap, we have considered three critical components of male neurophysiology: testosterone, serotonin, and the amygdala. Together, they determine what it means to be masculine and why boys are a "breed apart." Having considered what might be viewed as the downside of these features, I must hasten to say that boys and men have their share of neurological advantages, too. Because of the specialization of their brains, males are typically better than females at math, science, spatial relations, logic, and reasoning. This is why most architects, mathematicians, and physical scientists are men. It is also interesting that males are more responsive to stories than women. When they get together, they share experiences that convey emotional meaning for them, whereas women almost never do this. Women talk more openly about their feelings rather than playing the game called "Can you top this?" In short, the sexes are very, very different in ways that may never be fully understood.

How about it then? Is masculinity good or bad? right or wrong? Are boys biologically defective? At first blush, it would appear that girls have all the right stuff. On average, they make fewer mistakes, take fewer risks, are better students, are more thoughtful of others, and are less impulsive than boys. Was testosterone one of God's great mistakes? Would it be better if boys were more like girls and if men were more like women? Should men be feminized, emasculated, and "wimpified"? That is precisely what some feminists and other social liberals seem to think and want us to believe. As we have seen, some of them are trying to reprogram boys to make them less competitive, less aggressive, and more sensitive. Is that a good idea? Most certainly not. First, because it contradicts masculine nature and will never succeed, and second, because the sexes were carefully designed by the Creator to balance one another's weaknesses and meet one another's needs. Their differences didn't result from an evolutionary error, as it is commonly assumed today. Each sex has a unique purpose in the great scheme of things.

How incredibly creative it is of God to put a different form of dominance in each sex so that there is a balance between the two. When they come together in marriage to form what Scripture calls "one flesh," they complement and supplement one another. Wouldn't it be boring if men and women were identical, as the feminists have claimed? It just ain't so, and thank goodness it isn't.

Consider again the basic tendencies of maleness and femaleness. Because it is the privilege and blessing of women to bear children, they are inclined toward predictability, stability, security, caution, and steadiness. Most of them value friendships and family above accomplishments or opportunities. That is why they often dislike change and resist moving from one city to another. The female temperament lends itself to nurturance, caring, sensitivity, tenderness, and compassion. Those are the precise characteristics needed by their children during their developmental years. Without the softness of femininity, the world would be a more cold, legalistic, and militaristic place.

Men, on the other hand, have been designed for a different role. They value change, opportunity, risk, speculation, and adventure. They are designed to provide for their families physically and to protect them from harm and danger. The apostle Paul said, "If anyone does not provide for his relatives, and especially for his immediate family, he has denied the faith and is worse than an unbeliever" (1 Timothy 5:8). This is a divine assignment. Men are also ordained in Scripture for leadership in their homes, to be expressed within the framework of servanthood. Men are often (but not always) less emotional in a crisis and more confident when challenged. A world without men would be more static and uninteresting. When my father died, Mom said with a tear in her eye, "He brought so much excitement into my life." That characteristic is often attractive to women.

When these sex-linked temperaments operate as intended in a family, they balance and strengthen one another's shortcomings. For example, a man will sometimes get excited about an entrepreneurial venture or idea that presents itself. He may throw all the family's resources impulsively into a single roll of the dice. His wife, on the other hand, sees the risks. She is more skeptical and cautious. Her reluctance is based on a certain ability to perceive danger or negative outcomes. She is especially good at reading the character of people. A woman will say, "There's something about Clark (or

Jack or Marty) that I don't like. I just don't trust him." She might not be able to explain why she feels that way, but her intuition is often right. And any man who doesn't at least consider the perspective of his wife is depriving himself of valuable information.

On the other hand, if a woman has to endorse an idea before it flies, her husband may miss genuine opportunities that are there for the taking. There are times when his spirit of adventure should trump her skepticism. In short, neither the woman nor the man has a corner on truth. Their individual temperaments are designed to moderate each other, not only in business pursuits, but also in almost every aspect of life. I talked to a married couple recently who understood these contrasting inclinations very well. They said that he was the "pedal" and she was the "brake." Both are vital to the safe operation of an automobile. If they only have a throttle, they are certain to crash. If they only have the ability to stop, they will never move.

My mother and father were like "yin and yang." They disagreed, respectfully, on nearly everything—from how to pack the car for a trip to which hotel to select. Fortunately, they used their differing perspectives to advantage. As Dad said, "Any proposal that gets past both of us must be pretty good."

That brings us back to our understanding of boys. Remember that they are men-in-training. Their aggressive nature is designed for a purpose. It prepares them for the "provision and protection" roles to come. That assertiveness also builds culture when properly channeled. I urge you as parents not to resent or try to eliminate the aggressive and excitable nature that can be so irritating. That temperament is part of a divine plan. Celebrate it. Enjoy it. Thank God for it. But also understand that it needs to be shaped, molded, and "civilized." That's where we're headed in the chapters to come.

QUESTIONS AND ANSWERS

Our pediatrician told us he believes our son may have attention deficit hyperactive disorder (ADHD). Can you tell us what is known about this problem?

ADD, or attention deficit disorder, appears to be an inherited neurological syndrome that affects approximately 5 percent of children in the United States.[16] It refers to individuals who are easily distracted, have a low tolerance for boredom or frustration, and tend to be impulsive and flighty. Some of them are also hyperactive, and hence they are said to have ADHD (attention deficit hyperactivity disorder).

These children have a pattern of behavior that sets them up for failure in school and conflict with their parents. They have difficulty finishing tasks, remembering details, focusing on a book or assignment, or even remaining seated for more than a few minutes. Some appear to be driven from within as they race wildly from one thing to another. They are often very bright and creative, yet they're seen as lazy, disruptive, and terribly disorganized. ADD and ADHD children often suffer from low self-esteem because they have been berated as goof-offs and anarchists who refuse to follow the rules. They sometimes have few friends because they can drive everyone crazy—even those their own age.

How can I know if my son has ADHD?

It is unwise for a parent to attempt to diagnose his or her own child. There are many other problems, both psychological and physical, that can cause similar symptoms. Disorders of the thyroid, for example, can make a child hyperactive or sluggish; depression and anxiety can cause the distractibility associated with ADD. Therefore, you must have assistance from a physician, a child developmentalist, or a psychologist who can confirm the diagnosis.

If you see in your child the symptoms I've described, I urge you to have him seen professionally. Again, you should *not* try to diagnose your own child! The sooner you can get that youngster in to see a professional who specializes in this disorder the better.

What causes attention deficit disorder?

It is believed to be inherited. Russell Barkley of the University of Massachusetts Medical Center estimates that 40 percent of ADD (and, by implication, ADHD) kids have a parent with similar symptoms, and 35 percent have an affected sibling. If one identical twin is affected, the chances are between 80 and 92 percent that his or her sibling will be also. ADD is two to three times more likely to be diagnosed in boys as in girls.[17]

The cause of ADD is unknown, but it is probably associated with subtle differences in brain structure, its neural pathways, its chemistry, its blood supply, or its electrical system. As of this writing, some interesting hypotheses are emerging, although definitive conclusions are yet to be drawn.

I've heard that ADD is controversial and that it may not even exist. You obviously disagree.

I do disagree, although the disorder has become faddish and tends to be overdiagnosed. But when a child actually has this problem, I assure you that his parents and teachers don't have to be convinced.

Does ADD go away as children grow up?

We used to believe the problem was eliminated with the onset of puberty. That's what I was taught in graduate school. Now it is known that ADD is a lifelong condition, usually influencing behavior from the cradle to the grave. Some ADD adults learn to be less disorganized and impulsive as they get older. They channel their energy into sports activities or professions in which they function very well. Others have trouble settling on a career or holding a job. Follow-through remains a problem as they flit from one task to another. They are particularly unsuited for desk jobs, accounting positions, or other assignments that demand attention to detail, long hours of sitting, and the ability to juggle many balls at once.

Another consequence of ADD in adolescence and adulthood is the thirst for high-risk activity of the type we have described in this chapter. Even as children, people with ADD are accident prone. As they get older, rock climbing, bungee jumping, car racing, motorcycle riding, white-water rafting, and related activities are among their favorite activities. Adults with ADD are sometimes called "adrenaline junkies" because they are hooked on the "high" produced by the adrenaline rush associated with dangerous behavior. Others are more susceptible to drug use, alcoholism, and other addictive behaviors. Approximately 40 percent of people with ADD will have been arrested by eighteen years of age.[18]

Some of those who have ADD are at higher risk for marital conflict too. It can be very irritating to a compulsive, highly ordered husband or wife to be married to a "messie"—someone whose life is chaotic and who forgets to pay the bills, fix the car, or keep records for income-tax reports. Such a couple usually needs professional counseling to help them learn to work together and capitalize on each other's strengths.

What kind of treatment is available?

Treatment involves a range of factors, beginning with education. The adult with ADD is often greatly relieved to learn that he or she has an identifiable, treatable condition. Dr. Robert Reid from the University of Nebraska calls it the "label of forgiveness." He said, "The kid's problems are not his parents' fault, not the teacher's fault, not the kid's fault."[19] That is good news to the person who has been told all his life that he's dumb, stupid, lazy, obnoxious, and disruptive.

The first step in rebuilding the self-concept of an adult, then, is to get an understanding of the forces operating within. My advice to that individual and to his family is to read, read, read!

Do you worry about Ritalin and other drugs being overprescribed? Should I be reluctant to give them to my very hyperactive ten-year-old?

I do worry about giving these drugs capriciously and for the wrong reasons. There are reports of some classrooms where up to 10 percent of the kids are taking them.[20] That is a huge red flag. Prescription drugs have been used as a cure-all for various forms of misbehavior. That is unfortunate. I suspect that some parents and teachers medicate their unruly kids because they have failed to discipline them properly or because they prefer to have them sedated. Every medication has undesirable side effects and should be administered only after careful evaluation and study. Ritalin, for example, can reduce the appetite and cause insomnia in some patients. It is, nevertheless, considered remarkably safe.

If your child has been evaluated and diagnosed with ADD by a professional who is experienced in treating this problem, however, you should not hesitate to accept a prescription for an appropriate medication. Some dramatic behavioral changes can occur when the proper substance is identified for a particular child. A boy who sits and stares off into the distance or one who frantically climbs the walls is desperately in need of help. To give that individual a focused mind and internal control is a blessing. Medication often works just that way when the child is properly diagnosed.

One more thought. I personally believe that some of the boys who are suspected to have ADD and ADHD do not have the disorder. Rather, their symptoms are caused by the fact that they were pulled out of the safety of their homes and put into structured learning situations before they were ready. They are developmentally unprepared for the demands made on them there. If we would let these immature boys stay at home for a year or two longer, I think the incidence of fidgety-flighty boys would decrease.[21]

WOUNDED SPIRITS

SOME OF MY readers may be wondering at this point, *Why only boys? Why not also consider the needs of girls?* The answer is that boys, even more than girls, are in serious trouble today. We have been hearing for three decades about girls being discriminated against, sexually harassed, disrespected, and given short shrift in school. There is some validity to those assertions, and steps are being taken to address them. But a chorus of social scientists is warning now of a crisis among males like nothing we have seen before. While many kids are coping adequately, a sizable minority is struggling with perplexing social pressures and forces that yesterday's kids didn't have to face. For some, just trying to survive emotionally can best be described as overwhelming. Let's look at the findings that have led us to conclude that many males are foundering today—and the vast majority of them are being negatively influenced by the culture.

Boys, when compared to girls, are six times more likely to have learning disabilities, three times more likely to be registered drug addicts, and four times more likely to be diagnosed as emotionally disturbed. They are at greater risk for schizophrenia, autism, sexual addiction, alcoholism, bed wetting, and all forms of antisocial and criminal behavior. They are twelve times more likely to murder someone, and their rate of death in car accidents is greater by 50 percent. Seventy-seven percent of delinquency-related court cases involve males.[1]

There is more. Boys younger than fifteen years of age are twice as likely

33

to be admitted to psychiatric hospitals[2] and five times more likely than girls to kill themselves.[3] Fully 80 percent of suicides involve males under twenty-five years of age.[4] Suicide among black adolescent boys has increased 165 percent just in the past twelve years.[5] Boys comprise 90 percent of those in drug treatment programs and 95 percent of kids involved in juvenile court.[6]

Dr. Michael Gurian, psychotherapist and author of the best-selling book *The Wonder of Boys,* said masculine confusion and discontent are especially evident in public education.

> From elementary grades through high school, boys receive lower grades than girls. Eighth-grade boys are held back 50 percent more often than girls. By high school, boys account for two-thirds of the students in special education classes. Fewer boys now attend and graduate from college. Fifty-nine percent of all master's degree candidates are now women, and the percentage of men in graduate-level professional education is shrinking each year. When eighth grade students are asked about their futures, girls are now twice as likely as boys to say they want to pursue a career in management, the professions, or business. Boys experience more difficulty adjusting to school, are up to ten times more likely to suffer from "hyperactivity" than girls, and account for 71 percent of all school suspensions.[7]

Perhaps the most disturbing evidence of the crisis has involved the increase in violence among males, especially the terrifying school shootings in Littleton, Colorado; Jonesboro, Arkansas; Springfield, Oregon; Paducah, Kentucky; Ft. Gibson, Oklahoma; Santee, California; and El Cajon, California. Unfortunately, there will probably be other bloody incidents by the time this book is released. Most of the young killers to this point have been young white males who couldn't explain why they wanted to murder their classmates and teachers. When those who survived were asked to explain their motives, most simply said, "I don't know." Several referred to harassment by peers similar to what we adults experienced and learned to cope with as children.

One of the killers was a fifteen-year-old boy named Kip Kinkel in Springfield, Oregon. He murdered both his parents and then shot twenty-seven of his classmates at Springfield High School. Two of them died.

Here is a partial transcript of the interview with Kinkel, taken by investigators a few hours after he had killed his father and then his mother.

> **Unidentified Police Officer:** You walked up behind him and shot him in the head. Is that right?
> **Kinkel:** Basically, yeah.
> **Officer:** How many times did you shoot him?
> **Kinkel:** Once.
> **Officer:** And where did that bullet hit him?
> **Kinkel:** Right about the ear. . . . Oh, my God . . . I loved my dad; that's why I had to.
> **Officer:** You love him, so that's why you had to kill him?
> **Kinkel:** Yes. . . . Oh, my God. My parents were good people. . . . I didn't know what to do because . . . oh, my God, my mom was coming home. . . . Oh, my God.
> **Officer:** Did you know it was wrong?
> **Kinkel:** I had no other choice. It was the only thing I could do.[8]

Who can say for sure what motivated Kip to shoot his father, despite the love he professed? We do know, however, that there is a common denominator between him and many of the other young men who have massacred their peers. It is an inner rage that almost defies explanation. One researcher believes these kids typically don't know until the last minute whether they will commit homicide, suicide, or both.[9] Although there are millions of other teens out there today who will never resort to such extreme violence, they are also dealing with their own brand of alienation.

Clearly, something has gone terribly wrong in our day. How can we explain this cauldron of emotions that simmers within many boys, and who can possibly anticipate what it portends for the men they will become? And what accounts for the rising number of male adolescents who simply aren't making it in today's world? These are perplexing questions and their answers are varied and complex. I'll talk in subsequent chapters about the underlying factors and suggest what parents and teachers can do to help. But first, let's look more closely at the emotional life of kids today and the prevalence of a disturbing phenomenon called "wounded spirits."

Now, more than ever, boys are experiencing a crisis of confidence that reaches deep within the soul. Many of them are growing up believing they are unloved by their parents and are hated or disrespected by their peers. This results in a form of self-loathing that often serves as a prelude to violence, drug abuse, promiscuity, and suicide. It helps explain why both boys and girls do things that would otherwise make no sense, such as cutting their flesh, piercing sensitive body parts, tattooing themselves from head to toe, taking dangerous drugs, and/or identifying themselves with death, perversion, and satanic ritual. Some of them, it has been said, "cry with bullets."

For some kids, the wounded spirit syndrome begins very early, as a consequence of abuse and neglect. Tiny boys and girls whose basic needs remain unsatisfied may never fully recover. They go on to experience serious psychological and neurological impairment, as we will see in a moment. Why is this happening? Seventy-seven percent of parents who harm or neglect their children are abusers of their own bodies through excessive use of alcohol or addictions to other mind-altering substances.[10] One can hardly care for and love a child while drunk or stoned.

Not all abuse is related to the use of chemical substances, of course. Many parents are simply too busy and distracted or too immature and selfish to meet the pressing needs of babies and toddlers. Divorce, when it occurs, diverts the attention of adults away from children and focuses it on their own painful circumstances. This disengagement of parents in our fast-paced and dizzying world will show up repeatedly in our discussion of boys. It is *the* underlying problem plaguing children today.

Chronic neglect of boys and girls during the first two years of life is devastating psychologically and neurologically. The brain is a dynamic and interactive organ that requires stimulation from the outside world. When children are ignored, mistreated, or shuffled from one caregiver to another, terrible losses occur in thinking capacity. The more severe the abuse, the greater the damage that is done.

This understanding has been confirmed by hundreds of millions of federal dollars invested in medical and behavioral research, focusing not only on infants but on teens who were horribly abused as babies. Some of them stood in cribs for days while wearing dirty diapers that burned their bottoms, or they were beaten or scalded by mentally ill or cocaine-addicted parents. Extreme neglect or rejection of this nature, researchers say, causes a child's body to produce significant quantities of the hormones cortisol and adrenaline. These chemicals move through the bloodstream to targeted areas of the brain responsible for compassion and conscience. The damage done there to critical neural pathways never repairs itself and ultimately limits the individual's ability to "feel" for others later in life. That's why many of the most violent kids are "brain damaged," quite literally.[11]

These studies help explain why a growing number of teenagers appear to have no conscience about killing or maiming innocent victims. One fourteen-year-old boy shot a man who was sitting in his car at a stop sign. When asked why he did it, he said it was because the man "looked at him funny." Another kid stood outside a 7-Eleven store and murdered a customer just for the fun of watching him die.[12] These young killers, almost all of whom are boys, typically express no remorse or regret for their brutality. Robin Karr-Morse, coauthor of *Ghosts in the Nursery: Tracing the Roots of Violence*, said a nation of ignored and emotionally neglected babies "has created an assembly line [of children] leading straight to our jails."[13]

There are other factors that wound the spirit, of course. One of them is the extreme emphasis on body image that now invades the souls of very young children. Life can be difficult for a boy who is odd or different in an obvious way—whose nose is crooked, or whose skin is pock-marked or acned, or whose hair is too curly or too straight, or whose feet are too big, or who has one crossed eye, or whose ears protrude, or whose behind is too large. Those with red hair can be teased unmercifully from the preschool years. In fact, a youngster can be physically perfect except for a single embarrassing feature, yet under a barrage of taunts, he or she will worry about that one deficiency as though it were the only important thing in life. For a period of time, it is precisely that.

Author Frank Peretti coined the term "wounded spirits" and used it as the title of his excellent book based on his own childhood experience. He was born with a tumor in his jaw that disfigured him and led to unmerciful taunting during his childhood. He saw himself as a "monster," because that is what he was called by other children.[14] Frank is joined by millions of others who have been through years of rejection and ridicule because of a physical abnormality or unsightly characteristic.

This vulnerability to one's peers has always been part of the human experience, but today's children and teens are even more sensitive to it. The reason is that popular culture has become a tyrannical master that demands ever-greater conformity to its shifting ideal of perfection. For example, if you have had an occasion to watch an old Elvis Presley movie, you must have noticed that the girls who were paraded in bikinis were slightly overweight and out of shape. There they were, "twisting" their corpulent behinds to the delight of Elvis and the other oversexed members of his band. But those actresses who seemed so luscious in 1960 could not make it on *Baywatch* today. Most of them would need to spend a year or two in the gym and undergo breast augmentation to make the grade. In Rembrandt's day, the women considered exceptionally beautiful were downright fat. Today, extreme thinness and "hard bodies" have become the ideal—sometimes bordering on masculinity. In short, the standard of perfection has shifted upward and been placed out of reach for most kids.

The media and the entertainment industry are largely responsible for the assault we are witnessing today. They laud images of bodily perfection, including "supermodels," "playmates," "babes," and "hunks." The net effect on children and teens is profound, not only in this country but around the world. We saw it illustrated dramatically when Western satellite TV transmission penetrated the islands of the South Pacific for the first time. It projected images of gorgeous, very thin actresses who starred on *Melrose Place, Beverly Hills 90210,* and other teen-oriented shows. Four years later, a survey of sixty-five Fijian girls revealed how their attitudes had been shaped (or warped) by what they had seen. Almost immediately, the girls began to dress and try to fix their hair like Western women. Dr. Anne Beecher, research director at the Harvard Eating Disorder Center, also observed serious changes in eating habits among the Fijian adolescents. Those who watched TV three times per week or more were 50 percent more likely to perceive themselves as "too big" or "too fat" than those who did not.[15] More than 62 percent had attempted to diet in the previous thirty days.[16]

A youngster does not have to be obese to feel this pressure. A study conducted at the University of California some years ago revealed 80 percent of girls in the fourth grade were attempting to diet because they perceived themselves as fat.[17] Another study, this one also out of date now, revealed that half of elementary-school children, ages eight to eleven, reported dissatisfaction with their weight.[18] It is my belief that the numbers would be even more shocking today. Dr. Mary Sanders and her colleagues at Stanford University School of Medicine speculated that the root causes of anorexia nervosa, bulimia, and other eating disorders might be found in these early experiences. She and her colleagues believe that today's youth "are immersed in a culture where messages about dieting are prevalent."[19] Guess why? Because messages about "fatness" are so incredibly threatening that even those who are thin become terrified by the prospect of gaining weight. No wonder eating disorders are rampant among the young.

This obsession with one's weight appears to have affected the late Princess Diana of the United Kingdom, whom some would say was the most glamorous and beautiful woman in the world. She certainly was one of the most photographed, as evidenced by the paparazzi that tracked her to the very final moment of her life. No other person generated the level of support for charities and causes quite like Diana, princess of Wales. Given her glamour and beauty and her enormous influence around the world, isn't it almost incomprehensible that Diana had a very poor body image—that she disliked what she saw in the mirror and that, for a time, she struggled with an eating disorder? How could a woman of such wealth and popularity descend into self-loathing and depression?

Perhaps Diana's damaged self-concept wasn't as strange as it might have seemed. Our value system is arranged so that few women feel entirely at ease with their physical bodies. Even Miss America or Miss Universe competitors will admit, if they're honest, that they are bothered by their physical flaws. If those who are blessed with great beauty and charm often struggle with feelings of inadequacy, imagine how your immature, gangly teenagers feel about the imperfect bodies with which they're born. The beauty cult is an international curse plaguing hundreds of millions of people, most of them young, with a sense of inferiority. Even the late princess fell victim to it.[20]

Now, the illustrations I've provided herein have focused primarily on girls and women. Why are they also of relevance to boys and men? Because this preoccupation with physical perfection and body image has become as serious a problem for males as for females. Research reveals that there is now no difference between the sexes in this regard.[21] Boys want desperately to be big, powerful, and handsome. By the age of four, they will flex their little biceps by holding up their arms, making a fist, and pointing to the bump where a muscle will someday grow (hopefully). "Feel it, Dad," they will say. "See how big it is?" "Yeah, Son," fathers are supposed to reply, "you are really strong."

Young boys wear Superman and Batman capes, cowboy clothes, and the funny little loincloths Tarzan wore to show that they are "bad"—meaning cool. This masculine "will to power" is why boys fight, climb, wrestle, strut, and show off. It is the way they are made. This is why when a boy is slow in developing or is smaller than his peers, he often suffers from self-image problems. Just put yourself in the position of a tiny boy who is taunted and shoved around by every other kid in his class—one who is even shorter than the girls, one who lacks the strength to compete in sports—and one who is called "Runt," "Squirt," "Gnat," or "Killer." After he runs that gauntlet for a few years, his spirit begins to bleed.

I remember sitting in my car one day at a fast-food restaurant eating a hamburger and french fries. (This was before a heart attack took the joy out of eating!) I happened to look in the rearview mirror in time to see a scrawny, dirty little kitten walking on a ledge behind my car. It looked so pitiful and sick. I've always been a sucker for an underdog—or in this case, an undercat—and I couldn't resist this one. I got out, tore off a piece of my hamburger, and tossed it to the kitty. But before the kitty could reach the morsel, a huge tomcat sprang from the bushes and gobbled it down. I felt sorry for the little guy, who turned and shrank back into the shadows. Although I called and offered him another bite, he was too afraid to come out again. I was immediately reminded of my years as a junior-high teacher. I saw teenagers every day who were just as needy—just as deprived, just as lost as that little kitten. It wasn't food they were after; they needed love, attention, and respect. Some were almost desperate to get it. When they dared to open up and "reach for a prize," such as asking for a date or going out for a team sport, one or more of the popular kids would intimidate them and send them scurrying back to the shadows, frightened and alone. It happens routinely on every campus.

A mother called me a few weeks ago to say she was extremely concerned about her twelve-year-old son, Brad. She had found him crying two nights earlier and pressed him to tell her why. The boy reluctantly admitted through his tears that he didn't want to live and that he had been looking for a way to kill himself. He had read that toothpaste could be harmful if swallowed, so he was considering eating an entire tube. This family is one of the strongest and most impressive I have had the privilege of knowing, yet right under the parents' noses, their precious son was considering suicide. Brad had always been a good boy who had many friends, yet he had encountered a problem with which he couldn't cope. After working their way through the crisis, the parents learned that a boy at school had been making fun of Brad's ears because they protruded a bit. The bully had made him feel like the most stupid-looking person in school. When they passed in the hall, the harasser would put his hands behind his own ears and press them forward.

Some of my readers might consider Brad's personal crisis to be silly. I've heard some people say in similar situations, "Come on. This is just kid stuff. He'll get over it. We've all been through moments like that." They are right. Most of us have been taunted or ridiculed by our peers. But we must never underestimate the distress that can occur in what looks like "no big deal" to an adult, especially for kids who are already wounded from other sources. In Brad's case, it even took away his desire to live. Parents should never brush off an experience of this nature, nor should threats of suicide be taken lightly. Even if you are raising your children in a healthy, safe, loving environment, you must keep your eyes and ears open during their teen years. Adolescent emotions are volatile, and they can lead to dangerous developments that materialize out of nowhere. Boys, far more often than girls, turn to antisocial behavior when they are backed into a corner.

So what are you to do when you see a child being besieged by his peers? In Brad's case, I advised his mom to talk to the mother of the bully. Rather than attacking her son verbally, which would have invited instant retaliation and greater trouble, I suggested that Brad's mother explain that *she* had a problem and would appreciate the other mom's help in handling the situation. She did just that. The two women talked together and discussed their mutual concerns. Although the other boy's mom was somewhat defensive, the bullying stopped and the issue was laid to rest. Brad's family also sought professional counseling to help their son deal with the deeper self-image problems and personal insecurities that had arisen.

I also suggested to this mother (and now to you, at the risk of seeming self-serving) that she get a copy of my book and cassette-tape series entitled *Preparing for Adolescence*. They are intended not for parents but for pre-teens. The first chapter and tape deal with the assault on self-worth that is almost certain to occur in the early adolescent years. They also tell a boy or girl how to brace themselves for these experiences. If we as adults know these difficult days are coming and don't make an effort to get our kids ready for them, we are not doing our job. The details are all in the book and tapes. I hope you will find them helpful.

By the way, the advice I gave Brad's mom was somewhat risky. I knew she could pull it off, because she is such a wise and nonthreatening lady. But her conversation with the other woman about her son was difficult and could have backfired. Mother bears can be shockingly cranky when someone is criticizing their cubs. Furthermore, some moms have no control over their unruly kids and couldn't resolve the conflict even if they wanted to. In those cases, other approaches may be tried. Some of them are not so helpful. When I was a school psychologist, I knew a mother who became so angry over the bullying of her son that she managed on her own to corner the perpetrator. She worked him over like a marine sergeant going after a recruit. I saw the bully a few days later and he was still ashen. I asked, "What did Mrs. Jordan say to you?" He said, "She . . . she . . . told me if I didn't leave her son alone she was gonna kill me." Obviously, that was not the best solution. But I will tell you this. Mrs. Jordan got her point across and the bullying went quietly into the night.

There has to be a better way to preserve the spirit of your son. It may require extraordinary and inconvenient measures. As for me, I would not permit my child to stay in an abusive environment if I perceived it as more than the usual bickering between kids. If peers begin to gang up on your youngster and are ripping into his heart day after day, I would get him out of there. I would find a magnet school, or a Christian school, or I would even move to another city if necessary. (By the way, bullying on Christian campuses can be just as prevalent as in public schools.) Whenever the deck is stacked against your child, a change of scenery might be in order. We'll talk presently about homeschooling, which is another excellent option for some. Whatever the approach taken, you must protect the spirit of your child. I have seen firsthand what a pack of wolves can do to a defenseless lamb.

Speaking of wolves, let me share another animal story with you that I think is relevant. Our dog Mindy was neither a purebred nor a champion.

Her daddy had been a travelin' man, so we didn't know much about her ancestry. She was just a scared pup who showed up at the front door late one night after being abused by her owners and thrown out of a car. We didn't really need another dog, but what could we do?

We took Mindy in, and she quickly grew to become one of the finest dogs we had ever owned. But she never lost the emotional fragility that had been brought on by abuse. She couldn't stand to be criticized or scolded when she accidentally did something wrong. She would actually jump in your lap and hide her eyes. One summer, we went away for a two-week vacation and left her in the backyard. The neighbor boy gave her food and water, but otherwise, Mindy was alone during that time. We obviously underestimated what this isolation would do to her. When we returned, we found her lying next to the house on a blanket. Surrounding her were about seven of our daughter's old stuffed animals, which she had found stored in the garage. Mindy had carried them one by one to her bed and ringed herself with these little friends.

If an old dog needs love and friendship in this way, how much more true is it of every child who walks the earth? It is our job as adults to see that each one of them finds the security he or she needs. We must never forget the difficulties of trying to grow up in the competitive world in which a child lives. Take a moment to listen, to care, and to direct such a youngster. That may be the best investment of your life.

One reason I feel strongly that adults should protect children from each other is because I have a very good memory. After enjoying a happy and secure childhood, I entered junior high and took some heavy flak from several older students. I remember crying all the way home from school one day because of what two boys and a girl had said to me. It threw me into a crisis of confidence that my dad had to help me deal with. Having seen so many kids struggle with the same pressures I faced, I often tell those in middle school that if they can survive their thirteenth and fourteenth years, they will be able to handle anything life throws at them thereafter. I am only half kidding.

Referring again to my father "being there" for me when I was in despair, my experience illustrates the importance of having a strong and loving family to help a kid survive the pressures of adolescence. One of the reasons some teenagers react violently and stupidly is that there is no one at home to "talk them down" from the precipice. Everything circles around, sooner or later, to the quality of family life. That is the big problem.

I eventually learned how to defend myself from attack. During my third year in high school, my family moved and sent me to a new high school. Almost immediately, I had to deal with several bullies who saw me as an easy mark. One of them followed me down the hall between classes, taunting and picking on me. I had had enough. I wheeled around and threw my books in his face. By the time he could see me again I was on top of him. Fortunately, I was six foot two and able to hold my own. That was the end of our conflict. Word quickly got around to the other bullies and they left me alone. But if I had weighed thirty pounds less and been about eight inches shorter, I would have been the continued target of these big dudes. That is the world in which adolescent boys live. As Little Orphan Annie sang in the Broadway production, "It's a hard-knock life."

Let me admit, in passing, that I also thought it would be fun to bully someone at one point. I was an immature ninth grader who had been through a difficult year of harassment as described earlier. It seemed reasonable that I pass along the pain to someone else. I selected who I thought was a good candidate and began giving him grief. Denny was about my size but I took him for a sissy. One day right before class, I was on his case big time. Unfortunately, he turned out to be much tougher than I thought. Denny suddenly hit me with about six sharp blows to the head before I knew what was happening. He really rang my bell, which was one of the greater shocks of my life. I gave up my bullying career then and there. My heart just wasn't in it.

Why do boys harass and intimidate each other this way? Angela Phillips explained it like this: "The effect of intimidation is to drag other children down to the same level of powerlessness, through fear. A child who lives in fear is unable to learn. The bully has then reduced his victim to his own dysfunctional level."[22] That is exactly what I was trying to do with Denny. I just picked the wrong victim, that's all.

Here's another reason why bullies bully. *The Journal of Developmental Psychology* reported a study of 452 boys in the fourth, fifth, and sixth grades. It revealed that those who taunted weaker peers and were aggressive and rebellious at school were often the most popular with their classmates. Raw power and audacity in boys are the characteristics kids tend to admire. Dr. Phillip Rodkin of Duke University explained why. He said, "These boys may internalize the idea that aggression, popularity, and control naturally go together, and they may not hesitate to use physical aggression as a social strategy because it has worked in the past."[23] In other words, bullies are rewarded socially for harassing kids who are below them in the pecking order, which probably explains why many of them do it. By the way, other studies showed that bratty and rebellious behavior among girls did not result in greater popularity. Only boys are admired for breaking the rules. One or more of them could belong to you!

Whatever the reason, there are plenty of young bullies around to do their dastardly work. A study by psychologist Dorothy Espelage revealed that 80 percent of students take part in bullying, and 15 percent of seventh and eighth graders say they bully someone regularly.[24] In an older study, boys were found to be four times as likely as girls to be responsible for physical attacks and far more likely to be victims of attacks.[25] In a study sponsored by the Kaiser Foundation, 74 percent of eight- to eleven-year-olds, and 86 percent of teens, report being teased or bullied by their peers.[26] One child in five is frightened in the classroom.[27] It is a major problem for boys on campuses today. It also plays a significant role in the bloody violence that continues to distress the nation. In the past four decades, there has been a 500 percent increase in the rates of homicide and suicide.[28] I am convinced that many of those who kill themselves, and who kill others, suffer from wounded spirits. Andy Williams, the young gunman who killed two of his classmates at Santee High School, was taunted relentlessly for having an "anorexic body."[29] Some kids can pass off this kind of ridicule, but for others it turns into a rage that lasts for a lifetime.

Those who turn violent or behave in other antisocial ways often come from the bottom of the social pyramid. Adrian Nicole LeBlanc, author of an article entitled "The Outsiders," provided some valuable insight for us about bullying as follows:

> The traditional hierarchies operate [in school]: the popular kids tend to be wealthier and the boys among them tend to be jocks. The Gap Girls-Tommy Girls-Polo Girls compose the pool of desirable girlfriends, many of whom are athletes as well. Below the popular kids, in a shifting order of relative unimportance, are the druggies (stoners, deadheads, burnouts, hippies or neo-hippies), trendies or Valley Girls, preppies, skateboarders and skateboarder chicks, nerds and techies, wiggers, rednecks and Goths, better known as freaks. There are troublemakers, losers and floaters—kids who move from group to group. Real losers are invisible.
>
> To be an outcast boy is to be a "nonboy," to be feminine, to be weak. Bullies function as a kind of peer police enforcing the social code. The revenge-of-the-nerds refrain—which assures unpopular boys that if they only hold on through high school, the roster of winners will change—does not question the hierarchy that puts the outcasts at risk. So boys survive by their stamina, sometimes by their fists, but mainly, if they're lucky, with the help of the "family" they've created among their friends.[30]

LeBlanc continued with revealing excerpts from an interview with a boy named Andrew, who was at the bottom of the heap:

"First people harassed me because I was really smart," Andrew says, presenting the sequence as self-evident. "I read all the time. I read through math class." Back then, in middle school, he had the company of Tom Clancy and a best friend he could talk to about anything. He says things are better now; during school, he hangs out with the freaks. Yet the routine days he describes sound far from improvement— being body-slammed and shoved into chalkboards and dropped into trash cans headfirst. At a school dance, in the presence of chaperones and policemen, R. lifted Andrew and ripped a pocket off his pants. "One day I'll be a 'faggot,' the next day I'll be a 'retard,'"Andrew says. One girl who used to be his friend now sees him approaching and shouts, "Oh, get out of here, nobody wants you!"

Andrew joined the cross-country team but the misery trailed him on the practice runs. He won't rejoin next year although he loves the sport. Recently he and some other boys were suspended for suspected use of drugs. According to Andrew, he used to earn straight A's; now he receives mostly C's and D's. He does not draw connections between the abuse and the changes in his life.

Neither does Andrew tell his parents. He believes they think he is popular. "If I try to explain it to my parents," he says, "they'll say: 'Oh, but you have plenty of friends.' Oh, I don't think so. They don't really get it." His outcast friends, however, do.

One of them is Randy Tuck, a 5-foot-4-inch sophomore with a thick head of hair and cheeks bright red with acne. He rescued Andrew from a "swirly" (two boys had him ankle up, and headed for the toilet bowl).

Andrew says that the ostracizing "does build up inside. Sometimes you might get really mad at something that doesn't matter a lot, kinda like the last straw." He could understand the killers, Dylan Klebold and Eric Harris, if their misery had shown no signs of ending, but Andrew remains an optimist. After all, there are some people who have no friends.[31]

It is not difficult to understand how boys with wounded spirits—the freaks and the geeks and the nerds and the dorks and the dweebs—can break loose under intense pressure and do unthinkable harm to others. I'm not excusing or justifying their behavior, of course. Most students journey through this difficult time without resorting to violence. Some, however, harbor such hatred that they shoot not only those who have taunted them but everyone else in sight. Then they turn the guns on themselves as the ultimate act of self-hatred. In nearly every instance of random violence on school campuses, young perpetrators have been ridiculed and harassed by their peers. As mentioned by Andrew, this is what happened at Columbine High School in Littleton, Colorado, on that tragic afternoon in April 1999. Twelve students and a teacher were murdered before the two seventeen-year-old gunmen committed suicide.[32] While they bear the full responsibility for the massacre, one cannot study the underlying circumstances without seeing evidence of rejection by the more popular kids. As they were killing their classmates, Klebold reportedly shouted, "This is for everyone who teased us." Harris said, "Your children have humiliated me. They've embarrassed me. They will all be dead, [blankety-blank-blank], they will all be dead. I am God and I determine what is true."[33] Pent-up anger obviously boiled over and resulted in many deaths. It is becoming a familiar pattern.

Another key factor is the prevalence of violence in the media, which has taught kids the wrong way to deal with tormentors. Teens, including those with wounded spirits, live every day with images of killing, poisoning, maiming, decapitating, knifing, crashing, and exploding. It is everywhere, from the theater to cable television to music videos and the Internet. One of the most popular movies a few years ago was *Scream,* produced by Miramax—a subsidiary owned, it is sad to say, by the Disney Corporation. The film opened with the brutal killing of a young girl. Her body was then disemboweled and left hanging on a clothesline to be discovered by her mother.[34] Millions of teenagers saw this movie during their most impressionable years. *Scream 2* and *Scream 3* have come along since. Thanks, Disney, for doing this to our kids. Your founder would roll in his grave if he knew what you are doing with his good name. So go ahead. Take the money and run. But as you go, remember that the blood of innocent victims will stain your hands forever. I deeply resent this demoralization and exploitation of the young that Disney Chairman Michael Eisner and other movie and television moguls have perpetrated at the expense of the most impressionable among us.

Given the pervasiveness of violence in the media, why are we surprised when kids who have seen and heard it throughout childhood sometimes act in violent ways? Children are taught that killing is the way they are supposed to act when insulted or frustrated. "Come on," they shout when taunted, "make my day!" followed by the *rat-a-tat-tat* of an automatic rifle.

Many people blame school violence on the availability of guns, leading them to crusade passionately against firearms. There's no doubt that adolescence and guns make a volatile cocktail, but that will not explain what is occurring today. Rabbi Daniel Lapin, president of Toward Tradition, said there was a time when boys in most American schools brought guns with them to their classrooms. They left them in the cloakrooms until the afternoon, when they retrieved them to go hunting. The firearms were not a problem.[35] Now there is violence in almost every school, not because the guns have changed but because the boys have changed. And why have they changed? Because popular culture has taught them that violence is manly. Wasn't Sylvester Stallone violent in *Rambo?* Wasn't Bruce Willis violent in *Die Hard?* Wasn't Arnold Schwartzenegger violent in *Commando?* Aren't our boys learning from these role models to get even or to kill those who get in their way?

Protecting the family from this culture of violence is very difficult for parents. It's like trying to hold back the falling rain. Nevertheless, we *must* shield our kids from it as much as possible, especially when they are young. Four prestigious national organizations have linked violence in television, music, video games, and movies to increasing violence among children. They are the American Medical Association, the American Academy of Pediatrics, the American Psychological Association, and the American Academy of Child and Adolescent Psychiatry. Their joint statement reads, in part, "[The] effects [of violence] are measurable and long lasting. Moreover, prolonged viewing of media violence can lead to emotional desensitization toward violence in real life."[36]

An even stronger statement was issued singly by the American Academy of Pediatrics. It was reported by Steve Rubenstein of *The San Francisco Chronicle,* who wrote, "Turn off the TV, moms and dads, the health of your little tyke is at stake. Children younger than 2 should not watch TV because it can interfere with 'healthy brain growth,' according to a new policy issued this week by the American Academy of Pediatrics. 'Pediatricians should urge parents to avoid television viewing for children younger than 2. Research on early brain development shows that babies and toddlers have a critical need for direct interactions with [people] for healthy brain growth,' the policy stated."

The report continued, "In previous issues of the association's medical journal, *Pediatrics,* doctors have warned that TV viewing by children can lead to violent behavior, obesity, apathy, lower metabolism, decreased imagination, constipation, and even death—in the event that the TV should topple over and fall on the child. But this is the first time the association has called for an outright ban. The study also said that the average child is subjected to 14,000 sexual references on TV a year and is exposed to $2 billion worth of alcohol ads in other media annually."[37]

Common sense told us decades ago that regular viewing of graphic images of blood and gore were harmful to kids, but only recently has there been enough credible scientific evidence to prove it. Now the authorities on child development are in agreement. The entertainment industry has put our kids at risk. The response from Hollywood, unfortunately, has been little more than a yawn. We'll talk more about sex and violence in the media in a subsequent chapter.

Let me offer some advice now to mothers and fathers of wounded spirits about what you can do to prevent them. As I said earlier, I have been urging parents and teachers for the past thirty years to intervene on behalf of hurting children. One of your most important assignments as a parent is to preserve the mental and physical health of your kids. You wouldn't think of letting someone injure them physically if you could prevent it. Why, then, would you stand by and watch the spirit of your boy or girl being warped and twisted? The damage to the self-concept that occurs during adolescence can haunt an individual for the rest of his life.

As a teacher, I made it clear to my students that I wouldn't put up with teasing. If anyone insisted on ridiculing another of my students, he was going to have to deal with me. I wish every adult would do the same. When a strong, loving teacher comes to the aid of the least-respected child in the class, something dramatic occurs in the emotional climate of the room. Every child seems to utter an audible sigh of relief. The same thought bounces around in many little heads: *If that kid is safe from ridicule, then I must be safe too.* By defending the least-popular child in the classroom, the teacher is demonstrating that she respects everyone and that she will fight for anyone who is being treated unfairly.

Children love justice and they're very uneasy in a world of injustice and abuse. Therefore, when we teach children kindness and respect for others by insisting on civility in our classrooms and in our homes, we're laying a foundation for human kindness in the world of adulthood to come. Sadly, the opposite philosophy is evident in many schools today. It needs to change. Don't tell me that we as adults can't put a stop to bullying. Of course we can. We know who the defenseless kids are. We can rescue them. We just need the determination to intervene when a child shows signs of distress. It is our profound obligation to get this job done.

Here's the tricky part. While you are working behind the scenes to protect your child from abuse, you must not make him feel victimized beyond the immediate circumstance. It is very easy to give a boy the idea that the world is out to get him. That overarching sense of victimization is terribly destructive. It paralyzes a person and makes him throw up his hands in despair. Once he yields to the insidious notion that he can't win—that he is set up for failure—he becomes demoralized. The will to overcome adversity is weakened. Talk to your boys not about the wider world that is stacked against them, but teach them how to deal with the isolated situation that has arisen. I hope this is clear. You must never make your child think you believe he is destined for failure and rejection. He will believe you!

We must also identify the children and teenagers who appear to be experiencing self-hatred or are harboring deep resentment and anger. The symptoms to look for include overreactions to minor frustration, fear of new social situations, experimentation with drugs or alcohol, difficulty sleeping or eating, extreme isolation and withdrawal, chewing the fingernails, inability to make friends, disinterest in school activities, and the bullying of others. Watch also for signs of threatened suicide. Be especially vigilant when a child who has mentioned killing himself suddenly seems carefree and happy. That sometimes means he has decided to go through with the death wish and is no longer struggling with what has been bothering him. In each of these cases, I urge you to obtain professional help for those kids. Do not console yourself with the notion that "he'll grow out of it." That youngster may be in desperate need of assistance. Don't miss the opportunity to provide it.

The above comments relate to teens; let me focus now on children. It used to be believed that most kids were basically happy and carefree. That is changing. According to psychologist and author Dr. Archibald Hart, we are now seeing more signs of serious depression in children, even as young as five years old.[38] If a five-to-ten-year-old is depressed, he may show signs of lethargy: he may not want to get out of bed in the morning; he may mope around the house; he may show no interest in things that would normally excite him. Sleep disturbances and stomach complaints are also warning signs. Another symptom can be open anger, hostility, and rage. He may lash out suddenly or unexpectedly at people or things around him. If you suspect that your child is depressed, you should help him put his feelings of sadness or frustration into words. Make yourself available to listen without judging or belittling the feelings expressed. Simply being heard can go a long way toward lifting a child's depressed mood. Most important, you need to look for the root cause that is behind the distress. What is happening in your child's school may hold the answer.

Finally, I'll turn to columnist Kathleen Parker to provide the concluding advice about how to raise healthy boys in our shock-wave world. She said it can by accomplished "by being reasonable, smart and fully awake: Reduce boys' exposure to violence, be there when they return from school, help them with homework, ask them about their day, let them cry if need be, support them when they're down, help them to see options, teach them to handle guns safely if you have them, reward good behavior, provide meaningful consequences for unacceptable behavior, make reasonable demands, express moral expectations, talk to their teachers, [and] hug those boys every chance you get. Don't ask them to be men when they're just little boys, but show them how to be real men by demonstrating the thing we as a society seem to have lost: self-control. It's the greatest gift, and it isn't even rocket science. It's just good parenting."[39]

QUESTIONS AND ANSWERS

Can you give me some more specific advice about how to tell if my son is at risk for suicide?

The Family Research Council provided the following checklist that may be helpful to you. Ask yourself these questions:

- Has your son's personality changed dramatically?
- Is he having trouble with a girlfriend? Or is he having trouble getting along with other friends or with parents? Has he withdrawn from people he used to feel close to?
- Is the quality of his schoolwork going down? Has he failed to live up to his own or someone else's standards when it comes to school grades, for example?
- Does he always seem bored, and is he having trouble concentrating?
- Is he acting like a rebel in an unexplained and severe way?
- Is he having trouble coping with a major life change, such as a move or the separation with a parent?
- Has he run away from home?
- Is your teenager abusing drugs and/or alcohol?
- Is he complaining about headaches, stomachaches, and other symptoms that may or may not be real?
- Have his eating or sleeping habits changed?
- Has his appearance changed for the worse?

- Is he giving away some of his most prized possessions?
- Is he writing notes or poems about death?
- Does he talk even jokingly about suicide? Has he said things such as, "That's the last straw," "I can't take it anymore," or "Nobody cares about me"? (Threatening to kill oneself precedes four out of five suicidal deaths.)
- Has he tried to commit suicide before?[40]

If you are seeing a pattern of these characteristics in your son, I urge you to seek professional help for him immediately. Many suicides come as a complete shock to bewildered parents. You are wise to remain vigilant for the signs and symptoms that might otherwise escape notice. Having a strong and involved family is *the* most effective preventative, not just for potential suicide but also for most other antisocial behaviors. Unfortunately, this kind of family is what millions of kids do not have.

My son has recently begun running around with some tough kids who have introduced him to marijuana. He doesn't deny what he is doing because he says it is harmless. Can you give me the facts?

Your son has been given some very bad information that is being passed around by those who are promoting the legalization of marijuana. It is a lie. Dr. Harold Voth, the senior psychiatrist for the Menninger Foundation in Topeka, Kansas, has set the record straight.

He said, first, that five marijuana cigarettes have the same cancer-causing capacity as one hundred and twelve conventional cigarettes. Second, the part of the brain that allows a person to focus, concentrate, create, learn, and conceptualize at an advanced level is still growing during the teenage years. Continuous use of marijuana over a period of time will retard the normal growth of those brain cells. Third, a study conducted at Columbia University revealed that female marijuana smokers suffer a sharp increase in damage to DNA, the genetic code. It was also found that reproductive eggs are especially vulnerable to damage by marijuana. Fourth, a second Columbia University study found that people who smoked a single marijuana cigarette every other day for one year had a white blood cell count that was 39 percent lower than normal, thus damaging the immune system and making the user far more susceptible to infection and sickness.[41] Smoking marijuana is a dangerous hobby.

I doubt if your son will be satisfied with this answer, even though you should share it with him. His motivation is probably related more to peer pressure than to his belief in the harmlessness of marijuana. The danger is that he will "graduate" from pot to something harder and more addictive. If I were you, I would bring all my energies to bear on getting my son away from the gang he is now running with, even if it required us to move. He is apparently at a critical juncture in his life.

The Essential Father

CHAPTER 5

WE HAVE SEEN that boys are in serious trouble today and that many of them are experiencing emotional pressure that contributes to violence, drug abuse, early sexual activity, and other forms of rebellious behavior. Even some teens who play by the rules and seem to be doing fine are struggling quietly with problems of identity and meaning. On behalf of them, and for the little boys who have not yet encountered these difficulties, we need to examine the specific forces that have created such an unhealthy environment for kids and, more important, what to do about them.

Chief among the threats to this generation of boys is the breakdown of the family. Every other difficulty we will consider has been caused by or is related to that fundamental tragedy. It can hardly be overstated. We have been emphasizing for years that stable, lifelong marriages provide the foundation for social order. Everything of value rests on those underpinnings. Historically, when the family begins to unravel in a given culture, everything from the effectiveness of government to the general welfare of the people is adversely impacted. This is precisely what is happening to us today. The family is being buffeted and undermined by the forces operating around it. Alcoholism, pornography, gambling, infidelity, and other virulent infections have seeped into its bloodstream. "No-fault divorce" is still the law of the land in most states, resulting in thousands of unnecessary family breakups. Clearly, there is trouble on the home front. And as we all know, it is the children who are suffering most from it. In cultures where divorce becomes commonplace or large numbers of men and women choose to live together or copulate without bothering to marry, untold millions of kids are caught in the chaos.

If I may be permitted to offer what will sound like a hyperbole, I believe the future of Western civilization depends on how we handle this present crisis. Why? Because we as parents are raising the next generation of men who will either lead with honor and integrity or abandon every good thing they have inherited. They are the bridges to the future. Nations that are populated largely by immature, immoral, weak-willed, cowardly, and self-indulgent men cannot and will not long endure. These types of men include those who sire and abandon their children; who cheat on their wives; who lie, steal, and covet; who hate their countrymen; and who serve no god but money. That is the direction culture is taking today's boys. We must make the necessary investment to counter these influences and to build within our boys lasting qualities of character, self-discipline, respect for authority, commitment to the truth, a belief in the work ethic, and an unshakable love for Jesus Christ. The pursuit of those objectives led me to undertake the writing of this book.

The devastating impact of family disintegration on children is indisputable. A special U.S. commission consisting of authorities on child development was convened in the 1990s to examine the general health of adolescents. This report, called *Code Blue,* concluded: "Never before has one generation of American teenagers been less healthy, less cared for, or less prepared for life."[1] Most of the characteristics the commission decried are even worse today. This is occurring, mind you, in one of the most affluent and privileged nations in the history of the world. It is a direct result of marital disintegration and related forces at work against the family.

I know I've thrown too many statistics at you this far, but the ones I will share now should be put in neon lights: Seventy percent of black babies and 19 percent of white babies in the United States are born out of wedlock. Most will never know their fathers or experience what it means to be loved by them. Only 34 percent of all children born in America will live with both biological parents through age eighteen. This is a recipe for trouble, especially when we consider the fact that 62 percent of mothers with children under three are employed. The number was half that in 1975! Fully 72 percent of mothers with children under eighteen currently hold jobs.[2] This busyness of mothers combined with the noninvolvement of fathers means that too often, there is *nobody home!* No wonder boys are in such a mess today!

Behavioral scientists have only recently begun to understand how critical fathers are to the healthy development of both boys and girls. According to psychiatrist Kyle Pruett, the author of *Fatherneed*, dads are as important to children as moms, but in a very different way. Here are other surprising findings that have emerged from careful research on the role of fathers:

- There is an undeniable linkage between fathers and babies beginning at birth.
- Infants as young as six weeks old can differentiate between a mother's and a father's voice.
- By eight weeks, babies can distinguish between their mother's and their father's caretaking methods.
- Infants are born with a drive to find and connect to their fathers. As they begin to speak, their word for "father" often precedes their word for "mother." The reasons for this are unknown.
- Toddlers are especially obvious in their assertions of fatherneed: they will seek out their father, ask for him when he's not present, be fascinated when he talks to them on the phone, and investigate every part of his body if allowed.
- "Teenagers express fatherneed in yet more complex ways, competing with their father and confronting his values, beliefs, and, of course, limits. For so many sons and daughters, it is only at the death of the father that they discover the intensity and longevity of their fatherneed, especially when it has gone begging."[3]

While children of all ages—both male and female—have an innate need for contact with their fathers, let me emphasize again that boys suffer most from the absence or noninvolvement of fathers. According to the National Center for Children in Poverty, boys without fathers are twice as likely to drop out of school, twice as likely to go to jail, and nearly four times as likely to need treatment for emotional and behavioral problems as boys with fathers.[4]

Repeatedly during my review of the latest research for this book, I came face-to-face with the same disturbing issue. Boys are in trouble today primarily because their parents, and especially their dads, are distracted, overworked, harassed, exhausted, disinterested, chemically dependent, divorced, or simply unable to cope. As indicated above, all other problems plaguing young males flow from (or are related to) these facts of life in the twenty-first century. Chief among our concerns is the absence of masculine role modeling and mentoring that dads should be providing. Mothers, who also tend to be living on the ragged edge, are left to do a job for which they have had little training or experience. Having never been boys, women often have only a vague notion of how to go about rearing one. Boys are the big losers when families splinter.

The National Center on Addiction and Substance Abuse at Columbia University found that children living in two-parent families who had only a fair or poor relationship with their fathers were at 68 percent higher risk of smoking, drinking, and drug usage than teens having a good or excellent relationship with dads. By comparison, children growing up in a home headed by a single mother who had an excellent relationship with their mothers had a 62 percent lower risk of abusing substances than children living in a two-parent family with a fair or poor relationship with their father.[5] The influence of a good father can hardly be overemphasized.

Dr. William Pollock, Harvard psychologist and author of *Real Boys,* concludes that divorce is difficult for children of both sexes but it is devastating for males. He says the basic problem is the lack of discipline and supervision in the father's absence and his unavailability to teach what it means to be a man. Pollock also believes fathers are crucial in helping boys to manage their emotions. As we have seen, without the guidance and direction of a father, a boy's frustration often leads to varieties of violence and other antisocial behavior.[6]

Numerous researchers agree that losing a dad (or never having had one) is catastrophic for males. Thirty years ago it was believed that poverty and discrimination were primarily responsible for juvenile crime and other behavioral problems. Now we know that family disruption is the real culprit. Despite all the red flags that warn us of the dangers, cavalier attitudes abound with regard to premarital pregnancy, divorce, infidelity, and cohabitation.

Don Elium, author of *Raising a Son,* says that with troubled boys, the common theme is distant, uninvolved fathers and, in turn, mothers who have taken on more responsibility to fill the gap.[7]

Sociologist Peter Karl believes that because boys spend up to 80 percent of their time with women, they don't know how to act as men when they grow up. When that happens, the relationship between the sexes is directly affected. Men become helpless and more and more like big kids.[8]

These statistics and trends can't be appreciated fully until we see how they are translated into the lives of individuals. I was talking recently to such a person—a fifty-eight-year-old man who described the unhappy memory of his father. His dad had been a minister who was consumed by work and other interests. This father never came to sporting events or any other activities in which his son was a participant. He neither disciplined nor affirmed him. By the time the boy was a senior in high school, he was the starting guard on a winning big-school football team. When his team qualified for the state championship, this boy was desperate to have his dad see him play. He begged, "Would you please be there on Friday night? It is very important to me." The father promised to come.

On the night of the big game, the boy was on the field warming up when he happened to see his father enter the stadium with two other men wearing business suits. They stood talking among themselves for a moment or two and then left. The man who told me this story had tears streaming down his cheeks as he relived that difficult moment of so long ago. It had been forty years since that night, and yet the rejection and disappointment he felt as a teenager were as vivid as ever. A year after our conversation, this man's father died at eighty-three years of age. My friend stood alone before his dad's casket at the funeral home and said sorrowfully, "Dad, we could have shared so much love together—but I never really knew you."

Going back to the night of the football game, I wonder what that father considered more important than being there for his son. Was his "to do" list really more urgent than meeting the needs of the boy who bore his name? For whatever reasons, that man allowed the years to slide by without fulfilling his responsibilities at home. Although he is gone, his legacy is like that of countless fathers who were too busy, too selfish, and too distracted to care for the little boys who reached for them. Now their record is in the books. If only they could go back and do it differently. If only . . . ! If only . . . !

A father holds awesome power in the lives of his children, for good or ill. Families have understood that fact for centuries. It has been said, "No man stands so tall as when he stoops to help a boy." Another wise observer said, "Tie a boy to the right man and he almost never goes wrong." They are both right. When asked who their heroes are, the majority of boys who are fortunate enough to have a father will say, "It's my dad." On the other hand, when a father is uninvolved—when he doesn't love or care for his kids—it creates an ache, a longing, that will linger for decades. Again, without minimizing how much girls need their fathers, which we also acknowledge, boys are constructed emotionally to be dependent on dads in ways that were not understood until recently.

We now know that there are two critical periods during childhood when boys are particularly vulnerable. The most obvious occurs at the onset of puberty, when members of both sexes experience an emotional and hormonal upheaval. Boys and girls at that time desperately need their father's supervision, guidance, and love. Divorce at that time, more than at others, is typically devastating to boys. But according to Dr. Carol

Gilligan, professor at Harvard University, there is another critical period earlier in life—one not shared by girls. Very young boys bask in their mother's femininity and womanliness during infancy and toddlerhood. Fathers are important then, but mothers are primary. At about three to five years of age, however, a lad gradually pulls away from his mom and sisters in an effort to formulate a masculine identity.[9] It is a process known as "disconnection and differentiation," when, as Don Elium writes, "the inner urge of the male plan of development nudges him out of the nest of the mother over a precarious bridge to the world of the father."[10] It is typical for boys during those years, and even earlier, to crave the attention and involvement of their dad and to try to emulate his behavior and mannerisms.

I remember my son clearly identifying with my masculinity when he was in that period between kindergarten and first grade. For example, as our family prepared to leave in the car, Ryan would say, "Hey, Dad. Us guys will get in the front seat and the girls will sit in the back." He wanted it known that he was a "guy" just like me. I was keenly aware that he was patterning his behavior and masculinity after mine. That's the way the system is supposed to work.

But here's the rub: When fathers are absent at that time, or if they are inaccessible, distant, or abusive, their boys have only a vague notion of what it means to be male. Whereas girls have a readily available model after which to pattern feminine behavior and attitudes (except when they are raised by single fathers), boys living with single mothers are left to formulate their masculine identity out of thin air. This is why early divorce is also devastating for boys. Writer Angela Phillips believes, and I agree, that the high incidence of homosexuality occurring in Western nations is related, at least in part, to the absence of positive male influence when boys are moving through the first crisis of child development.[11] One of the primary objectives of parents is to help boys identify their gender assignments and understand what it means to be a man. We must return to that point when I talk in a later chapter about the antecedents of homosexuality.

I was blessed to have a wonderful father who was accessible to me from the earliest years of childhood. I'm told that when I was two years of age, my family lived in a one-bedroom apartment, and my little bed was located beside that of my parents. My father said later that it was very common during that time for him to awaken at night to a little voice that was whispering, "Daddy? Daddy?" My father would answer quietly, "What, Jimmy?" And I would say, "Hold my hand!" Dad would reach across the darkness and grope for my little hand, finally just engulfing it in his own. He said the instant he had my hand firmly in his grip, my arm would become limp and my breathing deep and regular. I'd immediately gone back to sleep. You see, I only wanted to know that he was there!

I have a catalog of warm memories of my dad from the preschool years. One day when I was nearly three, I was at home with my mother and heard a knock on the front door.

"Go see who it is," she said with a little smile on her face.

I opened the door and there stood my dad. He took my hand and said, "Come with me. I want to show you something." He led me to the side of the house, where he had hidden a big blue tricycle. It was one of the wonderful moments of my life. On another day during that same year, I recall trotting beside my big dad (he was six foot four) and feeling very proud to be with him. I even recall how huge his hand felt as it held mine.

I also remember the delightful times I roughhoused with my father. Many moms fail to understand why that kind of foolishness is important, but it is. Just as wolf cubs and leopard kittens romp and fight with each other, boys of all ages love to rumble. When I was five years old, my dad and I used to horrify my mother by having all-out kick fights. That's right! *Kick fights!* He weighed 180 pounds and I tipped the scales at about 50, but we went at each other like sumo wrestlers. He would entice me to kick his shins and then, inevitably, he would block my thrust with the bottom of his foot. That made me go after him again with a vengeance. Then dad would tap me on the shin with his toe. Believe it or not, this was wonderful fun for me. We would end up laughing hysterically, despite the bumps and bruises on my legs. My mother would demand that we stop, having no clue about why I loved this game. It was just a guy thing.

Child-protection officers today would throw the book at a man who had kick fights with his kids. Some might say that this "violence" at home could lead to criminal behavior. Likewise, many have concluded that corporal punishment, even when administered in a loving environment, teaches kids to hurt others. They are wrong. It isn't roughhousing or measured discipline that predisposes boys to misbehavior. It is often the absence of a father who can teach them how to be men and correct them authoritatively when they are wrong.

Let me illustrate this principle with a recent finding from the world of nature. Other than dogs, which I have always loved, the animals that fascinate me most are elephants. These magnificent creatures are highly emotional and surprisingly intelligent. I suppose that's why it is disturbing to see them suffering the encroachment of civilization.

That is happening in the Pilanesberg National Park in northwestern South Africa. Rangers there have reported that young bull elephants in that region have become increasingly violent in recent years—especially to nearby white rhinos. Without provocation, an elephant will knock a rhinoceros over and then kneel and gore it to death. This is not typical elephant behavior and it's been very difficult to explain.

But now game wardens think they've cracked the code. Apparently, the aggressiveness is a by-product of government programs to reduce elephant populations by killing the older animals. Almost all of the young rogues were orphaned when they were calves, depriving them of adult contact. Under normal circumstances, dominant older males keep the young bulls in line and serve as role models for them. In the absence of that influence, "juvenile delinquents" grow up to terrorize their neighbors.[12]

I know it's risky to apply animal behavior too liberally to human beings, but the parallel here is too striking to miss. Let me say it one more time: The absence of early supervision and discipline is often catastrophic—for teenagers *and* for elephants.

Prisons are populated primarily by men who were abandoned or rejected by their fathers. Motivational speaker and writer Zig Ziglar quotes his friend Bill Glass, a dedicated evangelist who counseled almost every weekend for twenty-five years with men who were incarcerated, as saying that among the thousands of prisoners he had met, not one of them genuinely loved his dad. Ninety-five percent of those on death row hated their fathers.[13] In 1998, there were 1,202,107 people in federal or state prisons. Of that number 94 percent were males. Of the 3,452 prisoners awaiting execution, only forty-eight were women. That amounts to 98.6 percent males.[14] Clearly, as Barbara Jackson said, "it is far easier to build strong children than to repair broken men."[15]

Some years ago, executives of a greeting-card company decided to do something special for Mother's Day. They set up a table in a federal prison, inviting any inmate who so desired to send a free card to his mom. The lines were so long, they had to make another trip to the factory to get more cards. Due to the success of the event, they decided to do the same thing on Father's Day, but this time no one came. Not one prisoner felt the need to send a card to his dad. Many had no idea who their fathers even were.[16] What a sobering illustration of a dad's importance to his children.

Contrast that story with a conversation I once had with a man named Bill Houghton, who was president of a large construction firm. Through the years, he had hired and managed thousands of employees. I asked him: "When you are thinking of hiring an employee—especially a man—what do you look for?" His answer surprised me. He said, "I look primarily at the relationship between the man and his father. If he felt loved by his dad and respected his authority, he's likely to be a good employee." Then he added, "I won't hire a young man who has been in rebellion against his dad. He will have difficulty with me, too." I have also observed that the relationship between a boy and his father sets the tone for so much of what is to come. He is *that* important at home.

As I have been writing the words of this chapter, my thoughts have turned repeatedly to the single mothers who are rearing boys on their own. I'm sure that the findings I've reported about fathers and about divorce have been deeply disturbing to some. Forgive me for that. Your circumstances are tough enough without my making them more difficult. The overriding question for you is, "How can I compensate for the absence of a father who should be there to teach my boys the essence of manhood?" That is not an easy question, but there are answers for it.

Despite everything I've shared, there is hope for women who are raising boys alone. Admittedly the task is terribly difficult, but millions of mothers have done it admirably, overcoming serious limitations and obstacles. We will talk more about those concerns in future chapters, but for now, let me simply say that family life is almost never ideal. That is why each of us has to cope with unique challenges and problems. Some parents are confronted every day with sickness, some with poverty, some with an alcoholic spouse, and some with a disabled child or parent. In those situations and many more, families must evaluate their circumstances and decide how to make the most of them. I urge those of you who are single parents to take this considered approach to your family. God loves your children even more than you do, and He will help you raise them. There are also ways to substitute for an absent father, and I have offered some of those ideas and suggestions in chapter 16. I hope you will find them helpful.

Before moving on, I want to share a letter sent to me a few years ago from a mother who had lost her husband. I am enclosing it for the benefit of the fathers who are reading along with us. It illustrates the vital role men play in the lives of their children and why it is important to contribute what you can to your children while you have the opportunity. Here is the letter that came from Mrs. Karen Cotting:

Dear Dr. Dobson:

Since listening to your broadcast you always encouraged your listeners to write in. Our family never has until now. We have a story to tell.

My husband, Cliff, had been a pilot with a major airline for the last eleven years. On a four-day trip last October, and with some time on his hands before the third day began, he decided to go jogging. Unfortunately for us, that would be his last run. While jogging, he had a fatal heart attack. He was a young 38 and in the best of health. He always ate well and was always exercising. There were no warning signs. So when I received the call from the Vice President of Operations at the airlines, I was in utter shock. Our family was so unprepared for this. My husband was in the prime of his life. Our three daughters were all under six. How could God do this to our family? How could He take away my best friend and the head of our household? In the months that followed his death and every day I breathe, God is revealing some of the answers as I trust His faithfulness.

Cliff was a very loving and caring person. He adored his family. Our three daughters, Nicole, Anna and Sarah, and I were the apples of his eye. We hated to see him go to work as we'd be without him from anywhere from two to four days. But we anticipated his return and he was always greeted with elated screams of joy from the girls (and even an howl or two from our German Shepherd, Tess). Of all the memories I can think of, the one that stands out the most is his playfulness with our girls. He'd always end with exhaustion and a playful question, "What's the most important thing in the world?" And the girls would shout out, "Knowing God." Cliff would be satisfied in his daughters' knowing that a personal relationship with Christ was the foundation for their eternity.

God has revealed some things to me that I never knew about my husband. At his funeral, we allowed time for anyone who wanted to share his or her memories of Cliff. I was amazed at the number of airline staff that filled the church. Just about everyone shared how great a friend he was, how he could always be counted on to lend a helping hand. But I learned he often spoke when he was at work of me and the children and of his love for God. I never knew Cliff to be this bold in sharing his faith with others. I always assumed he talked of office policies or golf while on the job.

Almost seven months have passed since he went home to be with our Lord, and I finally got the nerve to look in his flight bag. On it was the date, October 9, 1999, the day he went jogging for the last time. I cried thinking about how serious he took his responsibility as a pilot, how prepared he always was, from getting shirts ironed the night before an early "show" to knowing his schedule for each day. He was prepared and ready to work on October 9th. But most importantly, I heard God whisper to me through my tears, "He was prepared to meet Me."

That thought comforted my family. The spirit and flesh battle within me every day. I miss him terribly as I work through the tears of sadness in his absence. He was my backbone in many ways. Yet my spirit is comforted with the truth that Cliff is in the presence of our holy Father and he walks with Christ today. Cliff was prepared for the most glorious day he'd ever experience.

I am learning that through what can seem like a devastating experience, we are to lean on God for strength even when we don't think we "feel" His presence. The Bible has comforted our family with Psalm 27:5: "For in the day of trouble he will keep me safe in his dwelling; he will hide me in the shelter of his tabernacle and set me high upon a rock." Even with Cliff absent from us, God showed me He would never abandon our family as in Jeremiah 29:11-14: "'For I know the plans I have for you,' declares the Lord, 'plans to give you hope and a future. Then you will call upon me and come and pray to me, and I will listen to you. You will seek me and find me when you seek me with all your heart. I will be found by you,' declares the Lord."

As God reveals many wonderful things about His character and how much He loves our family, we want to encourage your listeners who may not know Christ in a personal way. He will "never leave you, nor forsake you." We all have eternal life. It's a matter of where we choose to spend it and if we are prepared to meet our Maker. Do not hesitate.

Our family has always received much encouragement from your broadcast and your monthly magazine. God bless you, your staff, and families.

Sincerely,
Karen S. Cotting[17]

I have shared this letter primarily for the benefit of the young fathers among my readers. If you are among them, let me remind you that only God knows how long you will be on this earth. Life can be unexpectedly short. Do not squander today's opportunities to relate to your children or to teach them about your faith. Don't let your career absorb your every resource and make you a virtual stranger at home. May the memories you leave behind, whether you live an hour longer or many more decades, be as warm and loving as those created by Cliff Cotting. His record is in the books; yours is yet to be written.

QUESTIONS AND ANSWERS

I know that divorce is tough on kids when it happens. But what are the long-term implications of a family breakup? Don't children quickly "get over" it?

I wish I could say that children quickly bounce back after their parents separate, but research tells us otherwise. It is indisputable now that emotional development in children is directly related to the presence of warm, nurturing, sustained, and continuous interaction with both parents. Anything that interferes with the vital relationship with either parent can have lasting consequences for the child. For example, one landmark study revealed that 90 percent of children from divorced homes suffered from an acute sense of shock when the separation occurred, including profound grieving and irrational fears. Fifty percent reported feeling rejected and abandoned. And indeed, half the fathers never came to see their children three years after the divorce. One-third of the boys and girls feared abandonment by the remaining parent, and 66 percent experienced yearning for the absent parent, with an intensity that researchers described as "overwhelming." Most significant, 37 percent of the children were even more unhappy and dissatisfied five years after the divorce than they had been at eighteen months.[18] In other words, time did not heal their wounds.

The above statistics came from the research findings of Dr. Judith Wallerstein, the foremost authority on the subject of children of divorce. She began studying boys and girls twenty-five years ago and has followed them to this time. Her recent book revealed that 40 percent of her subjects never married, compared with 16 percent of children from intact families.[19] Children of divorce, she found, had less chance at college, were more likely to use drugs and alcohol before age fourteen, and displayed less social competence. Girls whose parents divorced had earlier sexual experiences. Clearly, the impact of family breakups is a lifelong affair.

There is one more factor that will be of interest. Recent studies have shown that divorce is related to promiscuous behavior during adolescence. Researchers from the Oregon Social Learning Center tracked the behavior of two hundred junior high and high school boys who lived in higher-crime areas. They found that the boys who had sexual intercourse at an early age tended to be those who had experienced two or more parental transitions—divorce, remarriage, repartnering, and so on. Only 18 percent of those promiscuous boys came from intact families. By contrast, 57 percent of the virgins came from homes where divorce had not occurred.[20] A similar study found that a strong correlation existed between young women who bore babies out of wedlock and those who had been through a change in family structure when growing up.[21] It was concluded that the stresses of divorce and remarriage on children directly impacted out-of-wedlock childbearing.

Again, we are seeing now that divorce, single parenting, and family disruption are terribly hard on children. This is not to criticize those who find themselves in these difficult circumstances, but neither can we deny that intact, two-parent families are the most healthy for kids and that they contribute directly to a stable society.

Anyone who knows anything about boys can see that they need warm and loving relationships with their dads. But why make that case again? Surely everyone knows and accepts that fact by now.

How I wish! Unfortunately, some learned university professors and psychologists are attempting to discredit the belief that fathers are essential to boys and girls. Karla Mantilla, a radical feminist author, said this, "I am highly suspicious of the upsurge of praises of fatherhood and the necessity of kids to have a male role model. I come by this suspicion after much experience with my own two kids and their male role model, their father." She continued, "The propaganda that children, especially boys, need fathers I think, has contributed incalculably to the misery of children all over the world. Contrary to all the pro-father rhetoric of late, to the extent that we value fathers precisely for their 'discipline' and 'toughening up' qualities, we create children (especially boys) who are less empathic and caring. If we want kinder, gentler (and less violent) adults, we need to focus on kinder, gentler parenting."[22]

Two academics, Carl Auerbach and Louise Silverstein, both from Yeshiva University, published a terrible article in 1999 in the scholarly journal *American Psychologist*. It was a blatant piece of feminist/gay/lesbian propaganda entitled "Deconstructing the Essential Father." In it the authors claimed that divorce does not irretrievably harm the majority of children and, in fact, a child who has never known his dad would not be the worse for it. If anything, they contended, fathers are actually detrimental at home because of the amount of family resources they consume. "Who needs 'em?" was the message. Women could do the job of raising boys more effectively without the involvement of their husbands (or "partners"). For that matter, mothers were not considered essential either. Nonbiological caregivers would do the job even better! In other words, traditional families are not only unnecessary to children, but kids are healthier without them.[23]

This article was passed off as credible scientific research in a prestigious journal published by the American Psychological Association. This, mind you, despite the acknowledgment by the authors that "our reading of the scientific literature supports our political agenda. We are interested in encouraging public policy that supports the legitimacy of diverse family structures, rather than a policy that privileges the two-parent, heterosexual, married family."[24]

Parents should be very skeptical of what they read about family life in the press and even in scientific journals. If the findings of a particular study sound nonsensical to you, the chances are that they *are* nonsensical. There are influential professionals out there who despise the traditional family, and they are producing contrived evidence to weaken it. Just in recent years, we've seen reports of research in the media that claimed sexual abuse of children isn't all that harmful, that parents don't have much influence on their kids, that any effort to help homosexuals deal with their sexuality is damaging, that abortion results in a reduction of crime, that children must be exposed to specialized brain stimulation by age three or it is all over, and that 10 percent of all adults are homosexuals (this off-the-wall statistic and many others were "created" out of thin air by Alfred Kinsey). Such phony research has been used effectively by liberals to advance their agenda. Don't let your approach to child rearing be victimized by their manipulation. And don't let *anyone* tell you that boys do just as well without the influence of a man to guide their journey.

FATHERS AND SONS

CHAPTER 6

WHEN I WAS seventeen years old, the state of Texas granted me a license to drive. It was a bad decision. My dad had recently bought a brand-new Ford, and he let me take it out for a spin during lunchtime one day. That was another big mistake. Hundreds of my fellow students were milling around my school as I drove by, which gave me a great opportunity to show off. I also wanted to test a theory that had intrigued me. In our little town, there were huge dips on both sides of certain intersections to handle the flash floods that occasionally swept down our streets. I reasoned that if I hit the bumps at high speed, my car would sail over them. I was a big fan of Joey Chitwood, who was the Evel Knievel of that day, and I had seen him catapult his car over obstacles at the state fair. If Joey could do it, . . . why not me?

Obviously, there was much that I didn't understand about the physics of three thousand pounds of steel hurtling down the road. I approached the intersection helter-skelter and careened into the first dip. There was a violent reaction. *Kaboom!* went the bottom of the car! Then I blasted into the second canyon. *Kabang!* My head hit the headliner and the car convulsed up and down like a gigantic yo-yo. My entire life passed in front of my eyes. But my Texas friends were awestruck. They said, "Wow! Look at tha-yet. He got ar under his tars."

A few weeks later, my good ol' dad came to me and said, "Uh, Bo," (that's what he called me) "I just took the car to the mechanic, and he said

67

all four shocks have blown out. It's the craziest thing. Shocks usually wear out little by little, but the car is new and they're already shredded. Do you have any idea how this could have happened?"

The only thing that saved me was a momentary lapse of memory. At that second, I honestly didn't recall that I had hit the bumps, so I said no! He accepted my denial and I escaped with my life. A few weeks later, I was driving near our home when the steering column broke, sending the Ford into the curb. Fortunately, no one was killed. It was years later before I realized that I had blown the shocks and probably cracked the steering post during "the great physics experiment." Who knows what other damage I did to Dad's new car on that day.

By the time I admitted to myself that I was the guilty party, the statute of limitations had expired on my crime. My dad had forgotten about the episode and he never mentioned it again. Nor did I. My father went to his grave unaware of the stupid thing I had done. So Dad, if you're watching from up there, just know that I'm sorry and I won't ever do it again. I'll save my allowance for six years to pay for the damage. It was the only time I ever got "ar under my tars."

Boys have a way of frustrating and irritating the very souls of us dads. They leave our best tools out in the rain or they scramble them on the workbench. They lose our binoculars and they drop our cameras. Many of them are sassy, irresponsible, and hard to handle. Or they do things that make absolutely no sense to the rational mind, such as little Jeffrey hiding under the bed while his family ran through the neighborhood shouting his name. Of course, we fathers shouldn't complain. We were boys once who drove our own dads crazy too, so we should cut our sons some slack. Despite all the challenges associated with raising a rambunctious kid, one of the greatest privileges in living is to have one of them hug your neck and say, "I love you, Dad."

General Douglas MacArthur, one of my heroes, would agree with that sentiment. He was among the greatest military leaders of all time. He led the Allied armies to victory over the Imperial Japanese army in World War II and then commanded our United Nations forces in Korea. His surprise landing at Inchon was one of the most brilliant maneuvers in the history of warfare. These accomplishments on the battlefield explain why MacArthur is revered today, many decades after his death.

But there is another reason for my admiration of this man. It can be traced to a speech he gave in 1942, after he had been given an award for being a good father. This is what he said on that day: "Nothing has touched me more deeply than [this honor given to me] by the National Father's Day committee. By profession, I am a soldier and take great pride in that fact.

But I am prouder, infinitely prouder, to be a father. A soldier destroys in order to build. The father only builds, never destroys. The one has the potentialities of death, the other embodies creation and life. And while the hordes of death are mighty, the battalions of life are mightier still. It is my hope that my son, when I am gone, will remember me not from the battle, but in the home."[1] That is precisely the way I feel about my son and daughter.

Let's look a little more closely at what it means to be a father of boys. In the previous chapter, we discussed the importance of the father-son relationship and why the bond between them is essential to masculine development. Now I want to focus on the two primary ways a dad's influence is transmitted at home, beginning with modeling. If character training is a primary goal of parenting, and I believe it is, then the best way to instill it is through the demeanor and behavior of a father. Identification with him is a far more efficient teacher than lecturing, scolding, punishing, bribing, and cajoling. Boys watch their dads intently, noting every minor detail of behavior and values. It is probably true in your home, too. Your sons will imitate much of what you do. If you blow up regularly and insult your wife, your boys will treat their mother and other females disrespectfully. If you drink to excess, your kids will be at risk for chemical substance abuse. If you curse or smoke or fight with your coworkers, your boys will probably follow suit. If you are selfish or mean or angry, you'll see those characteristics displayed in the next generation.

Fortunately, the converse is also true. If you are honest, trustworthy, caring, loving, self-disciplined, and God-fearing, your boys will be influenced by those traits as they age. If you are deeply committed to Jesus Christ and live by biblical principles, your children will probably follow in your footsteps. So much depends on what they observe in you, for better or worse.

Someone said, "I'd rather see a sermon than hear one." There is truth to this statement. Children may not remember what you say, but they are usually impacted for life by what you do. Consider the task of teaching your boys to be honest, for example. Yes, you should teach what the Scripture says about truthfulness, but you should also look for opportunities to live according to that standard of righteousness. I'm reminded of something that happened several years ago in the state of Georgia, when the Bulldogs of Rockdale County High School overcame a big deficit to win the state basketball championship. Coach Cleveland Stroud couldn't have been more proud of his team. But then a few days later, while watching the game films of the playoffs, he noticed that there was an ineligible player on the court for forty-five seconds during one of the games. He called the Georgia High School Association and reported the violation, costing the school the title and the trophy. When asked about it at a press conference, Coach Stroud said, "Some people have said that we should have kept quiet about it. That it was just forty-five seconds, and that the player wasn't really an impact player. But you gotta do what's honest and right. I told my team that people forget the scores of basketball games. They don't ever forget what you're made out of."[2]

You can be certain that every member of the Bulldogs' team will remember the character of Coach Stroud. A letter to the editor of the local newspaper summed it up well. "We have scandals in Washington and cheating on Wall Street. Thank goodness we live in Rockdale County, where honor and integrity are alive and being practiced."[3]

Your boys and girls need to see you doing what is right, even when it is inconvenient to do so.

This raises a question about the other characteristics you are trying to model for your sons. Have you thought that through? Do you know exactly what you're trying to accomplish at home? If you're not sure who you are as a man or what you are trying to say with the "message of your life," your boys (and girls) will have no consistent example to follow. Such a plan should begin, I believe, with a personal commitment to Jesus Christ, who will guide your steps in the days ahead. Unless you know Him, your efforts to model righteousness will be inadequate and hollow.

Building upon that foundation, the goal is to become "a good family man." Dr. David Blankenhorn, head of the Institute for American Values, points out in his writings that this phrase almost has gone into obscurity.[4] It was once widely used in our culture to designate a true badge of honor. The rough translation would be "someone who puts his family first." Look at those three words that make up the phrase. *Good,* referring to widely accepted moral values; *family,* which points to purposes larger than the self; and *man,* which acknowledges a norm of masculinity. It seems that contemporary culture no longer celebrates a widely shared ideal of such a man who puts his family first. Where do we see responsible masculinity represented? Bill Cosby modeled it on TV for a few years, but who else has been portrayed in the media as a good family man? There just aren't many. No, we're more likely to hear about wayward athletes or womanizers or entrepreneurs who sacrificed all, including their wives and children, to make their start-up company a success. In the absence of good husbands and fathers, impressionable boys are often left to follow very flawed models.

Let's look more closely at what constitutes "a good family man" in today's world. To put that in perspective, it might be helpful to examine four traditional roles that men have played at home. The first is **to serve as the family provider.** No one disputed fifty years ago that it was a man's primary responsibility to be the "breadwinner." This is less clear today, which is unfortunate. Even though the majority of wives and mothers work outside the home, it is still a man's charge to assure that the financial needs of the family are met.

The second contribution a father has made historically is **to serve as the leader of the clan.** This role became highly controversial with the rise of the women's movement, but it was rarely challenged before the 1960s. It was often said in those days that "two captains sink the ship," and "two cooks spoil the broth." Dad was the final arbitrator on issues of substance. Admittedly, this "headship" role was sometimes abused by selfish men who treated their wives with disrespect and their children like chattel, but that was never the way the assignment was intended to function. Scripture, which seems to ordain this leadership responsibility for men, also spells out the limits of their authority. Husbands are told to love their wives as their own flesh, being willing to give their lives for them. They are also warned not to treat their children harshly or inconsiderately. That system generally worked well for thousands of years.

The third contribution made by a father is **to serve as protector.** He shielded his family members from the outside world and taught them how to cope with it successfully. He was the one family members came to when they felt anxious or threatened. If another man tried to abuse or insult his wife, Dad would defend her honor. It was his responsibility to see that the house was safe at night and that the children were home at a reasonable time. Each member of the family felt a little more secure because he was there.

Finally, the fourth contribution made by an effective dad was **to provide spiritual direction at home.** Although he often failed in this role, it was his obligation to read the Scriptures to his children and to teach them the fundamentals of their faith. He was the interpreter of the family's moral code and sacred rituals, and he made sure the children went to church every week. Admittedly, not many men in years past performed each of these four duties adequately. But there was a broad consensus in the culture that this was what they were *supposed* to do.

Okay, you can throw your rocks and bottles at me now. I'm sure some of my readers are bristling at even the implication that this is how men should function now. With all due respect, however, there is timeless wisdom in these traditional roles. Each of them is rooted in biblical teachings. Yep, it is old-fashioned stuff all right, but men have been defined by these responsibilities for millennia.

Unfortunately, each of these four roles has been ridiculed and attacked by postmodernists and their allies in the media. As a result, many fathers have a poor concept of what they are supposed to do or how to get it done. Some of them have surrendered their authority at home and are either altogether uninvolved or they are trying to nurture their children in ways that are more characteristic of mothers. They have been told they need to be more sensitive and to learn to express a full range of emotions—from rage to fear. In effect, men are being pressed to be more like women, and women are supposed to be more like men. This role reversal is terribly confusing to boys.

It is not inappropriate for a man to feel things deeply or to reveal his inner passions and thoughts. Nor must he present a frozen exterior to the world around him. But at the same time, there is a definite place in manhood for strength and confidence in the midst of a storm, and that role falls more naturally to men. As a huge oak tree provides shelter and protection for all the living things that nest in its branches, a strong man provides security and comfort for every member of his family. He knows who he is as a child of God and what is best for his wife and children. His sons need such a man to look up to and to emulate. They disrespect wimpy dads who are intimidated by their wives or whose emotions hang on their sleeves. Does that sound corny and contrary to everything you have heard? So be it. Men were designed to take care of the people they love, even if it involves personal sacrifice. When they fulfill that responsibility, their wives, sons, and daughters usually live in greater peace and harmony.

Good illustrations of traditional and biblical masculinity are hard to come by, but there is one example from my previous writings that I want to reprise. It describes my grandfather, who died a year before I was born. This account was included in my book *Straight Talk to Men,* but its relevance at this point warrants another look.

During the 1969 Christmas season, my father's two surviving brothers and his sister gathered in California for a family reunion. And on that happy occasion, they spent the better part of five days reminiscing about their childhood and early home life. One of the grandchildren recorded the discussions on cassette tapes, and I was privileged to obtain a complete set. What a rich heritage this provided, granting insight into my grandparents' home and the early experiences of my dad.

While all the conversations were of interest to me, there was a common thread that was especially significant throughout the week. It focused on the respect with which these four surviving siblings addressed the memories of their father (my grandfather). He died in 1935, a year before my birth, yet they spoke of him with unmistakable awe thirty-four years later. He still lived in their minds as a man of enormous character and strength. I asked them to explain the qualities that they admired so greatly but received little more than vague generalities.

"He was a tower of strength," said one.

"He had a certain dignity about him," said another, with appropriate gestures.

"We held him in awe," replied the third.

It is difficult to summarize the subtleties and complexities of the human personality, and they were unable to find the right words. Only when we began talking about specific remembrances did the personality of this patriarch become apparent. My dad provided the best evidence by writing his recollection of Grandfather Dobson's death, which I've reproduced below. Flowing throughout this narrative is the impact of a great man on his family, even three decades after his demise.

The Last Days of R. L. Dobson

The attack that took his life occurred when he was sixty-nine years of age and resulted ultimately in the breakup of the family circle. For many years after his death, I could not pass Tri-State Hospital without noting one particular window. It stood out from the rest, hallowed because it represented the room where he had suffered so much. The details of those tragic days and nights remain in my memory, unchanged by the passage of time.

We had been three days and three nights practically without sleep, listening to him struggle for breath, hearing the sounds of approaching death, smelling the smells of death. Dad lay in a deep coma. His heavy breathing could be heard up and down the corridor. We walked the halls of that old hospital for hours listening to the ceaseless struggle, which now was becoming fainter and fainter. Several times the nurse had called us in and we had said the last good-bye—had gone through the agony of giving him up—only to have his heart rally, and then the endless vigil would begin all over again. Finally, we had gone into an adjoining room not prepared for sleep, but some in the chairs and some across the beds, we had fallen into the sleep of utter exhaustion.

At five minutes to four o'clock the nurse came in and awakened one of my twin brothers. Robert roused with a start. "Is he gone?" he asked.

"No, but if you boys want to see your dad one more time while he is alive, you'd better come now."

The word quickly passed around and we filed into the room to stand around his bed for the last time. I remember that I stood at his left side: I smoothed back the hair from his forehead and laid my hand on his big old red hand, so very much like my own. I felt the fever that precedes death: 105 degrees. While I was standing there a change came over me. Instead of being a grown man (I was twenty-four at the time), I became a little boy again. They say this often happens to adults who witness the death of a parent. I thought I was in the Union Train Station in Shreveport, Louisiana, in the late afternoon, and I was watching for his return. The old Kansas City Southern passenger train was backing into the station and I saw it come 'round the curve. My heart swelled with pride. I turned to the little boy standing next to me and said, "You see that big man standing on the back of the train, one hand on the air brake and the other on the little whistle with which he signals the engineer? That big man is my dad!" He set the air brakes and I heard the wheels grind to a stop. I saw him step off that last coach. I ran and jumped into his arms. I gave him a tight hug and I smelled the train smoke on his clothes. "Daddy, I love you," I said.

It all comes back. I patted that big hand and said, "Good-bye, Dad," as he was sinking fast now. "We haven't forgotten how hard you worked to send five boys and one girl through college: how you wore those old conductor uniforms until they were slick—doing without that we might have things that we didn't really need. . . ."

At three minutes to four o'clock, like a stately ship moving slowly out of time's harbor into eternity's sea, he breathed his last. The nurse motioned for us to leave and pulled the sheet over his head, a gesture that struck terror to my heart, and we turned with silent weeping to leave the room. Then an incident occurred that I will never forget. Just as we got to the door, I put my arm around my little mother and said, "Mama, this is awful."

Dabbing at her eyes with her handkerchief, she said, "Yes, Jimmy, but there is one thing Mother wants you to remember now. We have said good night down here, but one of these days we are going to say good morning up there."

I believe she did say good morning too, eleven years later, and I know he met her "just inside the Eastern gate."

His death was marked by quietness and dignity, just like the life he had lived. Thus came to an end the affairs of R. L. Dobson, and thus ended, too, the solidarity of the family.

The old home place was never the same again. The old spirit that we had known as children was gone forever!

Again, this illustration reveals few of the specific characteristics that made R. L. Dobson such a powerful influence in his family; it does tell us how his son felt about him. I happen to know some of the other details. He was one of the oak trees I mentioned—a man of strength and integrity. Although not a Christian until shortly before his death, he lived by an internal standard that was singularly uncompromising. As a young man, for example, he invested heavily in a business venture with a partner whom he later discovered to be dishonest. When he learned of the chicanery, he walked out and virtually gave the company to the other man. That former partner built the corporation into one of the most successful operations in the South and became a multimillionaire. But my grandfather never looked back. He took a clean conscience with him to his grave.

There were other admirable traits, of course, and many of them were transmitted to my dad. These two men personified much of what I'm trying to convey in this examination of manhood. Then they passed those values down to me. If men today were as certain of their masculine identity as my father and grandfather, there would be far fewer lost boys who search vainly for role models in street gangs or in popular culture.

My point through this discussion has been to urge those of you who are young fathers to provide that modeling on which your boys can build their masculine identities. As you carry out the traditional roles we have described, or some version of them, your sons will observe who you are and thereby learn to serve in a similar way when they are grown. That's why any advice to dads about raising boys must begin with an examination of their individual demeanor and character.

I mentioned earlier that there were *two* primary ways fathers influence their boys. If modeling is the first, the second deals with the specific instruction that dads should transmit to their sons. That subject could fill many books, but I'll focus on the subtopic of what a father should teach his boys specifically about girls and women. They are unlikely to learn it anywhere else.

I'm going to throw some suggestions at you now in rapid succession, assuming you are a father of one or more boys. Here we go: If you speak disparagingly of the opposite sex, or if you refer to females as sex objects, those attitudes will translate directly into dating and marital relationships later on. Remember that your goal is to prepare a boy to lead a family when he's grown and to show him how to earn the respect of those he serves. Tell him it is great to laugh and have fun with his friends, but advise him not to be "goofy." Guys who are goofy are not respected, and people, especially girls and women, do not follow boys and men whom they disrespect. Also, tell your son that he is *never* to hit a girl under any circumstances. Remind him that she is not as strong as he is and that she is deserving of his respect. Not only should he not hurt her, but he should protect her if she is threatened. When he is strolling along with a girl on the street, he should walk on the outside, nearer the cars. That is symbolic of his responsibility to take care of her. When he is on a date, he should pay for her food and entertainment. Also (and this is simply my opinion), girls should not call boys on the telephone—at least not until a committed relationship has developed. Guys must be the initiators, planning the dates and asking for the girl's company. Teach your son to open doors for girls and to help them with their coats or their chairs in a restaurant. When a guy goes to her house to pick up his date, tell him to get out of the car and knock on the door. Never honk. Teach him to stand, in formal situations, when a woman leaves the room or a table or when she returns. This is a way of showing respect for her. If he treats her like a lady, she will treat him like a man. It's a great plan.

Make a concerted effort to teach sexual abstinence to your teenagers, just as you teach them to abstain from drug and alcohol usage and other harmful behavior. Of course you can do it! Young people are fully capable of understanding that irresponsible sex is not in their best interest and that it leads to disease, unwanted pregnancy, rejection, etc. In many cases today, no one is sharing this truth with teenagers. Parents are embarrassed to talk about sex, and, it disturbs me to say, churches are often unwilling to address the issue. That creates a vacuum into which liberal sex counselors have intruded to say, "We know you're going to have sex anyway, so why not do it right?" What a damning message that is. It is why herpes and other sexually transmitted diseases are spreading exponentially through the population and why unwanted pregnancies stalk school campuses. Despite these terrible social consequences, very little support is provided even for young people who are desperately looking for a valid reason to say no. They're told that "safe sex" is fine if they just use the right equipment. You as a father must counterbalance those messages at home. Tell your sons that there is no safety—no place to hide—when one lives in contradiction to the laws of God! Remind them repeatedly and emphatically of the biblical teaching about sexual immorality—and why someone who violates those laws not only hurts himself, but also wounds the girl and cheats the man she will eventually marry. Tell them not to take anything that doesn't belong to them—especially the moral purity of a woman.

Also, tell your boys that sex is progressive in nature. Kissing and fondling will lead inevitably to greater familiarity. That is just the way we are made. If guys are determined to remain moral, they must take steps to slow down the physical progression early in the relationship. Tell them not to start the engine if they don't intend to let it run. Finally, make it clear that sexual morality is not just right and proper; it is one of the keys to a healthy marriage and family life.

Begin these and other conversations early, geared to the age and maturity of the child. They must be well planned and carried out as the years unfold. Haven't you heard grown men say with conviction, "My father always told me . . ."? This is because the things emphasized during childhood often stay with a person throughout life, even if they haven't appeared to "stick" at the time. In short, this kind of specific instruction is the substance of your responsibility to affirm, recognize, and celebrate your son's journey into manhood.

Admittedly, as I've said, some of the ideas I've suggested sound like "yesterday." But they still make sense to me because most of them are biblically based. They also contribute to harmonious relationships between the sexes, which will pay dividends for those who will marry. Dr. Michael Gurian said it best: "Every time you raise a loving, wise, and responsible man, you have created a better world for women. Women [today] are having to bond to half-men, with boys who were not fully raised to manhood, don't know how to bond, don't know what their responsibilities are to humanity, and don't have a strong sense of service."[5] Today's fathers have an opportunity to change that.

I know the suggestions and ideas I have offered in this chapter put great pressure on us to be superdads, but that's just the way it is. I felt it too when our kids were small. Frankly, raising kids was a scary responsibility for Shirley and me. We knew we were inadequate to handle the job and that no one is capable of guaranteeing the outcome of that task. That's why we began praying diligently for the spiritual welfare of our children. Thousands of times through the years, we found ourselves on our knees asking for wisdom and guidance.

Then we did the very best we could at home. Somehow, that seems to have been enough. Both of our children love the Lord today and are wonderful human beings. Shirley deserves most of the credit for the outcome, but I gave it my best effort too. Fortunately, parents do not have to be perfect in order to transmit their values to the next generation.

Our heavenly Father will also answer your prayers for your kids if you turn to Him. He will guide them through the storms of adolescence. But He will not do for you what you can and must do for yourself, and that is what we are here to talk about.

QUESTIONS AND ANSWERS

My thirteen-year-old son is in the full bloom of adolescence. I'm suspicious that he may be masturbating when he's alone, but I don't quite know how to approach him about it. Should I be concerned, and if so, what should I say to him?

I don't think you should invade that private world at all unless there are unique circumstances that lead you to do so. I offer that advice while acknowledging that masturbation is a highly controversial subject and Christian leaders differ widely in their perspectives on it. I will answer your question but hope you understand that some Bible scholars and ministers will disagree emphatically with what I will say.

First, let's consider masturbation from a medical perspective. We can say without fear of contradiction that there is no scientific evidence to indicate that this act is harmful to the body. Despite terrifying warnings given to young people historically, it does not cause blindness, weakness, mental retardation, or any other physical problem. If it did, the entire male population and about half of females would be blind, weak, simpleminded, and sick. Between 95 and 98 percent of all boys engage in this practice—and the rest have been known to lie. It is as close to being a universal behavior as is likely to occur. A lesser but still significant percentage of girls also engage in what was once called "self-gratification," or worse, "self-abuse."

As for the emotional consequences of masturbation, only four circumstances should give us cause for concern. The first is when it is associated with oppressive guilt from which the individual can't escape. That guilt has the potential to do considerable psychological and spiritual damage. Boys and girls who labor under divine condemnation can gradually become convinced that even God couldn't love them. They promise a thousand times with great sincerity never again to commit this "despicable" act. Then a week or two passes, or perhaps several months. Eventually, the hormonal pressure accumulates until nearly every waking moment reverberates with sexual desire. Finally, in a moment (and I do mean a *moment*) of weakness, it happens again. What then, dear friend? Tell me what a young person says to God after he or she has just broken the one thousandth solemn promise to Him? I am convinced that some teenagers have thrown over their faith because of their inability to please God on this point.

The second circumstance in which masturbation might have harmful implications is when it becomes extremely obsessive. That is more likely to occur when it has been understood by the individual to be "forbidden fruit." I believe the best way to prevent that kind of obsessive response is for adults not to emphasize or condemn it. Regardless of what you do, you will not stop the practice of masturbation in your teenagers. That is a certainty. You'll just drive it underground—or under covers. Nothing works as a "cure." Cold showers, lots of exercise, many activities, and awesome threats are ineffective. Attempting to suppress this act is one campaign that is destined to fail—so why wage it?

The third situation around which we should be concerned is when the young person becomes addicted to pornographic material. The kind of obscenity available to teenagers today has the capacity to grab and hold a boy for the rest of his life. Parents will want to intervene if there is evidence that their son or daughter is heading down that well-worn path. I will discuss that danger in a subsequent chapter.

The fourth concern about masturbation refers not to adolescents but to us as adults. This habit has the capacity to follow us into marriage and become a substitution for healthy sexual relations between a husband and wife. This, I believe, is what the apostle Paul meant when he instructed us not to deprive or "defraud" one another as marital partners. The apostle Paul wrote, "Do not deprive each other except by mutual consent and for a time, so that you may devote yourselves to prayer. Then come together again so that Satan will not tempt you because of your lack of self-control" (1 Corinthians 7:5).

As for the spiritual implications of masturbation, I will have to defer to the theologians for a more definitive response. It is interesting to me, however, that Scripture does not address this subject except for a single reference in the Old Testament to a man named Onan. He interrupted sexual intercourse with his sister-in-law and allowed his semen to fall on the ground to keep from producing offspring for his brother, which was his "duty" (Genesis 38:8-9). Although that verse is often cited as evidence of God's disapproval of masturbation, the context doesn't seem to fit.

So, what should you as a father say to your thirteen-year-old son about this subject? My advice is to say nothing after puberty has occurred. You will only cause embarrassment and discomfort. For those who are younger, it would be wise to include the subject of masturbation in the "Preparing for Adolescence" conversation I have recommended on other occasions. I would suggest that parents talk to their twelve- or thirteen-year-old boys, especially, in the same general way my mother and father discussed this subject with me. We were riding in the car, and my dad said, "Jim, when I was a boy, I worried so much about masturbation. It really became a scary thing for me because I thought God was condemning me for what I couldn't help. So I'm telling you now that I hope you don't feel the need to engage in this act when you reach the teen years, but if you do, you shouldn't be too concerned about it. I don't believe it has much to do with your relationship with God."

What a compassionate thing my father did for me that night in the car. He was a very conservative minister who never compromised his standards of morality to the day of his death. He stood like a rock for biblical principles and commandments. Yet he cared enough about me to lift from my shoulders the burden of guilt that nearly destroyed some of my friends in the church. This kind of "reasonable" faith taught to me by my parents is one of the primary reasons I never felt it necessary to rebel against parental authority or defy God.

Those are my views, for what they are worth. I know my recommendations will be inflammatory to some people. If you are one of them, please forgive me. I can only offer the best advice of which I'm capable. I pray that in this instance I am right.

My son is in his freshman year of college, and it looks like he's found a girl that he thinks he loves. He came home at Christmastime, and we talked about the kind of family he wanted to have. He was worried, however, about the high divorce rate that threatens every new marriage and asked me how he could lower the risk of having that happen to him and his future wife. What advice would you have given?

The answer to that question could go six hundred different ways, but I'll be content to offer just one suggestion. You need to explain to your son how women are different from men and how that uniqueness will affect his own marriage. It concerns what might be called "differing assumptions." Many men come into marriage laboring under the mistaken idea that their wives are going to be their cheerleaders, who will take care of the children and expect nothing in return. They believe that their greatest and perhaps only responsibility is to make money and to succeed professionally, even if it requires twelve hours a day to do it. The assumption of women, on the other hand, is that their marriage will be a wonderfully romantic affair. They anticipate candlelit dinners and walks in the rain and evenings of soul-to-soul conversations. Both of these expectations are illusions that bump along for a few years until they finally collide. Workaholic men and Cinderella women often destroy each other. I saw this pattern develop repeatedly with medical students who began their training with such enthusiasm that was shared by their spouse. But by the third year, the wife (assuming the student was a man) began to realize that her husband had a mistress. It was not another woman. He was in a lifelong love affair with medicine, and he would be captivated by that obsession for the rest of their lives together. When that reality sank in, divorce was not far behind, usually in the senior year.

I strongly urge fathers to tell their adolescent and college-age boys that girls are incurable romantics and that it will not be enough for them as husbands to be successful in their professional pursuits. That would have been sufficient in decades past. Today, something more is expected. If they are going to have strong marriages and families, they must reserve time and energy for the marital relationship, talking together and treating each other as sweethearts.

This is the one word of advice that I would like to give to every engaged or newly married couple. A simple understanding of these "differing assumptions" could prevent many painful divorces. I think you should share it with your son.

You mentioned the need to share the biblical basis for morality with our kids. Can you provide some specific scriptural references to help me teach it to them?

Yes, there are many sources, but those that follow should be helpful. Depending on the age of the child, begin by reading the first five chapters of Proverbs in a modern translation, where King Solomon gives fatherly advice to his son. There will be many points therein for you and your boy to stop and talk about righteous living. Then go on to the following verses:

- Matthew 15:19: For out of the heart come evil thoughts, murder, adultery, sexual immorality, theft, false testimony, slander.
- Romans 1:24: Therefore God gave them over in the sinful desires of their hearts to sexual impurity for the degrading of their bodies with one another.
- Romans 13:13: Let us behave decently, as in the daytime, not in orgies and drunkenness, not in sexual immorality and debauchery, not in dissension and jealousy.
- 1 Corinthians 6:18: Flee from sexual immorality. All other sins a man commits are outside his body, but he who sins sexually sins against his own body.
- 1 Corinthians 10:8: We should not commit sexual immorality, as some of them did—and in one day twenty-three thousand of them died.
- 2 Corinthians 12:21: I am afraid that when I come again my God will humble me before you, and I will be grieved over many who have sinned earlier and have not repented

of the impurity, sexual sin, and debauchery in which they have indulged.

- Galatians 5:19: The acts of the sinful nature are obvious: sexual immorality, impurity and debauchery.
- Ephesians 5:3: But among you there must not be even a hint of sexual immorality, or of any kind of impurity, or of greed, because these are improper for God's holy people.
- Colossians 3:5: Put to death, therefore, whatever belongs to your earthly nature: sexual immorality, impurity, lust, evil desires and greed which is idolatry.
- 1 Thessalonians 4:3: It is God's will that you should be sanctified: that you should avoid sexual immorality.
- Jude 1:7: In a similar way, Sodom and Gomorrah and the surrounding towns gave themselves up to sexual immorality and perversion. They serve as an example of those who suffer the punishment of eternal fire.

MOTHERS AND SONS

CHAPTER 7

OKAY, MOM. It's your turn. Let's talk about what it means to be a boy and how you might relate better to them. I have the highest respect and admiration for those who are blessed to be called mothers. There are few assignments in human experience that require the array of skills and wisdom needed by a mom in fulfilling her everyday duties. She must be a resident psychologist, physician, theologian, educator, nurse, chef, taxi driver, fire marshal, and occasional police officer. And if she succeeds in each of these responsibilities, she gets to do it all again tomorrow.

To understand the world in which a young mother lives, our male readers might want to join one of them on a midmorning visit to the pediatrician's office. After sitting for forty-five minutes with a cranky, feverish toddler on her lap, Mom and Baby are finally ushered into the examining room. The doctor checks out the sick child and then tells the woman with a straight face, "Be sure you keep him quiet for four or five days. Don't let him scratch the rash. Make certain he keeps the medicine down, and you'll need to watch his stool."

"Yeah, sure, Doc! Any other suggestions?"

"Just one. This disease is highly contagious. Keep your other four kids away from him. I'll see you in a week."

The amazing thing about mothers is that most of them would get this job done, and they would do it with love and grace. God made 'em good at what they do. And He gave them a passion for their children. Most of them would quite literally lay down their lives to protect the kids entrusted to their care. Despite that commitment, however, many women admit that raising boys has been a special challenge. As we mentioned earlier, they remember what it was like to be a frilly little girl, but they have only a vague notion of how their sons feel, think, and behave. Boys are bent on making messes, teasing the other siblings, racing through the house, and challenging every decision and order that comes their way.

One of my colleagues, Dr. Tim Irwin, shared his observation that women who have not grown up with brothers are often shocked by the sheer physicality of boys—by the sights and sounds and smells they generate. Some admit they are completely "clueless" in knowing how to deal with them. One obvious suggestion is to help boys release their excess energy by getting them involved in activities where fighting, laughing, running, tumbling, and yelling are acceptable. Soccer, karate, Little League, and football are a few possibilities. Moms also need to keep boys' little minds and hands busy. It's in their best interest to do so. My father once said about our energetic toddler, "If you let that kid get bored, you deserve what he's going to do to you." Shirley's stepfather, who has a South Dakota accent, once said after baby-sitting our kids for a week, "Oh, der good kids. You just gotta keep 'em out in da open." Good advice!

There's another characteristic of boys that I'll bet you've noticed. They ain't listening most of the time. They have a remarkable ability to ignore anything that doesn't interest them. Men are like that too. My wife can't understand how I am able to write a book, including this one, while a televised football game is blaring in the study. I don't actually watch and compose at the same time, but I can turn off the sound in my mind until I choose to hear it, such as when a replay appears on the screen. After watching for a moment, I go back to what I was doing. This is a "talent" that drives women crazy. Their husbands can read a report from the office and miss everything being said three feet away. One frustrated lady actually held a match to the bottom of the newspaper being read by her husband, which finally got his attention when it flamed up in his face. She said the only other way to have awakened him would have been to dance stark nude on the dining room table. I'm not even sure that would have worked.

Alas, boys have that same ability to ignore their moms. They honestly don't hear the words that are being poured into their ears. That is why I recommend that you as a mom reach out physically and touch your boys if you want to get their attention. When they turn to look at you, give them your message in short bursts. I'll talk more about communication with boys later, but for now, I want to discuss the various developmental milestones, beginning at birth.

We have been talking in previous chapters about the essential role that fathers play in boys' early development, but moms are on the hook too. There is no way to overstate the importance of what is called "infant bonding" between mother and child of either sex. The quality of that relationship will have lifelong implications and can even determine life or death. Mary Carlson, a researcher from Harvard Medical School, recently studied an overcrowded Romanian orphanage, where row upon row of babies lay neglected in their cribs. The staff was hopelessly overworked, so the babies were rarely touched, even when feeding. What struck Carlson was the oppressive silence in the nursery. There was no crying, no babbling, not even a whimper. Upon physical examinations administered at age two, Carlson found that the babies had unusually high amounts of a stress hormone in the blood called cortisol, which in large amounts is known to damage the brain. (We also mentioned this phenomenon in the fourth chapter.) Growth was stunted and the children acted half their age.[1] Even if they manage to survive, they will never fully recover.

But what are the implications of less tragic circumstances where the mother-boy relationship simply fails to jell? That specific question was studied at Harvard University. Researchers found that early bonding is vital. It is even related to physical health forty or fifty years later. Incredibly, 91 percent of college men who said they had not enjoyed a close relationship with their mothers developed coronary artery disease, hypertension, duodenal ulcers, and alcoholism by the midlife years. Only 45 percent of the men who recalled maternal warmth and closeness had similar illnesses. Even more surprising is the fact that 100 percent of participants in this study whose parents were cold and distant went on to suffer numerous diseases in midlife. In short, the quality of early relationships between boys and their mothers is a powerful predictor of lifelong psychological and physical health. When certain needs are not met in infancy, trouble looms down the road.[2]

Given the delicate nature of infants, perhaps it is understandable why I remain unalterably opposed to the placement of babies in day-care facilities unless there is no reasonable alternative. Children may appear to be dealing adequately with a series of temporary caregivers, but they were designed to link emotionally with a mother and a father and to develop securely within the protection of their arms. That belief was rarely challenged for some five thousand years, but many women today feel they have no choice but to get back to a job as soon as possible after giving birth. If you are one of them, let me say respectfully and compassionately that I understand the financial and emotional pressures you face. But to new mothers who have other options, I would strongly recommend that you not hand your babies over to child-care workers, many of whom are underpaid and untrained and who will not share your irrational commitment to that infant.

My opinion on this subject is based on hard data. The National Institute of Child Health and Human Development has conducted the most comprehensive study of this issue to date. More than 1,100 mothers and children at ten premier child-care sites across the United States were evaluated when the children were six, fifteen, twenty-four, and thirty-six months of age. Preliminary results were reported in *USA Today* as follows: "Working moms worry that if they leave their infants and toddlers in the care of others, relationships with their children will be affected. News from the federal government says they are right to be concerned. Longer hours spent in child care in the first three years of life tend to mean less positive interaction between mother and child."[3] Preliminary findings confirm that leaving a very young child in a day-care facility is associated with less sensitive mothering and child engagement. The child also tends to react less positively to the mother. In other words, the bond between mother and child is affected somewhat negatively by early day-care experience, especially if the mother tends by nature to be insensitive.

The data reported above were issued when the study was incomplete. When it was concluded in 2001, the researchers announced even more disturbing findings. They said that children who spend most of their time in child care were three times as likely to exhibit behavioral problems in kindergarten as those who were cared for primarily by mothers. These results were based on ratings of the children by their mothers, those caring for them, and by kindergarten teachers. There was a direct correlation between the amount of time spent in child care and traits such as aggression, defiance, and disobedience. The more time spent in these out-of-home settings, the greater the behavior problems. Dr. Jay Belsky, one of the study's principal investigators, said children who spent more than thirty hours a week in child care "are more demanding, more noncompliant, and they are more aggressive. They scored higher on things like gets in lots of fights, cruelty, bullying, meanness, as well as talking too much, demands must be met immediately."[4] This is not good news for the 13 million preschoolers, including 6 million infants and toddlers, who are in child care in the United States.

After the release of this study, there was a hue and cry from the liberal community that has told us for years that children actually thrive better in child-care centers. They attacked the methodology of the study and claimed its findings were invalid. Others demanded more federal money for quality child-care programs. No one doubts that better day-care options are needed by parents who must depend on them. However, I may have a better idea. Why not reduce the tax burden on parents so that mothers can do what most of them desperately want to do—stay at home with their children?

In a study conducted by Public Agenda, 70 percent of mothers of children under five wanted to leave the workforce. Seventy-one percent said day care was the option of "last resort." When asked what child-care arrangement is best for young children, 70 percent said one parent at home is preferable. Fourteen percent said having both parents work different shifts is best, and 6 percent favored a close relative. Only 6 percent thought the best option was a quality day-care center.[5] Deborah Wadsworth, president of Public Agenda, said, "When it comes to handing their child over to another adult they do not know, they are gripped by anxiety."[6]

What does this mean for public policy? Let me say it again. The U.S. Congress should provide tax credits and other economic incentives for mothers (or fathers) who choose to stay at home. Why have they not done so to this point? Because they want the tax revenues that come from two-income families and because they are lobbied heavily by feminists and others who want all the advantages to go toward the employed mother. It's time to balance the scales. I am not unsympathetic to the working mom who struggles mightily to do what is called "double duty." She needs our love and respect too. Many working moms are in the labor force because they feel they have no alternative financially.

When our firstborn was two years old, I was finishing my doctoral work at the University of Southern California. Every available dollar was needed to support my tuition and related expenses. Although we didn't want Shirley to work when Danae was young, we felt we had no alternative. Shirley taught school and our little girl was taken to a day-care center each morning. One day when we arrived at the facility, Danae began to cry uncontrollably. "No! No! No, Daddy!" she said to me. She clung to my neck as I carried her to the door and then begged me not to leave. Children at that age typically do not like to be left by parents, but this was something different. Danae had a look of terror in her eyes, and I suspected that she had been very upset the last time she was there. I could only imagine what had happened. I turned and walked back to the car carrying my precious daughter. When we were alone, I said, "Danae, I promise that you will never have to stay there again." And she never did.

Shirley and I talked about how we were going to keep my promise. We finally decided to sell and "eat" one of our two Volkswagens, which allowed her to stay home and take care of our daughter for a year. By the time the money was gone, I was out of school and we could afford for Shirley to be a full-time mom. Not everyone could do what we did, and certainly, there are millions of single parents out there who have no alternatives. If that is the case, you simply have to make the best of it. If a relative or a friend can keep your child during the day, that is better than a child-care facility, all things being equal. What is needed is continuity in the relationship between a child and the one who provides daily care.

The bottom line from many studies of infancy and early child development is consistent: babies have several essential emotional needs. Among them are touch, connection, permanence, nurturance, and reassurance. I ache for the many abused and neglected children out there today whose needs are tragically ignored. There is nothing sadder in life than an unloved child or one who feels unloved. Sometimes I wish babies were born with a sign around their necks that warns, "Caution! Handle with Care! Love me. Protect me! Give me a place in your heart."

Despite the importance of an early mother-child bond, it may seem strange that little boys begin to pull away from their moms during the period between fifteen and thirty-six months. Boys, even more than girls, become negative at that time and resist any efforts to corral or manage them. They say no to everything, even to things they like. They run when called and scream bloody murder at bedtime. They usually respond better to fathers—but not very much. Believe it or not, this is a moment of opportunity for Mom. She *must* take charge during these delightful but challenging days of toddlerhood. It is not sufficient to leave the discipline solely to Dad. Respect for her authority and leadership are rooted in this period, and opportunities that are lost will be difficult to recover later on. Just remember that boys desperately need to be supervised. They also need to be "civilized," quite literally. In the absence of firm but loving leadership, they tend to follow their own selfish and destructive inclinations, which can be harmful to a boy and to other members of the family. We'll focus more on principles of discipline in chapter 16.

What are the other implications for mothers during this period of disconnection and differentiation? For one thing, they should not allow themselves to feel rejected and wounded by their boys' gravitation toward fathers. Just remember that the behavior isn't personal. Boys are genetically programmed to respond that way. I remember feeling somewhat embarrassed by my mother's hugs and kisses when I was three years old. I told her one day that I thought it was "silly." Her wise response was, "I do too." I wanted and needed her love, but I was already aware of a strange tug toward my dad. Although most kids won't be able to articulate that urge, what is happening is a healthy process from which manhood will flower in time. Mothers should encourage their husbands to be there for their sons when the need is the greatest. Show them this section of my book, even if they won't read the rest of it. Men tend to be extremely busy during the early years of parenthood, and their minds are on other things. A gentle nudge will get their attention better than inundating them with bucket loads of guilt and criticism.

With the passage of time, the sexuality of boys will become more apparent. Never believe for a moment that they are asexual, even from earliest childhood. Some toddlers and preschoolers will hold or rub their genitals, which has inaccurately been called masturbation. It embarrasses and worries their mothers, but it has no developmental or moral implications. It simply indicates that the boy has discovered "the good-feeling place." He can be taught that there is a right and wrong time to touch himself, but he should not be shamed or punished for revealing that he is wired properly.

When I was five years old, I was in bed one night with my great aunt. She was an older woman who had some prudish ideas. I was almost asleep, and she was reading a book. Suddenly, she said with alarm, "What are you doing under the covers?" Believe me, I was doing *nothing* under the covers. I didn't even know there was anything interesting to be done under the covers. It is funny when I think back on that moment, but it confused me at the time. I wondered what she was worried about. Don't make a similar mistake with your boys.

During the early elementary years, boys sometimes fantasize about women or girls. Not that they think about intercourse, which few of them understand, but they often have vague thoughts about nudity or other sexual images of females. It's all part of the male experience.

I'm reminded of a friend who was driving in her car with her seven-year-old son. Suddenly, he began asking all the relevant questions about sex. He pressed her to tell him every detail about babies and how they are conceived. His mom was uneasy to have been confronted so early with questions that she hadn't expected to deal with for two or three more years. But there she was and she couldn't wiggle out. *Okay,* she said to herself, *here we go.* She told him everything. All the time she was talking, the boy sat staring ahead with eyes unfocused. When the lesson was over, he reached over and pressed the switch to lower the window, then stuck out his head. He said, "Oooohhhh! Sick! I'm gonna be sick. I don't even want to remember this!" A few weeks later when his cousin was born, he told his little brother where the baby came from. But he didn't get it quite right. "The mom and dad," he said, "had to do that spur thing" (meaning sperm thing).

Age ten for most boys is a lovable time. Some have called it an "angelic" period, when cooperation and obedience are at their peak. It will never be quite that way again. By eleven, the typical boy will probably be getting testy and cantankerous. He may irritate his mother, tease his younger brothers and sisters, and push the limits a little farther. That means testosterone is starting to flow and the adolescent upheaval is getting under way. Then come twelve and thirteen. For the next three years, it's "Hang onto your hat!"

The late counselor and author Jean Lush was my guest on *Focus on the Family* some years ago to discuss this subject of mothers and sons. Here is a portion of what she said about the onset of puberty:

> Of all the counseling I've done and from my reading I can say . . . oh, my, age thirteen can be a hard year. I'll give you an example from our family. This mother noticed her son was in a bad mood and she said, "Oh, do come over and see these photographs and help me choose which one I'll use for Christmas. They're photos of myself." The boy came over and said, "I don't like any of them. Your breath stinks. I'm going to my room." The mother said, "Oh, I was so hurt." But two hours later the boy came out and said, "I love you, Mom." He kissed her and went to bed. Now, this was a typical thirteen-year-old. A boy at that age will often be rude and nippy. He will scream at his parents, slam doors, and have mood swings. But all of a sudden, he will break out of it and is a lovely member of the family again. These kids between thirteen and fourteen are really hard to figure out.
>
> There's another thing: A little boy achieves male maturity over his mother's dead body. And don't forget it. He doesn't just kill her; he "stabs" her slowly. Let me explain. I think many little boys are afraid of the male thing ahead. Not all of them are like this, of course. Some just sail through but there are others that ask anxiously, "Will I ever become a proper male?" In those cases the mother is in his way. If she is too close, the child may feel swallowed up by her. After all, she is a woman. She stands between him and being a man. The boys who struggle most are sometimes the ones who have had the closest relationship with their mothers. So what do they do to get her out of the way? They have to "kill" her. Killing is the little boy who said, "Your breath stinks." This was his way of establishing his masculinity. That episode was very hard for the mother, who felt rejected and wounded by her son, but it was a transition they had to endure. Mothers whose sons suddenly go through this kind of alienation are inclined to ask

themselves, "What am I doing wrong? I don't know what to do. The kid is a little tyrant." Well, hang in there. Better days are coming.[7]

But what if better days don't come? What if Junior's attitude goes from bad to worse in adolescence? I'm sure that has happened, or eventually will happen, with one or more of your children. It is hormonally driven and occurs in the best of families. When hostility and rebellion begin to appear, how do you keep your boys (and girls) from blowing up and doing something stupid? I've addressed that subject in other books, but let me offer a recent finding that I haven't shared before. The National Longitudinal Study of Adolescent Health surveyed 11,572 teenagers to determine which factors were most helpful in preventing harmful behavior, such as violence, suicide, substance abuse, early sexual behavior, and teen pregnancy. Here's what the researchers found: The presence of parents is very beneficial at four key times of the day—early morning, after school, dinnertime, and bedtime. When that regular contact is combined with other shared activities between parents and kids, the most positive outcome is achieved. The researchers also observed that adolescents who felt a sense of connection with their parents (feelings of warmth, love, and caring) were least likely to engage in harmful behavior.[8]

Some of my readers might be asking, "How can I be with my teenagers morning, noon, and night? I have altogether too much work to do." Well, you simply have to decide what is most important to you at this time. It won't matter as much a few years down the road, but your availability right now could make the difference for your child between surviving or plunging off the cliff.

My father and mother were faced with the same difficult choice when I was sixteen years old. Dad was an evangelist who was gone most of the time, while my mother was home with me. During the adolescent years, I began to get testy with my mother. I never went into total rebellion, but I was definitely flirting with the possibility. I'll never forget the night my mom called my dad on the phone. I was listening as she said, "I need you." To my surprise, my dad immediately cancelled a four-year slate of meetings, sold our home, and moved seven hundred miles south to take a pastorate so he could be with me until I finished high school. It was an enormous sacrifice for him to make. He never fully recovered professionally from it. But he and Mom felt my welfare was more important than their immediate responsibilities. Dad was home with me during those two volatile years when I could have gotten into serious trouble. When I speak with reverence about my parents today, as I often do, one of the reasons is because they gave priority to me when I was sliding close to the brink. Would you do the same for your teenagers?

You may not be called upon to make such a radical change in your lifestyle. Sometimes the solution is much simpler, according to a study conducted by Dr. Blake Bowden of the Cincinnati Children's Hospital Center. He and his colleagues surveyed 527 teenagers to learn what family and lifestyle characteristics were related to mental health and adjustment. What they observed, once more, is that adolescents whose parents ate dinner with them five times per week or more were the least likely to be on drugs, to be depressed, or to be in trouble with the law. They were also more likely to be doing well in school and to be surrounded by a supportive circle of friends. The benefit was seen even for families that didn't eat together at home. Those who met at fast-food restaurants had the same result. By contrast, the more poorly adjusted teens had parents who ate with them only three evenings per week or less.[9]

Isn't it interesting how the two studies reported above came to the same conclusion? Parental involvement is the key to getting kids through the storms of adolescence. And here's another investigation geared to younger children. Dr. Catherine Snow, professor of education at Harvard's Graduate School of Education, followed sixty-five families over an eight-year period. She found that dinnertime was of more value to child development than playtime, school, and story time.[10] Clearly, there is power in "breaking bread" together.

What do these findings mean? Is there something magical about sitting down together over a meal? No, and those parents who believe as much are in for a disappointment. What Bowden's study shows is that family relationships are what matters to adolescents. When parents have time for their kids, when they get together almost every day for conversation and interaction—in this case, while eating—their teens do much better in school and in life. Bottom line? Families bring stability and mental health to children and teens.

With such strong evidence in support of family meals, it's unfortunate that only one-third of U.S. families eat dinner together most nights. The hectic world in which we live has pressed in on all sides and caused us to eat on the run. Some people "dine" more often in their cars or offices than they do at home, stuffing down a burrito or a hamburger while driving. Fortunately, it *is* possible for us to change this trend. With determination and planning, we should be able to intersect each others' worlds at least once every day or two. The most important ingredient is not what's on the table—we can serve a home-cooked meal or call for a pasta delivery. What *does* make a difference is that we regularly set aside time to sit down and talk together.

Eating can also provide the centerpiece for family traditions, which give identity and belonging to each member. To cite our own circumstances again, we have designated foods for every holiday. It's turkey at Thanksgiving and Christmas, it's red beans and ham on New Year's Day, it's baked ham on Easter, it's barbecued hamburgers (made of turkey) on the Fourth of July, and it's Chinese food on Christmas Eve (don't ask me why). There are many dimensions to the various traditions, which go far beyond the choice of foods. Each of us looks forward to those occasions, which are always filled with laughter, spontaneity, and meaning. Children love these kinds of recurring activities that bond them to their parents. I hope you have similar traditions of your own.

Finally, family mealtimes continue to be great settings in which to impart the truths of our faith. As the blessings of the day are recounted, children see evidence of God's loving, faithful care and the importance of honoring Him with a time of thanks. In our family, we never eat a meal without pausing first to express gratitude to the One who provides us with "every good and perfect gift" (James 1:17). I believe children of Christian parents should be taught to "say grace" every time meals are partaken. Parents can also use that talking time to discuss biblical principles at the table and apply them to personal circumstances. Jesus used the time of fellowship created around meals to present many of His teachings. Acts 2:46-47 gives us a glimpse of how significant sharing a meal was to the early church by describing how believers "broke bread in their homes and ate together with glad and sincere hearts, praising God."

The more your boys feel part of something loving and fun, the less they will need to rebel against it. That's not a promise, just a probability.

Before we leave the family table, there is a related health issue I should mention. With all this talk about the importance of food, we need to be careful not to contribute to early obesity. A recent medical study conducted at Columbia Children's Hospital in Ohio has confirmed that today's children are heavier and have significantly higher cholesterol and triglyceride levels than kids did even fifteen years ago. One of the researchers, Dr. Hugh Allens, said, "Unless these trends change, thirty million of the eighty million children alive today in the United States will eventually die of heart disease."[11] And what a depressing prediction that is. The problem is that high-fat junk food has replaced good nutrition, and even when healthy foods are consumed, kids are just not exercising enough to burn the calories off. Between television, carpools, computer games, and just hanging out at the pizza parlor, kids just don't run and jump like they used to. So Mom and

Dad should find activities to do together with kids, such as walking, bicycling, playing catch, or hiking. Children are busy forming habits for a lifetime, so eating right and exercising every day will contribute to greater health in the future. And once your children are on the right path, you just might want to move your own "bod" as well.

Well, perhaps I've spent too much time talking about food, but it is an important part of family life. We'll talk about other aspects of the mother-son relationship in the next chapter.

QUESTIONS AND ANSWERS

It is hard for me to admit that I have very little respect for my husband. He has never succeeded at much of anything, and he is not a leader in our home. I try to conceal that attitude toward him at home, but it is difficult. What can I do if I just don't think he is worthy of my admiration?

I think you already know what my answer will be, but I will share it anyway. You as a mother hold the keys to the relationship between your boys and their father. If you show respect to him as a man, they will be more inclined to admire and emulate him. If you think he is a wimp or a dope or a loser, those attitudes will translate directly into their interaction. In one of my earlier books, I shared a personal story written by Lewis Yablonsky that bears repeating because it graphically illustrates this point. This is what he wrote about his browbeaten dad in his book *Fathers and Sons:*

> I vividly recall sitting at the dinner table with my two brothers and father and mother and cringing at my mother's attacks on my father. "Look at him," she would say in Yiddish. "His shoulders are bent down, he's a failure. He doesn't have the courage to get a better job or make more money. He's a beaten man." He would keep his eyes pointed toward his plate and never answer her. She never extolled his virtues or persistence or the fact that he worked so hard. Instead she constantly focused on the negative and created an image to his three sons of a man without fight, crushed by a world over which he had no control.
>
> His not fighting back against her constant criticism had the effect of confirming its validity to her sons. And my mother's treatment and the picture of my father did not convey to me that marriage was a happy state of being, or that

women were basically people. I was not especially motivated to assume the role of husband and father myself from my observations of my whipped father.[12]

Obviously, Yablonsky's mother seriously damaged the image of his father, making her sons not want to follow him. That is the power a woman holds within the family. In a sense, she serves as a gatekeeper between kids and their dad. She can build the father-son relationship, or she can damage it beyond repair. Boys, especially, are born with a need to "be like dad," but they will look elsewhere for role models if "the old man" appears to be an insufferable oaf at home.

My mother, who made very few blunders at home, stumbled into a major mistake at this point—not because she disrespected my dad, but because she didn't allow my dad to have proper access to me when I was a baby. She took full possession of me from the beginning. I was her first and only child, having been born by C-section in the days when that was a risky delivery. She loved being a mom and threw herself into the task of caring for me. She admitted later, with regret, that she had prevented my dad and me from bonding in the early years. She apologized for hurting him by making him feel unnecessary in the child-rearing responsibility. Things would change as I grew, but Mom had to pull back a bit before they did.

To summarize, I urge you as the Great Gatekeeper to facilitate the access between your children and their father. That is especially important for boys, who will look to that man as the example to follow.

You mentioned that boys and men are usually not natural communicators. Boy, does that describe the "men" in my life! What can I do to keep everyone talking to one another?

Every family needs at least one highly communicative person in the home, and it looks like you are the one. Many boys are inclined to bottle up whatever frustration they are carrying inside. Unless you take the initiative to pull them out, some of them may withdraw within themselves and stay there emotionally. I urge you to do whatever is required to get into your son's world. Keep talking and exploring and teaching. Communication is the goal. Everything depends on it.

In 1991 Saddam Hussein and his Iraqi army invaded the tiny, oil-rich country of Kuwait and subjected its people to terrible brutality. Their troops were poised to attack Saudi Arabia and thereby control half the world's oil supply. U.S. president George Bush demanded repeatedly that Hussein withdraw his forces, but he stubbornly refused. Thus, on January 17 of that year, Operation Desert Storm was launched. Several hundred thousand allied troops attacked the Iraqi army from land, sea, and air. What do you think was the first objective of the battle?

You might expect it to have been Saddam's tanks, or his planes, or his frontline soldiers. Instead, the allies destroyed the Iraqi's communication network. Stealth bombers smashed it with smart bombs and other weapons. In so doing, our forces interfered with the ability of the Iraqi generals to talk to each other. They had no way to coordinate their effort or direct the movements of their army. The war ended a few weeks later.

What happened in Desert Storm has direct relevance for families. When the communicative link between members breaks down, they become disorganized and distant from each other. If husbands and wives stop talking to each other, or if parents and children grow silent, they slip into misunderstanding and resentment. Steel-reinforced barriers are erected, and anger prevails. For many families, this is the beginning of the end.

Let me urge you mothers to talk regularly to your sons (and, of course, to every other member of the family). It is a skill that can be taught. Work hard at keeping the lines of communication open and clear. Explore what your children and your spouse are thinking and feeling. Target your boys, especially, because they may be concealing a cauldron of emotion. When you sense a closed spirit developing, don't let another day go by without bringing hidden feelings out in the open. It's the first principle of healthy family life.

The greatest thrill of my life has been the privilege of bringing our two children into the world and raising them day by day. It is hard for me to understand those who are hostile to motherhood and think it is just a waste of a woman's time. What could be more rewarding than being someone's mom?

The Bible refers to children as a "blessing" from God, and it certainly is just that. Your comment reminds me of an inspirational letter I received recently from a physician friend that speaks to that point. He shows us how motherhood is not only a blessing, it is "sacred." I think you will enjoy reading it. The letter came from Dr. C. H. McGowen:

Dear Dr. Dobson,

While reading Augustine's Confessions *recently, I came across the adjective* sacral, *which he used in reference to something holy or sacred. Being a physician, we in the profession know the word* sacrum *to identify a bone at the lower spine or pelvis. As a Christian, I wondered if there had been some divine influence or inspiration placed* upon the ancient anatomists who were bestowing names on various parts of the skeleton. That led me to do a bit of research into the possible association of theology and anatomy where this particular bone is concerned. It was quite providential, I believe, that the portion of the human anatomy which stands guard over the birth canal in the female is called, in Latin, the os sacrum, literally meaning "holy or sacred bone." Why would the ancient anatomist (Galan about 400 A.D. or Vesalius about 1543 A.D.) have chosen this particular name for this bone?

The dictionary tells us that the word sacred means "belonging to God, holy, set apart for a special purpose, and properly immune from violence or interference." Now we see the connection with the sacrum. It guards the pelvis with its birth canal, which is the origin of physical life. It contains the organs that produce the "seeds" of life in the ovaries. They are the producers of eggs which, when fertilized by the sperm, become a living soul implanted by God. The body developing in the womb, also located in the pelvis, contains this soul from the moment of conception, and that soul is declared sacred because it belongs to God. Ezekiel 18:4 reads, "Every living soul belongs to me." The body is merely the house or tent for the soul.

The sacrum, then, is a holy bone with a very definite purpose. It lends structural support to the developing baby within the womb, an act that becomes increasingly more important as the baby grows and gains weight. In God's eyes, this sacred place should never be violated by the abortionist's curette, suction apparatus, or trochar (the latter in the process of partial birth abortion). Nothing should interfere during any stage of development with that precious life that is growing there. No pill or surgical "weapon" should violate that sacral domain. To enter this area for any other reason than to give aid to, or deliver the life of, that individual which temporarily resides therein, is not only a violation of that person's life; it is also a violation of and intrusion upon God's law. God has a purpose and plan for that life. He inspired David to write, "All the days ordained for me were written in your book before one of them came to be" (Psalm 139:16).

Thank you, Dr. Dobson, for taking the time to read this letter. The sacrum really is sacred.[13]

CHASING THE CATERPILLAR

CHAPTER 8

THE GREAT FRENCH naturalist Jean-Henri Fabre once conducted a fascinating experiment with processionary caterpillars, so called because they tend to march in unison. He lined them around the inner edge of a flowerpot and then monitored them carefully as they marched in a circle. At the end of the third day, he placed some pine needles, which is the favorite food of caterpillars, in the center of the pot. They continued walking for four more days without breaking rank. Finally, one at a time, they rolled over and died of starvation, just inches from their ideal food source.[1]

These furry little creatures remind me in some ways of today's moms. Most of them are trudging around in circles from morning to night, exhausted and harried, wondering how in the world they can get everything done. Many are employed full-time while also taking care of families, chauffeuring kids, fixing meals, cleaning the house, and trying desperately to maintain their marriages, friendships, family relationships, and spiritual commitments. It is a backbreaking load. Sadly, this overcommitted and breathless way of life, which I call "routine panic," characterizes the vast majority of people in Western nations.

Are you one of these harried women running in endless circles? Have you found yourself too busy to read a good book or take a long walk with your spouse or hold your three-year-old child on your lap while telling him or her a story? Have you taken time to study God's Word—to commune with Him and listen to His gentle voice? Have you eliminated almost every meaningful activity in order to deal with the tyranny of a never-ending "to do" list? Have you ever asked yourself why in the world you have chosen to live like this? Perhaps so, but it is not an easy problem to solve. We live our lives as if we're on freight trains that are rumbling through town. We don't control the speed—or at least we think we don't—so our only option is to get off. Stepping from the train and taking life more slowly is very difficult. Old patterns die very hard indeed.

When was the last time you had friends drop by unexpectedly for a visit? For many of us it's been entirely too long. There was a time when families made a regular habit of packing into the car and driving over to a friend's home for an afternoon of good conversation and a piece of banana-cream pie. It was one of life's special little pleasures.

I'll never forget the times as a boy when I would hear a knock on the door and scurry to see who was there. The screen would crack open a few inches and a familiar voice would echo through the house, "Is anybody home?" Mom would rush to put on a pot of coffee and for the rest of the afternoon we'd sit and talk with our friends—about nothing and about everything. Finally, it came time for our friends to leave, and we'd hug them good-bye, encouraging everyone to come again sometime. Sadly, that kind of spontaneous camaraderie is difficult to achieve in today's fast-paced world. The pressures and busyness of life have all but destroyed the sense of community that was once common among families and friends. We seldom—if ever—drop in on friends unannounced. And even if we did, they would probably have to cancel a string of appointments in order to be with us. Thus, we go about our days, careening through life, glancing at our watches, and wondering why we don't have very many close friendships.

Shirley and I were blessed in recent years to live next door to an eighty-year-old lady named Jenny, whom we came to love. She saw our comings and goings and knew of our many pressures. Jenny told Shirley repeatedly, "Honey, don't forget to take time for friends and family. You know, it's important not to get too busy for people." She was lonely and was speaking from her own need. We did visit with her and enjoyed dinner together on occasions. Shirley "took tea" with her one afternoon and had a delightful conversation. But it was difficult to give her what she needed. We were traveling in the fast lane of a freeway, and Jenny was meandering down a country road at that stage of her life.

Jenny is gone now, but her words echo in our minds. Were our daily activities really more important in those years than taking time to love a special lady or reaching out to the many others whose paths we crossed? When I think in these terms, I want to disconnect—disengage, pull back from all the entanglements that weigh me down. I would give anything to go back twenty-five years and live another day with the two kids who graced our home. It would have been costly, of course, to have moved at a slower pace. I could not have built an organization called Focus on the Family, which I felt God had called me to do, or written some of the books that bear my name. Given all that was placed before us, we did a pretty good job of preserving our family life and getting into the world of our children. But as I reflect, I can't help but ask, "Could we have found a compromise that would have permitted Shirley and me to have done even better?" I wonder.

We are not the only family with reason to ask that question. Robert D. Putnam, political-science professor at Harvard University, addresses the growing trend toward overcommitment and isolation in his important book *Bowling Alone: The Collapse and Revival of American Community*. He interviewed nearly five hundred thousand people over the past twenty-five years and concluded that we are increasingly distancing ourselves from each other. The very fabric of our social connections has plummeted, impoverishing our lives and communities. We know our neighbors less, socialize with friends less often, and even grow distant from our families. We belong to fewer organizations that actually meet, such as the Jaycees, Shriners, Elks, and other service clubs. Only mailing-list membership has continued to expand. The same number of people are bowling now as in the past (hence the title of Putnam's book), although more of them are doing it alone. Participation in bowling leagues has declined 40 percent since 1980. In politics, we remain reasonably well-informed spectators of public affairs, but many fewer of us actually partake in the game.[2] (During the national election in 2000 which pitted presidential candidates with dramatically different views of America and its future, only 31 percent of potential voters in the state of Arizona bothered to go to the polls, 39 percent in California, 40 percent in Hawaii.[3]) In religious life, "Americans are going to church less often than we did three or four decades ago, and the churches we go to are less engaged with the wider community."[4]

At the same time, the so-called "electronic church," referring to services broadcast on television, radio, or the Internet, is gaining popularity. While it reaches some viewers and listeners who would never attend a church, watching from afar is no substitute for the fellowship of believers that involves the church body. The apostle Paul wrote, "Let us not give up meeting together, as some are in the habit of doing, but let us encourage one another." (Hebrews 10:25). How can we encourage one another when we're worshiping in our family rooms on the Sabbath?

Putnam says that the most significant factor behind the growing isolation is the increase in the number of two-career families, thus distancing men and women from their traditional social networks. Bingo! There is simply no time for much of anything but work and maintaining a household. Television, the Internet, and other forms of electronic communication have also weakened the linkage between generations and interfered with the transmission of family traditions. When considered together, they take much of the meaning and enjoyment out of life. In short, Putnam says that the "social capital" of America is shrinking, resulting in more divisiveness and a general breakdown of mutual trust.[5]

Other studies confirm the same trends and conclusions. Overcommitment and isolation are pandemic. Oxford Health Plans of New York, New Jersey, and Connecticut found that one in six employees in the United States is so overworked that he or she can't even take the vacation time earned because of job demands. "Americans," the pollsters said, "are already the most vacation-starved people in the industrialized world, with an average of thirteen vacation days per year, compared with twenty-five or more in Japan, Canada, Britain, Germany, and Italy. The study revealed that 32 percent of those surveyed said they work and eat lunch at the same time, and another 32 percent said they never leave the building once they arrive at work. Some 34 percent said they have such pressing jobs that they have no breaks or downtime while on the job. Nineteen percent say their job makes them feel older than they are, and 17 percent say work causes them to lose sleep at night. Seventeen percent said it is difficult to take time off or leave work even in an emergency, and 8 percent said they believe if they were to become seriously ill, they would be fired or demoted.[6] We are working ourselves to death.

I can't overstate how important these findings by Putnam and others are from my perspective. The harried lifestyle that characterizes most Westerners leads not only to the isolation of people from each other in the wider community, it is also the primary reason for the breakdown of the family. Husbands and wives have no time for each other and many of them hardly know their children. They don't get together with relatives, friends, or neighbors because they are tyrannized by a never-ending "to do" list. Repeatedly during my research in writing this book, which took longer than anything I have ever written, I came face-to-face with the same sad phenomenon. Parents were simply too distracted and exhausted to protect and care for their children.

Pollster George Barna saw evidence of this trend too. He wrote, "It is becoming less common these days for a teenager to have time isolated for focused interaction with family members. Most of the time they spend with their family is what you might call 'family and time': family and TV, family and dinner, family and homework, etc. The lives of each family member are usually so jam-packed that the opportunity to spend time together doing unique activities—talking about life, visiting special places, playing games, and sharing spiritual explorations—has to be scheduled in advance. Few do so."[7]

I find that children and young people are starved today for family life as it used to be—but almost never is. My in-laws, Joe and Alma Kubishta, are eighty-nine and ninety years of age, and yet my daughter and her friends love to visit their home. Why? Because everything there is so much fun. They have time to play table games, laugh, eat, and talk about whatever interests the young people. Nobody is in a hurry. If they are ever called on the phone, they are always available to talk. One of their frequent visitors is an unmarried man named Charlie who loves the Kubishtas. When he had to move away, he drove sixty miles to their house with a rosebush that he planted in their backyard. He just wanted to make sure Joe and Alma didn't forget him. This elderly man and woman, whom I also love, provide something to those who are younger that is simply not available elsewhere. How sad.

I spoke at a White House conference some years ago at which the other speaker was Dr. Armand Nicholi, a psychiatrist from Harvard University. His topic that day, like mine, was the state of the American Family. Dr. Nicholi explained how a frazzled existence that isolates us from each other produces much the same effect as divorce. Parents in the United States spend less time with their children than those in almost any other nation in the world. The result: No one is at home to meet the needs of lonely preschoolers and latchkey children. Dr. Nicholi stressed the undeniable connection between the interruption of parent-child relationships and the escalation of psychiatric problems that we are now seeing. "And if the trend continues," he said, "serious national health problems are inevitable."[8] Ninety-five percent of all hospital beds in the United States will be occupied by psychiatric patients if the incidence of divorce, child abuse, child molestation, and child neglect continues to soar.[9]

Busyness and family isolation aren't new problems, of course. Moms and dads have struggled to control the pressures of living since World War II, but their approach has changed. Most mothers in the fifties and early sixties gave priority to their families, no matter what the cost. That's why so many of them stayed at home full-time to care for their children. They also served as "managers" of the home, keeping everything orderly and clean. With the arrival of the sexual revolution, however, mothers with more liberal perspectives began to reconsider their options.

An article published in the May 1981 issue of *Vogue* presented some of the revolutionary ideas gaining acceptance at that time. It was called "The

New Sanity—Mother's Lib," by Deborah Mason. According to Mason, mothers of the eighties no longer felt the need to live up to the "unrealistic" expectations of motherhood and would be the first generation to do away with the idea of "Supermother," the "saint/tyrant who is all things to her child—and whose child is all things to her." In the article, Mason interviewed Dr. Phyllis Chesler, a psychologist who encouraged mothers to pursue and protect their own individuality by becoming more "separate" from their children. Chesler believed the idea of the "ever-present mother" was a "relatively modern insanity" and urged moms to share their parental responsibilities with others, including grandparents, aunts, siblings, and neighbors. "My son, Ariel, always had four or five adults who were important to him," she said. "For a period of two years, [my assistant] was like a second mother to him."

In keeping with the philosophy of the times, the article urged mothers to be more open with their children, both emotionally and sexually. "The idea persists that somehow you have to give up sex in order to be a mother: you shouldn't do it in front of the children; you shouldn't do it instead of being with the children," she wrote. "There's the idea that once you're a mother, a sex life is frivolous, self-indulgent, and slightly decadent. But women are learning. . . . Married mothers are telling their children, for instance, that on Saturday mornings their parents' bedroom is off-limits until 10:00 A.M. Single mothers are allowing themselves the freedom to invite a man to spend the night."

I find myself in sharp disagreement with almost everything said about motherhood in this article. It is not that easy—or desirable—to become liberated from children. Dr. Chesler's comments in particular have a tinge of sadness to them. Concerning the assistant who became Ariel's "second mom," we can only guess what must have happened when the woman to whom he had become attached went on with her life and left the little boy in the care of his distracted mother. As for the parents' bedroom being off-limits until 10 A.M. on Saturday, I wonder who fixed breakfast for the child, what television programs he watched, and who kept him from doing something dangerous while Mom and perhaps a boyfriend were sleeping. In short, this article reveals the conflicts that were beginning to brew in the eighties and the illogical conclusions that sprang from them. Some women convinced themselves that their children could get along quite well without so much attention and that they actually did better when Mom was more disengaged. Angry mothers told me at the time that they resented the obligations of child rearing and didn't want kids hanging around their feet.

Please understand that I am not unsympathetic to the frustrations and pressures that produced those reactions. They were precipitated, in fact, by the same rat race I described above. And as I acknowledged in the previous chapter, many women *must* work outside the home today, whether for financial or emotional reasons. Still, I am here to express in the strongest possible terms the belief that mothers are just as necessary to healthy child development as they have ever been and that kids cannot raise themselves. They require enormous amounts of time and energy throughout childhood. Any effort to become liberated from them will be done at the children's expense.

Fortunately, there is growing evidence that mothers are questioning the assumptions of the eighties and nineties that led them and their husbands to run faster and buy more. That rethinking of old ideas was expressed in an article published in June 2000 in another women's magazine, *Cosmopolitan*, which, in my opinion, historically has espoused the ultraliberal line.

> According to a recent survey by Youth Intelligence, a market research and trend-tracking firm in New York, 68 percent of 3,000 married and single young women said they'd ditch work if they could afford to. And a *Cosmo* poll of 800 women revealed the same startling statistic: two out of three respondents would rather kick back *a casa* than climb the corporate ladder. "It's no fleeting fantasy—these women honestly aspire to the domestic life, and many will follow through with it," says Jane Buckingham, president of Youth Intelligence.

In this case, we find the other end of the universe from the views espoused by Dr. Chesler and the editors of *Vogue*. What a difference twenty years makes!

The contrast between Dr. Chesler's dislike of mothering in 1981 and *Cosmo*'s fantasy about staying at home in 2000 is humorous to me. One woman's ceiling is another woman's floor, as they say. Admittedly, the *Cosmo* article was more about having an easy life than about making an unselfish commitment to children and a husband. But the lure of full-time mothering was woven throughout. Helen Gurley Brown, longtime editor of *Cosmopolitan* and an avant-garde feminist, wrote a book in 1982 entitled *Having It All*. As with most of her other kooky notions, this one was off the wall. It asserted that women can do everything at once and not have to make tough choices. How interesting that Brown's successors in the new millennium are thinking, *Maybe we have bitten off more than we want to chew.*

There were other indications in the mid-nineties that a gradual sweep of the pendulum back toward the traditional family was occurring. According to a study conducted at that time by sociologists at Cornell University, nearly three-fourths of 117 middle-income couples in upstate New York were found to be scaling back their work assignments for the sake of the children. They were taking more time off and, when necessary, they were lowering their standard of living to accommodate the loss of income. Twice as many women in the study said they had disengaged from the workplace after the birth of their first child, making their husband's career the primary one. The men tended to press ahead with their professional commitments until they had achieved an "acceptable level of flexibility and autonomy in their careers."[12] Many families appeared to be recognizing that something was broken and needed to be fixed.

Women reported being fed up with the harried, exhausted, chaotic lifestyle that often characterized the two-career family. Some of them realized that very little money was left after taxes, child care, and related expenses. An article in *Barron's* estimated that 80 percent of a woman's salary goes for these work-related costs and concluded, "By the time she pays for everything from pantyhose to transportation—sometimes in the form of a second car—working could become an expensive hobby." Therefore, said *Barron's*, "[men and women are] refinancing their largest monthly obligation [their houses], not to take on more consumption, but to make a 'long-term lifestyle change.'"[13]

A related article in *Working Women* was titled "Superwoman's Daughters: They don't want your job. They don't want your life. All twenty-something women want is to change the way America works." It said women who are leaving the workplace can't be understood without considering how they were raised. "Generations are motivated by what they were deprived of as kids. For those under thirty years of age, they had far too little time with their parents. Therefore, younger women seem determined not to make that mistake with their own children." Continuing, "While Boomer women saw their fifties moms as trapped in domestic drudgery, [Busters] see themselves (or their friends) as victims of parental neglect; a whopping 40 percent were raised by divorced or separated parents. And while the conventional wisdom at the time may have been that if the parents were happier, the children would be too, the children say otherwise. 'I don't feel like I really had a family growing up,' says Cindy Peters, a 25-year-old San Francisco nanny. 'My parents divorced when I was two, and I saw my father maybe once or twice a year.'"[14]

Those were very exciting trends when they broke on the scene in the nineties. Unfortunately, they now appear to have stalled. The unprecedented prosperity and job opportunities enjoyed in Western nations may have been difficult for women to ignore. For whatever reason, the move back to homemaking and full-time mothering has not developed into a ground swell to date. Nor has the institution of the family staged a comeback. We will discuss more recent findings in the next chapter.

America's materialistic value system runs very deep within the culture. If the scale-back ever becomes a movement, however, it will portend well for the future of the family! It should result in fewer divorces and more domestic harmony. Children will regain the status they deserve, and their welfare will be enhanced on a thousand fronts. We haven't reached all those goals yet, but I pray that we will. I am convinced of this: most contemporary mothers care more about their families than they do about their careers. Marriage and parenthood still outrank everything else, especially to the generation that grew up in busy, dysfunctional, career-oriented households. They want something better for themselves and for those they love.

In closing, let me emphasize one more time that the trouble we are having with our children is linked directly to routine panic and the increasing isolation and detachment from you, their parents. Furthermore, boys typically suffer more from these conditions than do girls. Why? Because boys are more likely to get off-course when they are not guided and supervised carefully. They are inherently more volatile and less stable emotionally. They founder in chaotic, unsupervised, and undisciplined circumstances. Boys are like automobiles that need a driver at the steering wheel every moment of the journey, gently turning a half inch here and a quarter inch there. They will need this guidance for at least sixteen or eighteen years, or even longer. When left to their own devices, they tend to drift toward the center divider or into the ditch, toward misbehavior or danger. Yet 59 percent of today's kids come home to an empty house. It is an invitation to mischief or disaster for rambunctious males, and the older they get, the more opportunities they have to get into trouble. Today, when the culture is in a tug-of-war with families for control of our children, we can't afford to be casual about their care and training.

Your task as a mother, in conjunction with your husband, is to build a man out of the raw materials available in this delightful little boy, stone upon stone upon stone. Never assume for a moment that you can "do your own thing" without serious consequences for him and his sister. I believe this task must be your highest priority for a period of time. It will not always be required of you. Before you know it, that child at your feet will become a young man who will pack his bags and take his first halting steps into the adult world. Then it will be your turn. By all expectations, you should have decades of health and vigor left to invest in whatever God calls you to do. But for now, there is a higher calling. I feel obligated to tell you this, whether my words are popular or not. Raising children who have been loaned to us for a brief moment outranks every other responsibility.

Besides, living by that priority when kids are small will produce the greatest rewards at maturity.

I hope you know that I am not trying to tell you how to run your life. You and your spouse can discern what is best for your family. No one can tell you which road to take. Some women are emotionally geared for careers and would not want to be stay-at-home moms even if they had the resources to do so. They resent anyone criticizing them for having a career, and I don't blame them. It is a personal decision that is no one's business but their own. I do think, however, that there should be a way to avoid living in a state of perpetual chaos. It is hard on adults but creates havoc for children. From my perspective, almost anything is better than chasing the lead caterpillar endlessly around the flowerpot.

QUESTIONS AND ANSWERS

I am one of those women who would love to stay home with my children, but there is no way we can live on my husband's salary. Can you offer some suggestions for how I might "step off the train," as you called it, without facing bankruptcy?

There may be a way to get it done. Donna Partow, author of *Homemade Business,* has offered specific advice about starting your own business, which could involve desktop publishing, pet grooming, sewing, consulting, transcribing legal documents, or even getting into mail-order sales. Choosing the right business is the first of three preparatory steps. Consider taking a personal-skills-and-interest inventory to identify your abilities and to discover what you might enjoy doing. The second step is to do your homework. Begin by asking your librarian to help you research your chosen field. Look up books, magazines, and newspaper articles. Talk to other people who have done what you are considering. Join an industry organization and a network. Subscribe to industry publications. According to Mrs. Partow, the third step is to garner as much support as you can. Get your children, your spouse, and your friends on your side. Setting up a small business can be stressful, and you'll need as much encouragement as you can get. Then marshal your resources and go for it.[15] A home-based business might turn out to offer the very best of both worlds.

Before telling me why this alternative is impossible in light of your circumstances, let me tell you about the Van Wingerden family in Colorado Springs. They have twenty-two children, twelve of them adopted and ten born to Lynn, the mother. Theirs is one of the most impressive families I've had the opportunity to meet. They own a strawberry farm and all the children old enough to work are involved in it. Believe it or not, Mrs. Van Wingerden homeschools all the kids personally. The family is highly organized and structured, with the teenagers having specific and rotating responsibilities for routine tasks and for the care of the youngsters. Visiting their home is a delight. The Van Wingerdens prove that many things are possible for those who set their minds to it.

I hope you find an answer to the very important question you asked. I believe you will.

It seems to me that we are making our kids grow up too fast. Parents of my children's friends seem to be in a big hurry to make teenagers out of their kids. They arrange actual "dates" for their ten- or twelve-year-olds and give them adult materials to read. Am I right to resist this tendency to rush my children through childhood?

I agree with you wholeheartedly. Parents in the past had a better understanding of the need for an orderly progression through childhood. Kids in that day were given plenty of time to play and giggle and be themselves. There were cultural "markers" that determined the ages at which certain behaviors were appropriate. Boys, for example, wore short pants until they were twelve or thirteen. Now those markers have disappeared, or they have been moved downward. Children are depicted on TV as having more insight and maturity than their elders. They are rushed, ready or not, from the womb to the nursery school to the adult world at a breakneck pace. This scurrying to maturity leaves a child without a strong foundation on which to build because it takes time to build a healthy human being. When you rush the process, your kids have to deal with sexual and peer pressures for which their young minds are not prepared. There is another problem with making children grow up too quickly. When you treat them as though they are adults, it becomes more difficult to set limits on their adolescent behavior down the road. How can you establish a curfew for a thirteen-year-old rebel who has been taught to think of himself as your peer?

Besides, what's the big hurry, anyway? I think you are right to savor those childhood years and let the developmental process march to its own internal drumbeat.

My sixteen-year-old son wants to go on a supervised, three-week outing in a nearby national forest. The boys will eat off the land as much as possible and learn to deal with nature on its own terms. I am reluctant to let him go, however. It scares me to think of him being out there somewhere beyond my ability to help him if he got in difficulty. It just seems safer to keep him at home. Am I right to turn him down?

I'm sure you know that within a couple of years, your son will be gone off to college or to some other pursuit, perhaps the military, and he will be entirely beyond your reach. Why not give him a taste of that independence now, while he is still under your care? It will be better for him to ease away from your influence than to have it come to a sudden end.

There was a moment during my teen years when my mother and I had a similar debate. I was sixteen years old and had been invited to work on a shrimp boat during the summer. The captain and crew were tough dudes who didn't put up with any nonsense. It was a man's world, and I was drawn to it. My mother was very reluctant to grant permission because she understood that there could be dangers out there in the Gulf of Mexico for four days. She was about to say no when I said, "How long are you going to keep me as your little boy? I'm growing up, and I want to go." With that, she relented. It turned out to be a good experience during which I learned what it is like to work whether or not I felt like it and I began to understand better how the adult world works. I came back grimy and tired but feeling very good about myself. My mother later acknowledged that she had done the right thing, even though she worried the entire time.

Yes, I think you should let your boy go to the wilderness, especially since it is a supervised trip. "Letting go" works best as a gradual process. It's time to get started.

Your description of the caterpillar fits my family perfectly. We live an exhausting lifestyle but just can't seem to find a way to slow down. I am even depressed at times about how hard we work and how little time we have for ourselves. Do you have any last word of advice for us?

Let me share something that may help you and your husband make the tough choices on which a slower lifestyle could depend. Do you remember Vince Foster, who reportedly committed suicide during the early days of the Clinton administration? He was deputy counsel to the president before that tragic night of his death on July 20, 1993. Just eight weeks earlier, Foster had been asked to speak to students graduating from the University of Arkansas School of Law. This is what he told the students on that occasion:

> A word about family. You have amply demonstrated that you are achievers willing to work hard, long hours and set aside your personal lives. But it reminds me of that observation that no one was ever heard to say on a deathbed, I wish I had spent more time at the office. Balance wisely your professional life and your family life. If you are fortunate to have children, your parents will warn you that your children will

grow up and be gone before you know it. I can testify that it is true. God only allows us so many opportunities with our children to read a story, go fishing, play catch and say our prayers together. Try not to miss a one of them.[16]

Vince Foster's words now echo back to us from eternity. While you're climbing the ladder of success, don't forget your own family. Those years with your children at home will be gone in a heartbeat. Do whatever is necessary to grab those precious moments, whether it requires changing jobs, getting a smaller house, or turning down lucrative and exciting opportunities. Nothing is worth losing your kids. Nothing!

THE ORIGINS OF
HOMOSEXUALITY

A FEW YEARS AGO, I received the following scribbled note from a very troubled youth. He wrote:

Dear Dr. Dobson:

I've been putting this off for a long time so I'm finally writing you a letter.

I am a thirteen year old boy. I have listened to your tapes [Preparing for Adolescence] but not the complete set. I did listen to the one on sex though.

Getting to the point, I don't know if I have a serious problem or a passing? (I don't know the word for it).

All through my life (very short) I have acted and look much more like a girl than a boy. When I was little, I would always wear finger nail polish, dresses, and the sort. I also had an older cousin who would take us (little cousins) into his room and show us his genitals.

I'm afraid I have a little sodomy in me. It was very hard for me to write what I just did. I don't want to be homosexual but I'm afraid, very afraid. That was hard to write too. Let me explain further.

Through my higher grades in school (I'm in seventh grade) kids have always called me names (gay, fag etc.), and made fun of me. It's been hard. I have masturbated (I guess) but gone too far. When I was little (not that little) I tried to more than once to suck my own penis (to be frank). That sounds very bad and looks even worse to read it. I pray that nothing is wrong with me.

Very recently I have done such acts as looking (maybe lusting, I pray so hard that I wasn't) at my self in skimpy underwear. Whenever I wear it I feel a like sexual sensation.

Yesterday in the bathroom (in front of the mirror), I wiggled my body very rapidly, making my genitals bounce up and down. I get a little bit of that feeling mentioned above as I write this. After I did this, I immediately asked forgiveness of God, went in the shower but did it again there. I prayed more and felt very bad.

I talked with one of my pastors and told him at that point I probably preferred a man's body over a woman's. Now that was hard to say!

He said he didn't think anything was wrong with me (I don't know how else to say it. He apparently thought it was passing), but I feel very badly and want to know why.

The pastor mentioned above is one I go to for advice very often.

About my spiritual life; I came to Christ only about a year ago but have grown very much. I have also done lot's wrong. I am a Mennonite. What denomination are you? I have been baptized and am well liked in the church (I think).

I'm afraid if I am not straight (that's much easier to write) I will go to hell.

I don't want to be not straight.

I don't try to be not straight.

I love God and want to go to heaven. If something is wrong with me, I want to get rid of it.

Please help me.
Mark

I was deeply touched by Mark's letter. I know him well even though we have never met. He is representative of many other preteens and teens around the world who have awakened to something terrifying within—something they don't understand—something that creates enormous confusion and doubt. These kids often recognize very early in life that they are "different" from other boys. They may cry easily, be less athletic, have an artistic temperament, and dislike the roughhousing that their friends enjoy. Some of them prefer the company of girls, and they may walk, talk, dress, and even "think" effeminately. This, of course, brings rejection and ridicule from the "real boys," who tease them unmercifully and call them "queer," "fag," and "gay." Even when parents are aware of the situation, they typically have no idea how to help. By the time the adolescent hormones kick in during early adolescence, a full-blown gender identity crisis threatens to overwhelm the teenager. This is what Mark was experiencing when he wrote. And it illustrates why even boys with normal heterosexual tendencies are often terrified that they will somehow "turn gay."[1]

There is an additional dimension of pain for those who have grown up in a strong Christian home. Their sexual thoughts and feelings produce great waves of guilt accompanied by secret fears of divine retribution. They ask themselves, *How could God love someone as vile as me?* Mark even felt condemned for jumping up and down in the shower and for feeling the excitement it created. (That titillation by the sight of his own body is a classic symptom of narcissism, or a "turning inward" to fulfill his unmet gender-identification needs.) He either had to figure out how to control this monster within or, in his understanding, face an eternity in hell. There is no greater internal turmoil for a Christian boy or girl than this. At the top of Mark's letter he wrote, "I may sound very bad. I hope I'm not that bad."

Poor kid! Mark is in desperate need of professional help, but he is unlikely to get it. His parents apparently don't know about his travail, and the pastor he trusts tells him it will pass. It probably won't! Mark appears to have a condition we might call "prehomosexuality," and unless he and his entire family are guided by someone who knows how to assist, the probabilities are very great that he will go on to experience a homosexual lifestyle.

What do we know about this disorder? Well first, it *is* a disorder, despite the denials of the American Psychiatric Association. Great political pressure was exerted on this professional organization by gays and lesbians (some of whom are psychiatrists) to declare homosexuality to be "normal." The debate went on for years. Finally, a decision was made in 1973 to remove this condition from their *Diagnostic and Statistical Manual (DSM)*. It was made not on the basis of science but was strongly influenced by a poll of APA members, which was initiated and financed by the National Gay and Lesbian Task Force. The vote was 5,834 to 3,810.[2] The American Psychological Association soon followed suit.[3] Today, psychologists or psychiatrists who disagree with this politically correct interpretation, or even those who try to help homosexuals change, are subjected to continual harassment and accusations of malpractice.

The second thing we know is that the disorder is not typically "chosen." Homosexuals deeply resent being told that they selected this same-sex inclination in pursuit of sexual excitement or some other motive. It is unfair, and I don't blame them for being irritated by that assumption. Who among us would knowingly choose a path that would result in alienation from family, rejection by friends, disdain from the heterosexual world, exposure to sexually transmitted diseases such as AIDS and tuberculosis, and even a shorter lifespan?[4] No, homosexuality is not "chosen" except in rare circumstances. Instead, bewildered children and adolescents such as Mark find themselves dealing with something they don't even understand.

Third, there is no evidence to indicate that homosexuality is inherited, despite everything you may have heard or read to the contrary. There are no respected geneticists in the world today who claim to have found a so-called "gay gene" or other indicators of genetic transmission. This is not to say that there may not be some kind of biological predisposition or an inherited temperament that makes one vulnerable to environmental influences. But efforts to identify such factors have been inconclusive. Despite this lack of evidence, the gay and lesbian organizations and their friends in the mainstream media continue to tell the public that the issue is settled—that gays are "born that way." *Time* and *Newsweek* splashed "promising findings" to that effect on their covers. *Time* titled their story "Search for the Gay Gene,"[5] and *Newsweek* proclaimed, "Does DNA Make Some Men Gay?"[6] *Oprah* devoted several slanted television programs to the subject, and Barbara Walters said recently, "There is a growing body of opinion that says that people are born homosexual."[7] Even though entirely false, this politically motivated information (or *dis*information) has done its work. According to a Harris Poll in February 2000, 35 percent of the people polled believed homosexuality was "genetic."[8]

There is further convincing evidence that it is not. For example, since identical twins share the same chromosomal pattern, or DNA, the genetic contributions are exactly the same within each of the pairs. Therefore, if one twin is "born" homosexual, then the other should inevitably have that characteristic too. That is not the case. When one twin is homosexual, the probability is only 50 percent that the other will have the same condition.[9] Something else must be operating.

Furthermore, if homosexuality were specifically inherited, it would tend to be eliminated from the human gene pool because those who have it tend not to reproduce. Any characteristic that is not passed along to the next generation eventually dies with the individual who carries it.

Not only does homosexuality continue to exist in nations around the world, it flourishes in some cultures. If the condition resulted from inherited characteristics, it would be a "constant" across time. Instead, there have been societies through the ages, such as Sodom and Gomorrah and the ancient Greek and Roman empires, where homosexuality reached epidemic proportions. The historical record tells us that those cultures and many others gradually descended into depravity, as the apostle Paul described in Romans 1, resulting in sexual perversion in all its varieties. That ebbing and flowing with the life cycle of cultures is not the way inherited characteristics are expressed in the human family.

Finally, if homosexuality were genetically transmitted, it would be inevitable, immutable, irresistible, and untreatable. Fortunately, it is not. Prevention is effective. Change is possible. Hope is available. And Christ is in the business of healing. Here again, gay and lesbian organizations and the media have convinced the public that being homosexual is as predetermined as one's race and that nothing can be done about it. That is simply not true. There are eight hundred known former gay and lesbian individuals today who have escaped from the homosexual lifestyle and found wholeness in their newfound heterosexuality.

One such individual is my coworker at Focus on the Family, John Paulk, who has devoted his life to caring for and assisting those who want to change. At one time, he was heavily involved in the gay community, marched in "gay-pride" parades, and was a cross-dresser. Ultimately, John found forgiveness and healing in a personal relationship with Jesus Christ, and he has walked the straight life now since 1987. He is happily married to Anne, a former lesbian, and they have two beautiful children. Despite a momentary setback when he entered and was discovered in a homosexual bar, which delighted his critics, John did not return to his former life. There are hundreds of stories like this that offer encouragement to those who want out of the gay lifestyle but have no idea how to deal with the forces within. I would be less than honest if I didn't admit that homosexuality is not easily overcome and that those who try often struggle mightily. But it would be equally dishonest to say that there is no hope for those who want to change. Credible research indicates otherwise.

Psychologist George Rekers says there is considerable evidence that change of sexual orientation is possible—with or without psychiatric intervention. He wrote, "In a sizable number of cases . . . the gender-identity disorder resolves fully."[10]

Dr. Robert L. Spitzer, a psychiatric professor at Columbia University, created a firestorm in May 2001, when he released the results of his research at a meeting of the American Psychiatric Association. Spitzer, who had spearheaded the APA's decision in 1973 to declassify homosexuality as a mental-health disorder, says his findings "show some people can change from gay to straight, and we ought to acknowledge that."[11] This was not what his critics wanted to hear. We applaud Dr. Spitzer for having to courage to examine and then expose the myth of inevitability.

With that, let's return to Mark's story to explore what is going on within him and other boys who are experiencing prehomosexual urges. We also want to consider what causes their sexual identity disorder and what can be done to help. To get at those issues, we will turn to the very best resource for parents and teachers I have found. It is provided in an outstanding book entitled *Preventing Homosexuality: A Parent's Guide,* written by clinical psychologist Joseph Nicolosi, Ph.D. Dr. Nicolosi is, I believe, the foremost authority on the prevention and treatment of homosexuality today. His book offers practical advice and a clear-eyed perspective on the antecedents of homosexuality. I wish every parent would read it, especially those who have reason to be concerned about their sons. Its purpose is not to condemn but to educate and encourage moms and dads.

Dr. Nicolosi has permitted me to share some quotes from this book that will answer many questions. These are some of his words:

> There are certain signs of prehomosexuality which are easy to recognize, and the signs come early in the child's life. Most come under the heading of "cross-gender behavior." There are five markers to [diagnose] a child with "gender identity disorder." They are:
>
> 1. Repeatedly stated desire to be, or insistence that he or she is, the other sex.
> 2. In boys, preference for cross-dressing, or simulating female attire. In girls, insistence on wearing only stereotypical masculine clothing.
> 3. Strong and persistent preference for cross-sexual roles in make-believe play, or persistent fantasies of being the other sex.
> 4. Intense desire to participate in stereotypical games and pastimes of the other sex.
> 5. Strong preference for playmates of the other sex.
>
> The onset of most cross-gender behavior occurs during the pre-school years, between the ages of two and four. You needn't worry about occasional cross-dressing. You should become concerned, though, when your little boy continues doing so and, at the same time, begins to acquire some other alarming habits. He may start using his mother's makeup. He may avoid other boys in the neighborhood and their rough-and-tumble activities and prefer being with his sisters instead, who play with dolls and dollhouses. Later he may start speak-

ing in a high-pitched voice. He may affect the exaggerated gestures and even the walk of a girl, or become fascinated with long hair, earrings and scarves.[12] In one study of sixty effeminate boys aged four to eleven, 98 percent of them engaged in cross-dressing, and 83 percent said they wished they had been born a girl.[13]

The fact is, there is a high correlation between feminine behavior in boyhood and adult homosexuality. There are telltale signs of discomfort with . . . boys and deep-seated and disturbing feelings that they [are] different and somehow inferior. And yet parents often miss the warning signs and wait too long to seek help for their children. One reason for this is that they are not being told the truth about their children's gender confusion, and they have no idea what to do about it.

Perhaps you are concerned about your child and his or her "sexual development." Maybe your son or daughter is saying things like, "I must be gay," or "I'm bisexual." You've found same-sex porn in his room or evidence that he has accessed it on the Internet. You've found intimate journal entries about another girl in her diary. The most important message I can offer to you is that there is no such thing as a "gay child" or a "gay teen." [But] left untreated, studies show these boys have a 75 percent chance of becoming homosexual or bisexual.[14]

It is important to understand, however, that most of my homosexual clients were not explicitly feminine when they were children. More often, they displayed a "nonmasculinity" that set them painfully apart from other boys: unathletic—somewhat passive, unaggressive and uninterested in rough-and-tumble play. A number of them had traits that could be considered gifts: bright, precocious, social and relational, and artistically talented. These characteristics had one common tendency: they set them apart from their male peers and contributed to a distortion in the development of their normal gender identity.

Because most of these men hadn't been explicitly feminine boys, their parents had not suspected anything was wrong, so they had made no efforts at seeking therapy. Many clients have told me, "If only—back then when I was a child—someone had understood the doubts, the feeling of not belonging—and tried to help me."

But make no mistake. A boy can be sensitive, kind, social, artistic, gentle, and be heterosexual. He can be an artist, an actor, a dancer, a cook, a musician—and heterosexual. These innate artistic skills are "who he is," part of the wonderful range of human abilities, and there's no reason to discourage them. But they can all be developed within the context of normal heterosexual manhood.

In my opinion (and in the opinion of an increasing number of researchers), the father plays an essential role in a boy's normal development as a man. The truth is, Dad is more important than Mom. Mothers make boys. Fathers make men. In infancy, both boys and girls are emotionally attached to the mother. In psychoanalytic language, Mother is the first love object. She meets all her child's primary needs.[15]

Girls can continue to grow in their identification with their mothers. On the other hand, a boy has an additional developmental task—to disidentify from his mother and identify with his father. At this point [beginning about eighteen months], a little boy will not only begin to observe the difference, he must now decide, "Which one am I going to be?" In making this shift in identity, the little boy begins to take his father as a model of masculinity. At this early stage, generally before the age of three, Ralph Greenson observed, the boy decides that he would like to grow up like his father.[16] This is a choice. Implicit in that choice is the decision that he would not like to grow up like his mother. According to Robert Stoller, "The first order of business in being a man is, 'don't be a woman.'"[17]

Meanwhile, the boy's father has to do his part. He needs to mirror and affirm his son's maleness. He can play rough-and-tumble games with his son, in ways that are decidedly different from the games he would play with a little girl. He can help his son learn to throw and catch a ball. He can teach him to pound a square wooden peg into a square hole in a pegboard. He can even take his son with him into the shower, where the boy cannot help but notice that Dad has a penis, just like his, only bigger.

Based on my work with adult homosexuals, I try to avoid the necessity of a long and sometimes painful therapy by encouraging parents, particularly fathers, to affirm their sons' maleness. Parental education, in this area and all others, can prevent a lifetime of unhappiness and a sense of alienation. When boys begin to relate to their fathers, and begin to understand what is exciting, fun and energizing about their fathers, they will learn to accept their own masculinity. They will find a sense of freedom—of power—by being different from their mothers, outgrowing them as they move into a man's world. If parents encourage their sons in these ways, they will help them develop masculine identities and be well on their way to growing up straight. In 15 years, I have spoken with hundreds of homosexual men. I have never met one who said he had a loving, respectful relationship with his father.[18]

Many of these fathers loved their sons and wanted the best for them, but for whatever reason (perhaps there was a mismatch between the father's and son's temperaments), the boy perceived his father as a negative or inadequate role model. Dad was "not who I am" or "not who I want to be." A boy needs to see his father as confident, self-assured and decisive. He also needs him to be supportive, sensitive and caring. Mom needs to back off a bit. What I mean is, don't smother him. Let him do more things for himself. Don't try to be both Mom and Dad for him. If he has questions, tell him to ask Dad. She should defer to her husband anything that will give him a chance to demonstrate that he is interested in his son—that he isn't rejecting him.

But this natural process of gender identification can sometimes go awry. The late Irving Bieber, a prominent researcher, observed that prehomosexual boys are sometimes the victims of their parents' unhappy marital relationship.[19] In a scenario where Mom and Dad are battling, one way Dad can "get even" with Mom is by emotionally abandoning their son.

Some fathers find a way to get involved in everything but their sons. They lose themselves in their careers, in travel, in golf, or in any number of activities that become so all-important to them that they have no time for their boys—or for that "one particular son" who is harder to relate to because he does not share Dad's interests. Perhaps the activities this particular son enjoys are more social and less typically masculine.

I've even seen fathers who did not necessarily have other distracting interests but simply remained emotionally removed from the entire family. I saw one father—an immature and inadequate man who emphatically told his wife, before the son was born, that he did not want a boy—completely reject and ignore their son and dote on their daughter. Apparently threatened by the idea of having another "man in the house," this father made his displeasure so clear that, by the age of two, his son was (not surprisingly) wearing dresses and playing with a doll collection.

For a variety of reasons, some mothers also have a tendency to prolong their sons' infancy. A mother's intimacy with her son is primal, complete, exclusive; theirs is a powerful bond which can deepen into what psychiatrist Robert Stoller calls a "blissful symbiosis." But the mother may be inclined to hold onto her son in what becomes an unhealthy mutual dependency, especially if she does not have a satisfying, intimate relationship with the boy's father. She can put too much energy into the boy, using him to fulfill her own needs in a way that is not good for him. In reparative therapy [a psychologist's name for treatment of homosexuals], effeminate boys yearn for what is called "the three A's." They are: their father's affection, attention and approval.

If [a father] wants his son to grow up straight, he has to break the mother-son connection that is proper to infancy but not in the boy's interest after the age of three. In this way, the father has to be a model, demonstrating that it is possible for his son to maintain a loving relationship with this woman, his mom, while maintaining his own independence. In this way, the father is a healthy buffer between mother and son.

Recalling the words of psychologist Robert Stoller, he said, "Masculinity is an achievement."[20] [He] meant that growing up straight isn't something that happens. It requires good parenting. It requires societal support. And it takes time. The crucial years are from one and a half to three years old, but the optimal time is before age twelve. Once mothers and fathers recognize the problems their children face, agree to work together to help resolve them, and seek the guidance and expertise of a psychotherapist who believes change is possible, there is great hope.[21]

Once again, this short synopsis from Dr. Nicolosi's book is the most insightful material available on the subject. The bottom line is that homosexuality is not primarily about sex. It is about everything else, including loneliness, rejection, affirmation, intimacy, identity, relationships, parenting, self-hatred, gender confusion, and a search for belonging. This explains why the homosexual experience is so intense—and why there is such anger expressed against those who are perceived as disrespecting gays and lesbians or making their experience more painful. I suppose if we who are straight had walked in the shoes of those in that "other world," we would be angry too.

There is much more useful information in Nicolosi's book, of course. If you as a parent have an effeminate boy or a masculinized girl, I urge you to get a copy and then seek immediate professional help. Be very careful whom you consult, however. Getting the wrong advice at this stage could be most unfortunate, solidifying the tendencies that are developing. Given the direction the mental-health profession has gone, most secular psychiatrists, psychologists, and counselors would, I believe, take the wrong approach—telling your child that he is homosexual and needs to accept that fact. You as parents would then be urged to consider the effeminate behavior to be healthy and normal. That is exactly what you and your son don't need! You *do* need to accept the child and affirm his worth regardless of the characteristics you observe but also work patiently with a therapist in redirecting those tendencies. When deciding to seek that help, however, you must be aware that for many prehomosexual boys, the signs may be more subtle, such as an inability to bond with same-sex peers, feeling different and inferior, or a discomfort with one's gender. Sometimes a visit with a professional is needed just to determine whether or not a child is at risk.

To find a counselor who understands and accepts the perspective I have described, you might want to contact one of two outstanding organizations. They are:

Exodus International
P.O. Box 77652
Seattle, WA 98177
Phone: 206-784-7799 or 888-264-0877
Fax: 206-784-7872
Internet: www.exodusintl.org

National Association for Research and Therapy of Homosexuality (NARTH)
16633 Ventura Boulevard, Suite 1340
Encino, CA 91436
Phone: 818-789-4440
Internet: www.hnarth.com

It is the mission of these caring people to be of help to people such as you. Another resource is Focus on the Family, which has an outreach called Love Won Out. It offers seminars and information to those seeking help. If you are dealing with a child whose sexual identity is confused, I hope you will avail yourselves of these programs and resources.

There is another major cause of gender identity disorder that we must address. It results from early sexual abuse. One study indicated that fully 30 percent of homosexuals say they were exploited sexually as a child, many of them repeatedly. That experience can be devastating, and depending on when it occurs, it can be life changing. Despite the evil of abuse, there is a vigorous effort now to end the taboo against sex between men and boys. This campaign to change social attitudes is being talked about in gay and lesbian literature and is even beginning to appear in the mainstream press. For example, *The Weekly Standard* (January 1, 2001) featured a cover story entitled "Pedophilia Chic Reconsidered." Here is a quote from this very important and well-documented article written by Mary Eberstadt:

> This social consensus against the sexual exploitation of children and adolescents is apparently eroding. The defense of adult-child sex—more accurately, man-boy sex—is now out in the open. Moreover, it is on parade in a number of places—therapeutic, literary, and academic circles; mainstream publishing houses and journals and magazines and bookstores—where the mere appearance of such ideas would until recently have been not only unthinkable, but in many cases, subject to prosecution.

The article ended with this statement: "If the sexual abuse of minors isn't wrong, then nothing is."[22]

Is there further evidence that some members of the gay and lesbian movement are, in fact, seeking legal sexual access to very young boys? Yes. We see it in the growing influence of the North American Man/Boy Love Association (NAMBLA), which shamelessly promotes sex between adults and children. Its motto is "Sex before eight or else it's too late." Although this wretched organization has not been endorsed by most gay and lesbian publications, it has not been condemned by most of them either. That tells us a great deal.

There is also the vigorous effort by gays to infiltrate the Boy Scouts in the same way lesbians have done so successfully in the Girl Scouts, where 33 percent of their staff is said to be lesbian.[23] The purpose of this Boy Scout campaign is not to permit the sexual abuse of kids in most cases. It is to use scouting to teach and indoctrinate them. This explains the intensity of the debate and a lawsuit that went all the way to the U.S. Supreme Court. The case was decided by a razor-thin, five-to-four decision against homosexual interests.[24] Despite the loss, corporations have taken up the cause and are refusing to fund the Scouts.[25] Even some United Way chapters are withholding funds from this fine and desperately needed organization.[26]

There is other evidence of the desire to gain access to boys. It is seen in the worldwide effort to lower the age when a child can legally give his consent for intercourse with an adult. This effort has resulted in many intense legislative struggles in Western nations. I received a letter recently from Lyndon Bowring, a colleague in the U.K. who heads a profamily organization called Care Trust. This is what he wrote: "We are up to our eyes here in London with the rampant advances of the militant gay lobby. Our Parliament is planning to reduce the age of consent for homosexual intercourse between adult males from 18 to 16. Apart from a sovereign miracle of grace, we will not succeed in persuading them not to do so. We are doing everything in our power to prevent it and calling on His divine power to intervene on behalf of our young boys. There is hardly a place on the globe where similar struggles are not occurring, except where no fight remains in discouraged or outnumbered Christians."

Alas, Mr. Bowring and his coworkers lost that fight. The age of consent in the U.K. was lowered to sixteen.[27] It is fourteen in Canada,[28] fifteen in Sweden, fifteen in France, fourteen in Germany, Iceland, Italy, San Marino, and Slovenia, and twelve in Spain, Holland, Malta, and Portugal.[29] Isn't it utterly outrageous that twelve-year-olds in these latter countries, most of whom will not have reached puberty, can give their consent to older males who want to exploit them sexually? Furthermore, their parents can't legally prevent the exploitation. The question that jumps out at us is, "Why have gay and lesbian organizations worked feverishly to lower the age of accountability?" There can be only one answer.

The most shocking evidence of this targeting of children appeared in the following article written by Michael Swift, who worked for a publication called the *Gay Community News*. It was read during a congressional debate by former Congressman William Dannemeyer, who also entered it into the Congressional Record. Here is a short excerpt from that shocking statement:

> We shall sodomize your sons, emblems of your feeble
> masculinity, of your shallow dreams and vulgar lies. We
> shall seduce them in your schools, in your dormitories, in

your gymnasiums, in your locker rooms, in your sports arenas, in your seminaries, in your youth groups, in your movie theater bathrooms, in your army bunkhouses, in your truck stops, in your all-male clubs, in your houses of Congress, wherever men are with men together. Your sons will become our minions and do our bidding. They will be recast in our image. They will come to crave and adore us.

All laws banning homosexual activity will be revoked. Instead legislation shall be passed which engenders love between men. All homosexuals must stand together as brothers; we must be united artistically, philosophically, socially, politically, and financially. We will triumph only when we present a common face to the vicious heterosexual enemy.

The family unit—spawning ground of lies, betrayals, mediocrity, hypocrisy and violence—will be abolished. The family unit, which only dampens imagination and curbs free will, must be eliminated. Perfect boys will be conceived and grown in the genetic laboratory. They will be bonded together in a communal setting, under the control and instruction of homosexual savants.

All churches who condemn us will be closed. Our only gods are handsome young men. We adhere to a cult of beauty, moral and esthetic. All that is ugly and vulgar and banal will be annihilated. Since we are alienated from middle-class heterosexual conventions, we are free to live our lives according to the dictates of the pure imagination. For us too much is not enough.

We shall be victorious because we are filled with the ferocious bitterness of the oppressed who have been forced to play seemingly bit parts in your dumb, heterosexual shows throughout the ages. We too are capable of firing guns and manning the barricades of the ultimate revolution.

Tremble, hetero swine, when we appear before you without our masks.[30]

This article, which outraged conservative Christians and many other Americans, was greeted with a shrug by the general public and by members of Congress. Did these words represent one man's private views, or are they representative of a larger community? I don't know. Certainly not all homosexual activists would ascribe to them. It is clear, however, that our boys need to be protected from sexual abuse, whether it is homosexual or heterosexual in character. Guard them night and day when they are young. Don't send them into a public bathroom alone. Be very careful whom you trust in summer camp, in Sunday school, or in the neighborhood. Any sexual exploitation of a child, whether from a family member or the man next door, whether gay or straight, has the same deleterious effect.

I'll go a step further to make a controversial recommendation to you as parents. I don't think it is a good idea to leave your children of either sex in the care of teenage boys. Nor would I allow my teenage son to baby-sit. Why not? Because there is so much going on sexually within adolescent males. It is a preoccupation that invades every aspect of life. The sex drive in boys is at its lifetime peak between the ages of sixteen and eighteen. Under that influence, children have been severely damaged by "good kids" who meant no harm but who were enticed by curiosity to experiment and explore. I'm sure many of my readers will disagree with this position and may even be shocked by it. In the vast majority of cases, it would be safe to ignore my warning. But I simply would not take a chance during the vulnerable years. There is simply too much at stake. I have talked to too many parents who have regretted trusting someone they thought was okay. I make this recommendation knowing it will confuse and perhaps anger some of you. It is simply my opinion based on unfortunate incidents I have witnessed through the years.

Returning now to the issue of homosexuality, I am concerned not only about the sexual abuse of boys (and girls), but also about what they are being taught by the culture at large. Suddenly, everyone seems to be talking about a subject that I didn't know about until I was eleven years old. Now we seem determined to tell every five-year-old about this aspect of adult sexuality. Our public schools appear to be moving relentlessly in that direction.

Given what we have discussed in this chapter, can you see how this pervasive teaching will be terribly confusing to very young boys who are experiencing a gender-identity crisis? How about the other cultural influences, including television and movies, that are urging boys and girls to "think gay" and to experiment with role-reversal behavior? When combined with the absence or disengagement of fathers, we can begin to understand why the incidence of homosexuality appears to be rising and why more and more children and teens are reporting that they think they are homosexual.[31] As the institution of the family continues to unravel, we are laying the foundation for another epidemic like those that have occurred historically.

Moms and dads, are you listening? This movement is *the* greatest threat to your children. It is of particular danger to your wide-eyed boys, who have no idea what demoralization is planned for them. I would ask, "Is there anything more important than taking the time to protect your kids and to be there when they need you most?" I think not.

I'll close by referring again to Mark and other boys who appear effeminate, gender-confused, or chronically uncomfortable with same-sex peers. Parents, you have no time to lose. Seek professional help for those who appear to be in difficulty, and pray for them every day. Fathers, begin applying the principles outlined by Dr. Nicolosi, and by all means, give your boys what they most urgently need: YOU.

QUESTION AND ANSWER

My church tends to be on the liberal side of most social issues, and it teaches that since homosexuality is inherited and therefore involuntary, it should be affirmed and accepted by Christians. This is of importance to me because my son is seventeen and has announced that he is gay. Would you comment on the position taken by my church and how I can make sense out of the situation in our family?

First, the only way your church can validate its position is by ignoring the biblical passages that condemn the homosexual lifestyle. But let me answer your question on another level by asking two questions of my own. They are "What if?" and "So what?"

"What if" it could be demonstrated beyond a shadow of a doubt that homosexuality is, as activists claim, genetic, biochemical, and neurological in origin? We would still want to know, "So what?" As you said, the homosexual activist community would have us believe that because their behavior is genetically programmed and beyond their control, it is morally defensible. That is not supportable. Most men have inherited a lust for women. Their natural tendency is to have sex with as many beautiful girls as possible, both before marriage and after. Abstinence before marriage and monogamy afterward are accomplished by discipline and commitment. If men did what they are genetically programmed to do, most would be sexually promiscuous from about fourteen years of age onward. Would that make such behavior any less immoral? Of course not.

"What if" a pedophile (child abuser) could claim that he inherited his lust for kids? He could make a good case for it. Certainly his sexual apparatus and the testosterone that drives it are creations of genetics. Even if his perversion resulted from early experiences, he could accurately claim not to have chosen to be what he is. But "so what?" Does that make his abuse of children any less offensive? Should society accept, protect, and grant special civil rights to pedophiles? Is it blatant discrimination that they are tried, convicted, and imprisoned for doing what they are "programmed" to do? No! The source of their sexual preference is irrelevant to the behavior itself, which is deemed to be immoral and reprehensible by society.

"What if" it could be demonstrated conclusively that alcoholics inherit a chemical vulnerability to alcohol? Such is probably the case, since some races have a much higher incidence of alcoholism than others. But "so what?" Does that mean alcoholism is any less of a problem for those families and for society in general? Hardly!

I hope the point is clear. Being genetically inclined to do immoral things does not make them right. There are many influences at work within us, but they are irrelevant. I know of no instance in Scripture where God winked at evildoers because of their flawed inheritance or early experiences. In fact, the opposite is implied. In the book of Genesis we are told that an angel informed Ishmael's mother that the child she was carrying would be "a wild donkey of a man; his hand will be against everyone and everyone's hand against him, and he will live in hostility toward all his brothers" (Genesis 16:12). In other words, Ishmael was genetically inclined toward violence and rebellion. Yet there is no indication that he enjoyed a special dispensation from God that excused his sinful behavior. Each of us is accountable for what we do, without excuses and rationalizations. That's why we all need a Savior who died to eradicate our sins, regardless of their source.

There is one other "so what?" which I should address. If homosexuals can claim to be genetically predisposed to lust after their own sex, why does that make their circumstances different from unmarried heterosexuals? Single individuals are certainly programmed by heredity to desire fulfillment with the opposite sex, but they are called to a world of purity. I know that is a tough requirement—especially for those who will never marry—yet this is my understanding of Scripture. Promiscuity for unmarried heterosexuals is the moral equivalent of promiscuity for homosexuals. Liberal ministers who are revising church standards to sanction sexual expression by homosexuals must, I would think, extend the same concession to heterosexual singles. But before they do, some scriptural justification should be found to support the "new morality." I think none exists.

I hope this has been helpful. As for the situation in your family, I am sorry you are going through such difficult times. Since your son is seventeen years old, there is little you can do to require him to seek help. Your task at this time is to stay on your knees and ask the Lord to talk to him in the terms he needs to hear. Many seventeen-year-olds who think they are gay later return to the world of heterosexuality. I suggest that you maintain your relationship with the boy and that you be there for him when and if he comes back.

SINGLE PARENTS AND GRANDPARENTS

CHAPTER 10

MANY YEARS AGO when Shirley and I were newly married, she was at home alone late one afternoon. The doorbell rang unexpectedly and my wife went to answer it. Standing there on the porch was a poorly dressed young woman in her late teens. She immediately lumbered into a memorized sales pitch for a variety of household brushes.

Shirley let her talk for a few minutes and then said politely, "I'm really sorry, but we don't need any more brushes. Thank you for coming by."

The girl dropped her head and said, "I know. Nobody else wants them either."

Then big tears welled up in her eyes as she turned to leave.

"Wait," said Shirley. "Tell me who you are."

"My name is Sally," she replied. "I have a little boy, and I'm trying to earn a living for him. But it is so hard."

Shirley invited the young woman to come inside and get better acquainted. Coffee was served, and Sally began to talk. She turned out to be a single mother who had dropped out of high school at sixteen years of age. She had gotten pregnant and was hastily married to an immature boy. He soon abandoned Sally, leaving her with a baby and no visible means of support. Being desperate and having no marketable skills, she had taken the job as a door-to-door brush seller.

When I came home that evening, Shirley told me the story and expressed concern for her new friend. We got in the car and drove to the address Sally had given. She lived in an apartment building on a busy street. We climbed a flight of stairs at the side and knocked on the door. Sally appeared, holding her toddler, Sammy, and invited us to come in. After chatting a while, I asked what they had eaten for dinner. She took me to the kitchen and pointed to an empty can of SpaghettiOs. That was it. I opened the cabinets and the refrigerator. There was no more food in the apartment.

We packed Sally and Sammy in our car and drove to a nearby market. We bought several sacks of groceries and then returned them to their home. During the next few weeks we involved Sally in our church activities, and I helped her get a job at Children's Hospital, where I served on the pediatric staff. Gradually, she got on her feet and later moved out of the Los Angeles area.

It has been many years since I have seen Sally and Sammy, but I've thought of them often. What I remember thinking when I first met them is how incredibly difficult it must be to be poor, lonely, and stressed to the limit by the responsibilities of raising a child—or several of them. I can hardly imagine how very young moms in that situation are able to meet the challenges of everyday living. They have to locate available and safe child-care services, work for eight or more hours every day, pick up the kids, stop by the grocery store, then come home to cook dinner, wash the dishes, change the diapers, help with the homework, bathe the preschoolers, read a story, dry a tear, say a prayer, and tuck the kids in bed. Then, after perhaps sixteen hours of toil and mothering responsibilities, the household chores must be tackled.

Weekends are a blur of activity. Washing, ironing, vacuuming, and project work, such as cleaning the stove, must get done during those "off" hours. And who is there to help when the car won't run and the refrigerator burns out and the roof springs a leak? Finally, a mother must find a way to address her own needs to be loved and cared for and intellectually challenged. She's not a machine, after all. I'll tell you frankly that the task of the single mother, especially those who are young and poor, is the toughest job in the universe, and my greatest respect and admiration are reserved for those who do it superbly. Single fathers deserve our commendation as well, trying desperately to "mother" their needy kids. Our focus for this chapter, however, will be on moms because of the special problems they face in trying to raise boys.

We receive about 250,000 letters, phone calls, and e-mail responses at Focus on the Family every month, some of them coming from single mothers. Here is one of these impassioned notes:

I was married for 30 years but my husband died recently. Now I need your help. Tell me how I'm supposed to act as a single. I need to learn how to have fun alone; to know what to say, what to do and not do. Tell me how to come home to an empty house, not being needed, having no one to take care of and no one to share life with. How do I learn to enjoy life again? I married the second man I ever dated and he was my best friend, my lover, my companion. How do I find love again? Any man I would date would not want to talk about my husband, but I just can't put 30 years behind me and deny that they happened. Tell me, where do I go for answers, and do those answers exist?

Sincerely,
Kelly

This woman will learn to live again, but it will take a little time for her wounds to heal and her heart to mend. I have shared this letter and the other illustrations above to heighten the sensitivity of all of us to the plight of those who have suffered the loss of a loved one through death, abandonment, or divorce. It is one of the most traumatic experiences in living.

What we're describing here involves a huge number of people in the United States and around the world, and their ranks are growing exponentially. According to the census figures released in May 2001, the nuclear family has continued its downward spiral that began in the early seventies. Indeed, it is now in an unfettered free fall. Our local newspaper in Colorado Springs, *The Gazette,* shouted the news in seventy-two-point type: "Nuclear Family Fading."[1] *The Boston Herald,* in a column written by Don Feder, carried the headline "Nuclear Family in Meltdown."[2] Allan Carlson of the Howard Center for the family said, "We are moving toward a post-family society."[3] Sadly and ominously, these assessments are true. This God-ordained institution, which has prevailed in almost every culture on earth for more than five thousand years, is unraveling right in front of our eyes.

Here are some of the most disturbing findings from the report: Households headed by unmarried partners grew by almost 72 percent during the past decade, most of them involving people living together out of wedlock. Households headed by single mothers increased by more than 25 percent, and those led by single fathers grew by almost 62 percent.[4] For the first time ever, nuclear families dropped below 25 percent of households.[5] A third of all babies were born to unmarried women (33 percent), compared to only 3.8 percent in 1940.[6] From other studies we know that cohabitation has increased by 1,000 percent since 1960.[7] We are also seeing a growing number of unmarried women in their twenties and thirties who, like actress Jodie Foster, are choosing to bear and raise children alone.[8]

In essence, the old taboos against divorce and cohabitation are disappearing and the culture is abandoning its commitment to lifelong marriage. Indeed, I doubt if most young adults have any significant understanding of why previous generations defended the family so vigorously or why they were disdainful of those who blatantly "shacked up." It was because they violated biblical moral principles that were deeply ingrained within the culture. That belief system has almost disappeared. Now, the divorce rate is actually higher by a small margin among Christians than among those who profess to have no faith at all.[9] These social changes represent a growing decadence with far-reaching implications for the future.

It is predicted now, based on these trends, that more than half of the babies born in the 1990s will spend at least part of their childhood in single-parent homes.[10] Already the United States is the world's leader in the percentage of single parents,[11] and that number is skyrocketing. What will happen if marriage does indeed become obsolete or largely irrelevant in the days ahead? It portends a world where almost every child will have several "moms" and "dads," perhaps six or eight "grandparents," and dozens of half siblings. It will be a world where little boys and girls are shuffled from pillar to post in an ever-changing pattern of living arrangements—where huge numbers of them will be raised in foster-care homes or be living on the street (as millions do in Latin America today). Imagine a world where nothing is stable and where people think primarily about themselves and their own self-preservation. In short, the demise of families will produce a chaotic world that will be devastating to children.

Given the national crisis that appears to be on the horizon, one would think that the federal government would be trying desperately to support the institution of marriage and do everything possible to restore it to a position of health and vitality. Quite the opposite is true. Our political leaders have been shameless in their disregard for the institution of the family. When Margaret La Montagne, White House domestic policy advisor to President George W. Bush, was asked during a C-Span interview about her reaction to the census report, she replied, "I guess I would respond to say, you know, 'So what?'"[12] Her comment sets some kind of record for its ignorance. The nation's families are steadily disintegrating, yet La Montagne said, in effect, "Who cares?" The disturbing thing is that this woman sits at the highest level of government, offering advice and counsel every day to the most powerful man on earth. Lord, help us! Unfortunately, her flippant remark reflects the cavalier attitude toward families that is commonly expressed among officials in Washington. How long has it been since you've heard one of our prominent leaders talk about the pressures on marriages or the desperate need for government to lend a hand?

In the absence of assistance from our leaders or anyone else, the family continues to splinter. As it does, our children are the ones who are suffering most. Barbara Dafoe Whitehead, writing in her acclaimed article "Dan Quayle Was Right," said this about the stresses experienced by boys and girls when their families fall apart:

> All this uncertainty [in a single-parent home] can be devastating to children. Anyone who knows children knows that they are deeply conservative creatures. They like things to stay the same. So pronounced is this tendency that certain children have been known to request the same peanut butter and jelly sandwich for lunch for years on end. Children are particularly set in their ways when it comes to family, friends, neighborhoods, and schools. Yet when a family breaks up, all these things may change. The novelist Pat Conroy has observed that "each divorce is the death of a small civilization." No one feels this more acutely than children.[13]

Cynthia Harper at the University of California, San Francisco, and Sara McLanahan from Princeton studied the phenomenon of father-absence by conducting what came to be known as the "National Longitudinal Survey of Youth." The researchers identified 6,403 boys between fourteen and twenty-two years of age and then followed them until their early thirties. Here are a few of their salient findings:

1. The sons of single mothers are at greater risk for violence, apparently because they have spent less time with their fathers. A child born out of wedlock is two-and-a-half times as likely to serve time in prison.
2. Child support makes no difference one way or another in the likelihood that a boy will grow up to be a criminal. It appears that the economic status of a single mother is not the key factor. It is the absence of "Dad."
3. The third conclusion is even more surprising. The very small number of teenage boys in the study who lived with their single fathers were no more likely to commit crimes than were boys from intact families. Why? Perhaps it is because men who don't marry but care for their children single-handedly are unusually devoted fathers.[14]

Well, I know that is distressing news for single moms. I wish I could say that finding a new husband will offer the ultimate solution. Unfortunately, the research confirms that remarriage of a parent often makes things worse for boys. According to the study above, males living in stepparent families were almost three times as likely to face incarceration as those from intact families.[15] The odds for youths in stepparent families are similar to those who do not live with any parents. Apparently stepfathers and children frequently compete for the time, attention, and resources of the biological mother, creating conflict and bitterness.

Blending two families also poses some very unique and unsettling challenges. I can tell you that the Brady Bunch—the notion that a mom and dad with three kids each can create one big happy family without conflict or rivalries—is a myth. It just doesn't happen that way, although many blended families do eventually adjust to their new circumstances. During the first few years, at least, it is typical for one or more of the kids to see the new stepparent as a usurper. Their loyalty to the memory of their departed mother or father can be intense. So for them to welcome a newcomer with open arms would be an act of betrayal. This places the stepparent in an impossible bind.

Furthermore, it is common for one child to move into the power vacuum left by the departing parent. That youngster becomes the surrogate spouse. I'm not referring to sexual matters. Rather, that boy or girl begins relating to the remaining parent more as a peer. The status that comes with that supportive role is very seductive, and a youngster is usually unwilling to give it up.

There is an even more serious problem that occurs among reconstituted families. It concerns the way the new husband and wife feel about their kids. Each is irrationally committed to his or her own flesh and blood, while he or she is merely acquainted with the others. When fights and insults occur between the two sets of children, the parents are almost always partial to those they brought into the world. The natural tendency is for the blended family members to dissolve into armed camps—us against them. If the kids sense this tension between the parents, they will exploit it to gain power over their siblings. Unless there are some ways to ventilate these issues and work through them, some terrible battles can occur. Given these challenges, it is apparent why the probabilities of second and third marriages being successful are considerably lower than the first. It is possible to blend families successfully, and millions of people have done it. But the task is difficult, and if you choose that path, you may need some help in pulling it off. That's why I strongly suggest that those planning to remarry seek professional counseling as early as possible. It is expensive, but another divorce is even more costly.

There is another troubling problem that I am reluctant to mention to single mothers, who are probably discouraged already by the outlook I have described. But I must do it. According to a study by the Canadian researchers Martin Daly and Margo Wilson, preschool children in stepfamilies are forty times as likely as children in intact families to suffer physical or sexual abuse.[16] Whitehead points out that most of the sexual abuse is committed by a third party, such as a neighbor, a stepfather's male friend, or another nonrelative, but stepfathers are far more likely to assault nonbiological children than their own natural children.[17]

Since remarriage may or may not solve the problem of finding masculine influence for her boys, the single mother has to figure out other ways to meet the challenge. How can she teach them to shave, tie a tie, or think like a man? What can she tell them about male sexuality, and what can she do to get them ready to lead future families of their own? How can she find role models who will fill in for the missing dad? These are questions of monumental importance, but there are some approaches that may be helpful.

To every single mom who is on this quest, let me emphasize first that you have an invaluable resource in our heavenly Father. He created your children and they are precious to Him. How do I know that? Because He said repeatedly in His Word that He has a special tenderness for fatherless children and their mothers. There are many references in Scripture to their plight. For example:

- Deuteronomy 10:17-18: The Lord your God . . . defends the cause of the fatherless and the widow, and loves the alien, giving him food and clothing.
- Deuteronomy 27:19: Cursed is the man who withholds justice from the alien, the fatherless or the widow.
- Psalm 68:5: A father to the fatherless, a defender of widows, is God in his holy dwelling.
- Zechariah 7:10: Do not oppress the widow or the fatherless, the alien or the poor.

The message is very clear, isn't it? The Lord is watching over the oppressed, the poor, the downtrodden, and the child who has no father. And yes, He is concerned about your children too. He is waiting for you to ask Him for help. I have seen miraculous answers to prayer on behalf of those who have sought His help in what seemed like impossible situations.

My own wife, Shirley, was a product of a broken home. Her father was an alcoholic who abused the family and squandered their meager resources in a local bar. Soon, the marriage ended in divorce. At that critical moment,

Shirley's mom recognized that she was going to need help raising her two kids alone, so she sent them to a little evangelical church in the neighborhood. There they met Jesus Christ and found the stability they lacked at home. Shirley began praying in the quietness of her little bedroom that the Lord would send a father to love and take care of them. He did precisely that. Along came a wonderful thirty-seven-year-old man named Joe who had never been married. He became a Christian and a marvelous father to the two kids. Joe gave them stability through the rest of childhood and adolescence. He has been my father-in-law now for forty years, and I love him like my own dad. So you see, even though the probabilities and predictions are that remarriage is risky, anything is possible when you depend on God and look to Him for strength. I will leave it to you and your pastor to determine whether or not you have biblical grounds to remarry, which can be another thorny issue to be determined.

Until a good man like Joe comes along, you as a single mother must make an all-out effort to find a father-substitute for your boys. An uncle or a neighbor or a coach or a musical director or a Sunday-school teacher may do the trick. Placing your boys under the influence of such a man for even a single hour per week can make a great difference. Get them involved in Boy Scouts, Boy's Club, soccer, or Little League. Check out Big Brothers as a possibility. Give your boys biographies, and take them to movies or rent videos that focus on strong masculine (but moral) heroes. However you choose to solve the problem, do not let the years go by without a man's influence in the lives of your boys. If they have no nurturing male role models by which to pattern themselves, they will turn to whoever is available, such as gang members, or perhaps, to you, the mom. And as we know, it is not healthy for boys to model themselves exclusively after their mothers.

It would be a good idea to seek the help of organizations whose mission it is to give you a hand. There are hundreds of these ministries and nonprofit organizations that offer assistance of various sorts. My own bias is with Focus on the Family, which produces wonderful materials for kids. Chief among them is a series of high-quality recorded dramas designed for radio but now available on cassettes and CDs called *Adventures in Odyssey*. Kids love them. More than 470 of these value-based episodes are available now in albums, and each teaches masculine and feminine role modeling, family living, and principles of morality and ethics. Odyssey is one of the best ideas to come from our organization. There are many other ministries that will help in other ways as boys get older, including Young Life, Youth for Christ, and Youth Builders. For a more detailed list of possibilities, see the Web site provided at www.youthworkers.net.

Now let me offer some additional hope and advice to single mothers.

Even though the studies indicate that a higher percentage of kids from single families have problems, the great majority turn out fine. If you are a dedicated mom who gives priority to your children, they will do all right too.

Let's talk briefly about disciplining your boys, which will be discussed in more detail in chapter 16. You should train and guide your children in the same ways you would if your marriage was intact. Sometimes a single mom will feel guilty for not being able to provide adequately for her sons and daughters, and for the painful circumstances that accompanied the divorce. Therefore, she becomes permissive and namby-pamby. That is not in the best interest of your kids. It is especially risky for your boys. They need boundaries even more than the children of intact families. An authoritative but loving mother brings security to a child for whom everything seems insecure. Get in there and lead! Punish when punishment is needed. Hug them when they need reassurance. And make them think you know what you're doing and where you're going even when you may not have a clue.

I referred earlier to the child who has a tendency to move into the power vacuum created by the loss of a father and to become the "surrogate spouse" to the mom. Don't let that happen. The boy who is trying to be an instant adult is still a child and should not be burdened with grown-up responsibilities and cares. Don't tell him all your inner fears and anxieties, even if he seems able to handle them. Sooner or later, your abdication of the parental role will come back to haunt you when, perhaps in adolescence, you have to tell him no or confront him when he is straying. This substitute spouse may actually be female. It is not unusual for girls to also aspire to that role. Regardless, it is not a good idea for a child of either sex. Let them grow up as God intended—one day at a time.

And now some ideas for single mothers seeking to develop masculine characteristics in their boys. Debra Gordon, writing in *The Virginian-Pilot* (Norfolk, Va.), wrote an interesting piece about "natural aggression" called "Mama's Boys." You might find it helpful. An excerpt follows:

> This Christmas, Suzanne Rhodes did something she swore she'd never do—put toy guns under the tree.
>
> With four boys ranging in age from 9 to 15, Rhodes had decided early on that she'd never buy them guns, nor would she allow them into the house.
>
> Instead, she followed the politically correct, nonsexist agenda for raising boys in the '80s and '90s: buying them gender-neutral toys, like blocks and puzzles. When their friends

came over packing toy pistols, she made them park their weapons at the door.

"Didn't matter, though. There were lots of fingers smoking out there," the Chesapeake mother says.

But this year, after touring Civil War battlefields, reading books, and watching movies with her boys about this country's many wars, Rhodes changed her mind.

"I've done a lot of thinking about it," says Rhodes, who also has a 6-year-old daughter and whose husband is a naval officer. "They're out there playing war games; they're not out there killing for killing's sake. They're showing their aggression like boys do. There's just a connection to war games and war that men have. And I think you will never be able to breed it out of males because males and females are apples and oranges."

And therein lies the crux of the issue when you talk about mothers raising sons. Do we aspire toward the ultimate of non-sexist, gender-neutral childhoods, following the theory that we can mold a child primarily through environment and modeling, or do we accept that boys and girls are inherently different and teach our sons how to constructively channel and manage their inborn aggression, their "stick-beating gene," as one mother calls it?[18]

The best answer, in my opinion, is the latter.

GRANDPARENTS

Let me turn now to the people who are most likely to give you the help you need. I'm referring to maternal or paternal grandparents. They have a God-given responsibility to influence their grandkids, and most of them are more than willing to fit the bill. Our organization just published a helpful book that may stimulate some ideas. It is called *The Gift of Grandparenting,* by Eric Wiggen. Here are some excerpts from it that will, I hope, not only motivate single parents to look to their parents but will inspire grandparents to get more involved with grandkids. These are the considered words of Eric Wiggen:

> Young people who visit their grandparents, with few exceptions, do so because they want—often very badly—the companionship of their elders. The same grandmother who beat me at checkers when I was nine became a friend in whom

I could confide when I was 19. She wrote me letters, long and full of family news. When I came home from college, we talked. And you know what? Grandma wanted to listen to me! I soon found that she was fascinated with what I had to say, and she had more time to listen to me than my parents. For your teen or single young-adult grandchildren, perhaps the most important "entertainment" you can give them is to listen when they talk.[19]

A sage once remarked that the elderly slow down and stoop over so that they can see things as children once again, so that they can hold the hands of children who toddle along on inexperienced feet. That bug on the sidewalk, the snail under the cabbage leaf, the robin pulling the worm from the rain-moistened earth—these are the things small children and their grandparents notice.[20]

Our grandchildren live in imperfect homes, reared by imperfect parents: our sons and daughters who are married to our sons-in-law or daughters-in-law, all of them imperfect. Although we all made mistakes raising our children, the good news is that as godly grandparents, walking with the Lord, we can expect the Lord to use us. Because of our own immaturity when our children—now parents—were growing up, we may have disappointed them. But by keeping us alive to enjoy our grandchildren, the Lord is giving us a ministry to help fill in these gaps in our imperfect child-rearing.[21]

We grandparents must first firmly retake the lead, if not of society as a whole, at least of our own families. This is not as drastic a step as it may seem, for the pendulum has begun to swing the other way, and maturity is coming into fashion again.[22]

Writing to grandparents, columnist Evelyn Sullivan summarized a study of more than seven hundred students at Central Missouri State University. Sullivan cited Central Missouri professor of family studies Dr. Gregory E. Kennedy, who found that after a divorce these students felt the role of grandparents to be "even more important" in their lives than in homes that remained intact. Most grandparents, whether or not the parents have been divorced, do have regular interaction with their grandchildren, Dr. Kennedy's study found. Significantly, most students felt closer to their maternal grandparents than to their paternal grandparents. This is important to maternal grandparents, since in a divorce settlement the children are usually placed in the custody of the mother.[23]

As grandparents, we desire to help usher our Brandons and Meghans across the threshold of adulthood. We can best do this when we realize that these youth, who much of the time are carefree and happy, are also suffering through the most trying years of life—from puberty to young maturity. We gently criticize their behavior when we must. We set guidelines and expressions when they're entrusted to our care. Even as we wouldn't question another adult's toupée or hairdo, we avoid personal remarks about our emerging adult-teens whose souls may have been torn and trampled already in the school gauntlet or by conflicts at home. But most of all, we support, we listen, we pray. And we love.[24]

Grandparents today are not only needed in a supportive role to their daughters and sons, a surprising number of them have been given full custody of their grandchildren. They raised their children many years ago and thought their parenting job was done. Then when they should have been simply supplementary to the main event, they are faced with one of two very difficult choices: either accept the responsibility of raising another generation of kids, or watch them suffer from inadequate care or placement in a foster home. This is not the way families were designed to function. It represents another aspect of marital disintegration and children born out of wedlock. I would need another book, or many of them, to address that concern in depth, but it is one that deserves our prayers and creative thought.

I can't conclude this discussion without speaking directly, and perhaps boldly, to Christians who live in intact families. You have been reading in this chapter about the challenges faced by single parents. I hope you will consider the ways you might help. Men, how about taking the sons of single mothers with your own boys when you're going fishing or out to a ball game? Let those fatherless boys know that you care for them. Answer their questions and teach them how to throw a ball or how to block and tackle. This is not simply my own casual suggestion. It is a divine commandment. Remember the Scriptures I shared about God's compassion for fatherless children? Jesus conveyed that same love to the young. He took boys and girls on His lap and said, "Whoever welcomes a little child . . . in my name welcomes me" (Matthew 18:5).

To married moms, I hope you will reach out to the single mother such as Sally and help her cope with the child-rearing task. Baby-sit for her so she can get out every now and then. Share your financial resources with those who have less, and include them in your holiday activities. You might be able to keep a single mom from going over the edge by giving her just a little encouragement and assistance. The Lord will reward you, I believe, for caring for someone who is desperate for a friend.

With that, we will close our discussion of single parents and grandparents with two more simple thoughts. The first concerns the difficult task of letting go when the job is done. That can be a very emotional time, especially for a mom who has labored, sweated, prayed, cried, scrimped, saved, cooked, cleaned, taught, and shepherded her children through numerous crises without the help of a husband or a father for her kids. All of a sudden, at the other end of childhood, the reason for her existence and her passion in living has to be surrendered. Her children have grown up. The empty place inside as her sons and daughters leave home can be like a chasm. After all these years, she is alone again.

My office at Focus on the Family sits across the valley from the United States Air Force Academy. From there I can see the cadets as they train to be pilots and officers. I particularly enjoy watching the gliders soaring through the heavens. The only way those graceful yellow crafts can fly is to be tethered to a powered plane that takes them up to where they can catch a wind current. Then they disengage and sail free and alone until returning to land.

While watching that beautiful spectacle one day, I recognized an analogy between flying and child rearing as a single parent. There is a time when your children need to be towed by the "mother plane." If that assistance were not available, or if it were not accepted, the "glider" would never get off the ground. But, inevitably, there comes an appropriate moment for a young pilot to disengage and soar free and alone in the blue heavens. Both operations are necessary for successful flight. If you as a parent are not there for your kids when they are young, they are likely to remain "grounded" for life. On the other hand, if they stay tethered to you as young adults, they will never experience the thrill of independent flight. Letting go not only gives freedom to your grown son or daughter but allows you to soar as well. It's all part of the divine plan.

I will close this discussion of single parents and grandparents by sharing an inspirational thought from an old black-and-white movie. It starred Ginger Rogers and Robert Ryan and was titled *Tender Comrade*. It was set in 1943, when most husbands and fathers had gone off to war. Rogers was one of the many women who were raising a baby alone. One day, she received the dreaded telegram from the War Department that began, "We regret to inform you . . ." Her husband had been killed in action. Ginger immediately ran up the stairs to the nursery room, where her baby boy lay in his crib. She cradled him in her arms, and after a few quiet moments together, she tearfully spoke these touching words to the infant:

> Wake up, Chris. I am sorry to have to wake you up like this but I've got to talk to somebody. I can't talk to them downstairs because they're having a wedding down there. You're the only one I can tell it to. I guess this is just a private thing between you and me anyway. I suppose years from now I'll still be telling you about how I stood there beside the train. (Her voice trails off and a voice-over of a conversation she had with her husband at the train station is heard in the background.)
>
> Little guy (showing Dad's picture to the infant), this is your father. Chris, this is your son. You two aren't ever going to meet. Only through me will you ever know anything about each other. So now I am making my introductions. This is the kid you never wanted till you met me, Chris. This is your dad, young fella. I knew him when he wasn't much bigger than you. Oh, maybe a little bigger. You've got his eyes and that mop of hair, you know that one hair on your head that never stays in place. It's your dad coming out all right. Seems funny to call him your dad, he was such a baby himself. (Her voice trails off; a voice-over of a childhood memory she had with the father is heard in the background.)
>
> Just by having been brought up with him, I know everything that's going to happen to you. When you're seven, some girl is going to hit you over the head with a klinker; and when you're ten, you're going to cut her hair; and when you're fifteen, you're going to take her to her first dance and break her heart. You see, little guy, I know the ropes. (Her voice trails off, voice-over of the father telling about all the wonderful plans he has for his son.)
>
> Remember him, Son. Remember your father as long as you live. He was a fine man, Chris boy. He never made speeches, but he went out and died so that you could have a better break when you grew up than he ever had. Not the same break but a better one. Because he did a lot of thinking about you in his own way. Never forget it, little guy. Never forget it. He didn't leave you any money. He didn't have

time, Chris boy. No million dollars or country clubs or long, shiny cars for you, little guy. He only left you the best world a boy can ever grow up in. He bought it for you with his life. That's your heritage. A personal gift from your dad. (Her voice trails off; voice-over of the father talking about what the war is about is heard in the background.)

And one more thing: As long as you live, don't let anybody ever say he died for nothing because if you let them say it, you let them call your dad a fool. You let them say he died without knowing what it was all about. He died for a good thing, little guy, and if you ever betray it, if you ever let it slip away from you, if you ever let anyone talk you out of it, or swindle you out of it, or fight you out of it, you might as well be dead too. So hang on to it, sweet, latch on to it with those tiny little fingers; grab on to it, Chris boy, grab it right out of your dad's hands and hold it high, hold it proud.

(She stands up and talks to the picture of the father.) Don't worry, Chris. He'll grow up to be a good guy. Good night, Chris [to the picture]. Good night, Chris [to the baby].[25]

QUESTIONS AND ANSWERS

Hi, Dr. Dobson. My name is Christina and I am 9 years old. I love my grandmother and grandfather very much. I wrote a poem about where I like to go when I'm at my Nana and Papa's house. This is it.

There is a place were I like to hide.
There is a place with love inside.
It's my Nanas garden.
When it's all quiet I just stand still
and listen to the trees and whipperwhill.
There is a place where I like to hide.
There is a place with love inside.
It's my Nanas garden.
It's my Nana's garden.

Thank you, Christina. I loved your poem. You must have a very special grandmother and grandfather. I hope you will keep writing. You are very gifted. Jesus loves you Christina. So do I.

I have seven grandchildren that I think are just wonderful, but I don't know how to talk to them when we are together. It has been a long time since I was young. How can I engage these kids in conversation and draw them to me? What should I talk to them about?

Children love to talk about fun things and funny things. They love to play games and solve puzzles and look at pictures. When you interject yourself into their world at these and other points of interest, and if you aren't cranky and demanding, they will open themselves to you. All you have to do is give them your time and attention. Then you won't be able to keep them off your lap!

Now, concerning what you should talk about with your grandchildren: One of the most important contributions you can make is to teach them about your family's early history, about the obstacles your family overcame and what has made their stories unique. Education consultant and author Cheri Fuller applied the lyrics of an old African song to this responsibility. It included this line: "When an old person dies, it's as if a library burns down."[26] *You* are the "library" for your grandchildren, being able to connect them with their past. It is your obligation and privilege, I believe, to give them a sense of identity within the family.

My great-grandmother helped raise me during my early years. When I was just three or four years old, I remember her telling me stories about her life on the frontier. She told me how she would sit in her log cabin at night and hear the mountain lions come down from the hillside looking for the pigs. She would describe fascinating experiences that helped me understand how different life was then. The time we spent together bonded us to one another. The stories she told me then are still vivid in my memory. They helped open my mind to a love of history, a subject that still fascinates me to this day.

I suggest you gather your grandkids around and start telling them stories about your past—of your courtship with their grandmother, what she looked like, and why you fell in love with her. Then tell them how you came to a relationship with Jesus Christ and what that did for you. I think you'll find your little ones will be eating out of your hand.

"Let's Go for It!"

IF YOU HAVE a son, I would bet he is a natural competitor. He loves a challenge and nothing excites him quite like winning. Even if he lacks the skill to take on the world, he'll probably try to make a run at it. If you understand this aspect of his masculine temperament, much of his behavior will begin to make more sense.

One of my favorite stories was shared by a man named Bill Dolan who said, "I can remember the night at the dinner table when Tom wouldn't drink his milk and I made an issue out of it. I said, 'You're not leaving until you drink the milk.' He said, 'I don't want the milk.' I said, 'That's not the question. You're drinking the milk before you leave the table.' We were at a real Irish stalemate. So, finally it dawned on me that I know this kid, and I went and got a glass, and I filled the glass with milk. Then I said, 'I'll race you.' He said, 'Cool.' And we drank the milk, he put it down and said, 'Let's do two out of three.'"[1]

This competitive impulse is evident in "boys" of all ages. I've mentioned my father-in-law, Joe Kubishta, several times. He is eighty-nine years old but he still loves the thrill of victory. He plays golf four to five times a week and keeps track of his wins and losses against his younger buddies. He is especially good at a card game called hearts, which he played during off-hours when he was in the navy. He taught the game to me when Shirley and I were first married, and we played it every time we were together, but Joe never revealed the secrets of winning. Three years went by before I figured out how he was beating me. Joe just laughed and said, "Let's play again." Now I have a little secret of my own. When Joe has a good hand and is quietly trying to "run it," his neck turns red. I just watch that region below his ears and I can tell what he's trying to do. You see, Joe isn't the only one who loves to win.

It is impossible to understand why men do some of the things they do without considering their competitive nature. How else can we explain the bloody military campaigns that have raged through the ages? Vast armies led by the likes of Alexander the Great, Julius Caesar, Napoleon Bonaparte, or Adolf Hitler marched off to fight and die on foreign fields—not for the purpose of defending their homeland or advancing a particular cause, but simply to conquer and subjugate weaker peoples. Why did they do it? The motivation of the great generals is obvious: They came home with the spoils of war. But what about the lowly frontline troops? They endured terrible privation, low pay, bad food, devastating diseases, and the constant risk of injury or death. In return, most of them received nothing but a tiny share of the glory and the respect of their peers. Amazingly, that was enough. In 1862, after General Stonewall Jackson nearly drove the Yankee troops into the Rappahannock, Confederate General Robert E. Lee said, "It is a good thing war is so terrible; else we should grow too fond of it."[2]

This masculine thirst for conquest has led not only to numerous wars but also to daring and adventuresome feats that benefited humanity. It resulted in the discovery of the New World in the fifteenth and sixteenth centuries and other great exploits of that era. A more recent example is described in a wonderful book entitled *Endurance,* written by Alfred Lansing. It chronicles an expedition in 1914 to the bottom of the world. The ship on which the crew sailed, also called *Endurance,* eventually became locked in a sea of ice that crushed and sank the vessel. Men stood watching nearby on a floe as their only link with home slid out of sight.[3] This true story describes their desperate struggle to get back to England. It is a must-read. (I wrote the foreword to one version.)

In preparation for the journey, Captain Earnest Shackleton placed the following ad in local newspapers. It read, "Men wanted for hazardous duty. Small wages. Bitter cold. Long months of complete darkness, constant danger. Safe return doubtful. Honor and recognition in case of success." The response was phenomenal. More then five thousand men applied, of which twenty-seven were accepted. One stowaway also managed to make the journey. Again we have to ask, why were so many men willing to risk everything to be part of this perilous adventure? I think we know the answer.[4]

It is likely that your boy also possesses a measure of this competitive and adventuresome spirit. If you as a parent understand and respond to this nature, both you and your son will be more in sync. As a place to start, you need to teach him not only how to win but also how to lose gracefully. A good way to do that is by carefully supervising his participation in organized sports, using games as a stimulus for what you want to teach. Coaches and parents must model good sportsmanship, self-control, and teamwork. Not only should they exhibit these attitudes themselves, but they should teach them to their kids. The better athletes among them must not be permitted to taunt the boys who are smaller and less coordinated. Cruelty on the athletic field has no place in the world of the young, although it usually exists there. Finally, adults should resist vigorously the idea of "winning at any cost," which has become so common in children's organized sports. It is shameful the way some parents and coaches act in front of impressionable boys and girls. You would think a national championship was on the line.

A front-page article in *The New York Times* recently described the appalling behavior of parents whose youngsters are competing in soccer, baseball, and basketball. Referees, the writer said, are quitting in record numbers because of the abuse they are subjected to routinely. Moms and dads yell, jeer, spit, and brawl when decisions go against their sons and daughters. Their behavior has even been given a name: sideline rage. One ref who recently hung up his whistle said he was tired of spectators shouting, "Get your fat body down the field," "You're blind," "You're just in this for the money," and "My kid is heartbroken because of you." About 15 percent of youth games involve some sort of verbal abuse from parents or coaches, compared with only 5 percent five years ago. It is a disgraceful development.[5]

Your attitude as a parent will shape the future behavior of your boy. If he sees you acting like a spoiled kid, yelling at the umpire or referee, taunting other players, and throwing tantrums when things go wrong, your son will behave just as badly. You must remember what you are trying to accomplish through organized sports. Winning at this age is nothing; teaching your boy to deal properly with his anger, disappointment, and frustration is everything. This does not mean that you should belittle or ignore his feelings in difficult moments. In fact, you must never underestimate how bad your boy feels when he does poorly at something important to him. The issue is not just that he lost but that he embarrassed himself at having failed. It goes straight to his heart. Let your son talk about the experience and help him understand that there will be wins and losses for the rest of his life. Fathers should tell about times when they played well and other days when they flopped. In so doing, Dad will be modeling how to deal with each outcome. Rudyard Kipling, in his great poem "If," referred to both disaster and triumph as "impostors."[6] There is wisdom there. One's successes are not as wonderful as they appear, but neither are the failures as awful as they seem at the time.

The way you as parents respond to the painful moments will either make them better or worse. My friend Dick Korthals shared a story about his attendance at a dog show that illustrates the proper approach. As part of the competition, about a dozen dogs were commanded to "Stay!" and then were expected to remain in a statuelike manner for eight minutes while their owners left the ring. Judges scored them on how well they were able to hold their composure during their masters' absence. Well, about four minutes into the exercise, Dick noticed the dog on the end, a magnificent German Shepherd named Jake. He seemed to be losing his poise, sinking slowly toward the ground. By the time his trainer returned, poor Jake was lying flat on his stomach with his head on his paws. Now Jake immediately saw the disappointment in his owner's eyes and began crawling on his belly toward him. Everyone was expecting the trainer to scold the dog for his poor performance. But instead, he bent down and cupped the dog's head in his hands, and then he said with a smile, "That's okay, Jake. We'll do better next time." It was a very touching moment.

There's a lesson here for every parent, too, not only with regard to sports but everything else. Children are going to disappoint us. It's an inevitable part of being young. And when they do, our natural reaction will be to bark at them, "Why did you do that?" and, "How could you have been so stupid?" But if we're wise, we'll remember that they're just immature little human beings like we used to be. There are times to say with love and warmth, "That's okay, Son. You'll do better next time."

Here's an additional bit of advice that is bound to be controversial: I think it is a great mistake to ask boys to compete against girls in team sports. Sociologist George Gilder explains why. He believes coeducational sports demoralize and discourage the weaker boys without helping the girls. This view goes across the grain of what is happening in many American schools, where coeducational physical education is common. Gilder said, "[This is] just an idiocy that would amaze any anthropologist who might come from deep in the jungle to observe the peculiar behavior of Americans in our society."[7] I agree emphatically.

Let me hasten to say that girls need athletic opportunities as much as boys and that recent efforts in the United States to open those doors to girls and women have been well advised. Title IX funding by the federal government, which requires that a fair distribution of the money be allocated to each sex, has been a successful and beneficial initiative. At the same time, however, males have lost something valuable in the process. Sports have been the domain of boys for centuries. In the gym and on the athletic field, they found an outlet for their competitive impulses and a source for masculine identity and personal pride. Those avenues are still available to them, of course, but that world has been invaded, and in some ways, overtaken. Indeed, the sexes have begun attempting to outdo each other.

In 1999 after the American women won the World Cup in soccer, *Newsweek* carried a large banner on the cover of its July 19 issue proclaiming, "Girls Rule." It featured a photograph of a muscular Brandi Chastain at her moment of victory over the Chinese team, when she suddenly stripped off her jersey, fell to her knees, clenched her fists, and shouted in triumph. The cover story inside the magazine explained the headline: "From suburban soccer fields far and wide came a new battle cry: Girls Rule."[8] It also described ads sponsored by Gatorade that featured the theme "I can do better," pitting another player on the team, Mia Hamm against NBA star Michael Jordan. The two superstars squared off in a series of sports contests, from tennis to martial arts, with Mia matching Michael stride for stride. Rick Burton, a professor at the University of Oregon stated it this way: "You have the greatest icon of American sports put alongside this woman who's saying, 'I can beat you.'"[9]

I celebrated the U.S. soccer victory when it happened, and indeed, my wife and I were actually watching and cheering during the televised event. Mia and her teammates deserved the accolades that came to them from their accomplishment. There is, however, something unsettling to me about the way the match was reported. Positioning males and females against each other is a mistake. By proclaiming that "Girls Rule," we have to ask who they now rule over. Is it boys? The implication is that boys have been "dethroned," whatever that means. Our politically correct culture tells young males in a hundred ways that they are inferior.

How would I change this situation if I could? I don't know. I am conflicted over it. I am the father of a daughter who participated in track and other athletic events, and I recognize the value of these activities for girls and women. Organized sports would not have been available to them a decade or two earlier, and that would have been unfortunate. I just wish there were more things that guys could do to define their masculinity. One by one, former areas of unique mastery have disappeared until there is almost nothing remaining that identifies maleness. Not even combat is man's exclusive responsibility today. So many aspects of our culture have become unisexual. No wonder boys have only a vague idea what it means to be a man.

Let me conclude by providing an autobiographical article written by Raymond Lovett that appeared in *Esquire* magazine some years ago. I have kept it in my files because it helps us understand why sports and competition are so coveted by boys. I hope you will take the time to read it.

The Cut

"Don't hit it to me. Please don't hit it to me," I silently yell. My stomach hears the fear, punches itself. Magically, I expect my fervor to control the batter. "I bet he'll bat left—don't, oh, don't," I mutter the words into my untrustworthy, borrowed glove. I hope to get through the inning without fielding the ball.

Last chosen, I have been put in right field again. Today I suffer the humiliation of playing right field even though we have only seven on our side. A *vacant* center field is judged less harmful than having me in center. This judgment of my skill is more accurate than malicious, a fact that increases my fear.

"Don't hit it here, Bobby. Bat the other hand," I want to say to a muscle-bound Bobby Bodman, the only switch-hitter on the field, as he decides which way to bat. He chooses left. When he hits left-handed he usually hits a very high ball to right field. I dread the next few minutes. I do not have a long wait.

He tags the first pitch. I see it leave the bat and watch it. It is high. I hear the jeers.

"It's a home run, you hit it right to him."

"C'mon Raymo."

"Protect your head, Raymo."

"Go back, come up, to your right, to your left," someone teases.

The ball is coming down now. I have this one. I hold my fickle glove at my chest, give one punch of my empty hand into the mitt and wait for the ball to drop into my glove. It is moving back on me now. Back, back, back. I move with it. I stop. I ready the catch. At the last second the ball moves again. Leaping backwards, my glove touches it. The ball bounces up, then down into the mitt as I somersault backwards holding my glove to my chest. I jump up.

"I got it! I caught it!"

"Throw it! Throw it! Hard!"

Bodman is almost at third. I give myself a running start and whip the ball with all my might toward the infield in the best way I can: underhand. The ball falls far short of the first baseman and dribbles to a stop. As the first baseman gets to it,

Bodman is crossing the plate. The laughter is loud, the comments louder.

"Did you see that?"

"Nice throw."

"Great arm."

"Hey, Ramona, throw me one," someone yells in a falsetto voice.

"I . . . caught . . . it. . . ." The laughter submerges each successive word more deeply; hesitancy makes me mute.

"Yeah, sure you did," yells the first baseman.

I did catch it. My deriders and I are so accustomed to me dropping the ball we conspire not to accept my catch. They know my history in right field. I am too hurt to defend myself.

"Horseshoes. Horseshoes is his game."

"Roll me another one, Ramona."

The more it hurt, the harder I tried. The harder I tried, the worse I played. I blamed my sisters. They taught me to throw the way they did: underhand. I could not unlearn the lesson. The harder I tried, the more girl-like I looked. Each attempt at overhand resulted in more laughter. I would throw with my body and hand, my elbow glued to my side. This looked even more girlish. I had a choice between this flopping effort and the underhand. I chose the underhand and stayed with it through the long, taunting summer.

When they laughed at me, I wanted to hurt them back. At times I wanted to kill them. I wanted to inflict physical pain on each one until he begged for mercy. But my rage was spineless. The devastation of the group's laughter left me with a helplessness that drained the rage of any execution. I felt too devastated to throw a single punch.

I channeled my hurt into a vindictive desire. I would show them. Next year would I make the local team, I would be the new star of the South End Sluggers.

When the season ended I bought myself a pink ball for 39 cents. Through the fall leaves and into the slippery snow, I would throw my pink ball into the air, catch it, throw it again. Prompted by the longings of a scoffed-at right fielder, I practiced.

There, underneath my roof, I discovered my arm. Bringing my arm back was the key. If I brought my arm back,

153

I could throw farther. I learned to throw with a circular motion. I put the body and arm together. And I practiced daily. It came. I got it. I could throw overhand.

My skill delighted me. I moved on to imaginary games, then stardom. Underneath my roof I made outstanding catches in every major league park, saved home runs, threw out speedy runners as they tested my arm. The plate was a board between two windows on our gabled house. That spot dirtied with winter's grime as I bull's-eyed countless runners on their way home.

In addition to my new skills as thrower and fielder, I also got my very own glove. We were visiting my cousin and I saw it in the yard. I picked it up. Light brown in color, it had practically no padding in the fingers and less in the pocket, nor did it have a web. In truth, it resembled a loose-fitting ski glove as much as a baseball mitt. But it looked available. When I asked my father to ask my uncle for it, he refused. I told him I'd pay. Again he refused.

"You can get a glove when you learn how to play."

In a moment of courage, prompted by desperation, I called my uncle and asked about the glove. He gave it to me.

On the way home, I bought linseed oil. Oiling my glove I felt a new ecstasy: nothing could stop me now. I grabbed my pink ball and headed for the imaginary Fenway Park. The oil soaked through the flimsy leather covering my palm. The pink ball stung. I erased the fear that a hard ball might sting more. But no sting could rob me of my success. I could throw overhand, make great catches, had a strong arm, and now I had my own mitt. Under the eaves, pink ball in oiled glove, I began to see myself in a starring role as a South End Slugger.

I imagined every minute of the first practice. I would buy a baseball hat. I would travel on bike, glove on handlebar. I would be on time. I would warm up. I would win the speed races. I would make no errors in the field, catch what was hit my way, and show off my arm with accurate, powerful throws. I would make friends with the other players. No one would laugh at me. I would not have to try out for right field.

In my imagination nothing slipped through. I saw the blue sky, how I stood, where I stood, the ferocity of my line drives and the velocity of my baserunning. I felt the camaraderie of my friends, the joking and mutual admiration for skill and courage. I saw myself in uniform: number 8, batting third. At one point I even saw the score book of our first game; I was three for four (two doubles and a single), four RBIs. I knew what I would wear that day, what I would eat for breakfast. I could smell springtime on the field, see that center field would be wet, and especially that I would have fun, such great fun.

I began a watch of the bulletin board on March 1. My classmates, Mac and Henry, began talking about the first practice and about the team in the middle of March, but not to me. I'd ask a question. They would not answer. Or they would give the answer to one another. They ignored me, rec-reating my right-field feeling.

After school, Monday, April 4, I saw Mac and Henry speed by on their bikes, their gloves on the handlebars.

"Where ya going?" I yelled. They did not hear. A fear went through me: *Is it today?*

I reentered the school, bound up the stairs two at a time, then three, and ran to the board. I looked at the sea of notices, and there it was. On a small orange file card, thumbtacked to the middle of a cluttered board, in pencil:

Tryouts
South End Sluggers
14 and younger
Monday 3:30—South Park
B. Cummings, Coach

How did I miss it? I panicked. *I'm going! I'm going!* I ran the mile and a quarter to my house as fast as I could, stopping only once to catch my breath. I couldn't find my glove any-where. About to give up, I remembered where I left it every night, under my pillow. Joe DiMaggio, I think it was, slept with his glove when he was a boy. Sleeping with your glove increases your desire and makes you a better fielder. I snatched the glove and headed out for the field at a good clip.

I arrived at the field exhausted but only a few minutes late. I entered through the right-field gate and slowed down to a jog as I approached right field. As I stepped inside the foul line, my body stopped, and my expectations took a dive. I looked toward the plate and saw the coach. Henry, Mac, and others were warming up.

I felt alone, scared, needy. My history in right field overwhelmed me. A wave of self-doubt engulfed my hope and doused my exuberance. The territorial loneliness of the sandlot right fielder is hard to shake. Standing there I tried to forget. But I was not able. The fear of last summer's failure vied with the hope of my winter of practice.

I shook my head hard and *ran,* to kill the right fielder in my imagination. *This is a new season!* I yelled at my history.

Should I say hello to the coach? No. Not unless he looks me in the eye. I took off my jacket, placed it on the bench and headed for left field.

"Hey, kid, where are you going?" asked the coach.

"Out there. In the field. To practice."

"You trying out for the team?"

"Yes."

"What position do you play?"

"Me? I play out there. Field. Outfield mostly."

He looked at me and said nothing. His look was a pressure to say more.

"Out there," I pointed to right field. "I'm a right fielder."

"Okay," he said.

One look from the coach and I was back in right field.

The coach hit high, deep balls, the highest, deepest balls I had seen, to the outfielders. I had never caught a ball that high. Could I do it? I watched the others as he hit six or seven balls to each candidate. Each boy caught them with ease. One kid fell down, but everyone else caught each one and threw it in to second, showing off his arm. I was next.

As I stood there waiting for the coach to hit the first ball to me, I wished I was back under my eaves. He swung. The ball was high—so high and short, I thought. I ran in, and in, and in, faster, now at full speed. I dove for it. And caught it.

"Good hustle. Nice catch," he said.

I misjudged the next two and dropped the third, nullifying my good catch. Though I threw as hard as I could, my throws fell short. The ball was not pink.

In batting practice, I missed the first three pitches, hit one line drive and two pop-ups, and fouled off about twelve pitches. That is not how I planned it.

Waiting in the outfield during batting practice I tried to get in on the animated talk about the schedule, practice time, who would pitch the first game, and positions. When Henry told me that two kids would be cut, fear made me deaf. My enthusiasm was as dry as my mouth. I began to look for two kids who were worse than I. Not finding any standout inferiors, I began to exaggerate their slight mistakes. I gave silent tips to the coach:

See that, he swings late.

That guy is overweight.

He can't hit inside pitches.

I think he's moody.

As the practice wound down I found myself vainly trying to avoid the coach's look. He seemed to be looking at me constantly. Soon, with a head signal, I was called over.

The coach, forty-five, a giant of a man, World-Series serious, laid a hairy arm lightly on my shoulder. I wished I was somewhere else. With that noticeable effort of an abrupt man trying to be gentle, he told me he could keep only fifteen players. "You are not one of them."

He looked at me, and I at him. He started to say something. I interrupted him with the biggest lie of my twelve years, of my lifetime. Summoning the scantest remaining piece of dry courage in my broken soul, I said, "I understand. It's OK." Tears pushed my eyeballs from behind.

Don't cry. Don't cry.

I hid the inundating desire to be out of sight with an onstage casualness. I jaunted to the other side of the batter's box, picked up my glove and, summoning all my restraint, walked to the drinking fountain. I felt the eyes of the world watching. At the fountain I turned. No one was looking. I went behind the stands and slipped under the fence. I broke into a full-speed run, tearing through the woods, and onto the path toward my house. I ran fast, faster, fastest. My mind blank, I ran my race with disappointment. Exhausted, I stopped. My heart beat as hard as my heartbreak.

I sat down. Then laid on the grass. I looked directly into the sun, wishing for blindness. My stomach tightened.

A small tear escaped. I tried to stop it, but other tears followed. Now they grew, they fell, gushing up and out from an exploding well. I tried to stop, but I sobbed. Great swells of feeling shook through my body: anger, rage, disappointment and overwhelming hurt. My dream was murdered. My hope gasped for life. I could not stop sobbing.

I paid for wanting too much, for panting after the unattainable. It was a long time before I could feel that being cut judged only my baseball skill, not me. The powerful adolescent anguish of exclusion blinded me from this redeeming distinction.

I wish that the lesson—that another's judgment of my skill or power is not a judgment of my personal worth—had lasted a lifetime. But it did not. I still confuse judgments of my ability with judgments of myself. But now I know I can survive. Now I no longer whip myself as long or as hard. At times, when life cuts my dreams, I choose Popeye's wisdom over Coach Cummings' judgment. The realistic Popeye, homely but proud, says, "I yam what I yam." And that's enough.[10]

QUESTIONS AND ANSWERS

My son tried out for the basketball team when he was a sophomore in high school. When he didn't make it, Josh was so hurt and embarrassed that he has never competed again. This boy is a natural athlete and he could have been good in several sports, but he doesn't have the confidence to try. Got any suggestions?

The great baseball pitcher Orel Hershiser was a guest on our radio broadcast a few years ago and told a story about his first experience in competitive sports. You might want to share his story with your son as the background for a discussion about not giving up.

Orel said that when he was in junior high and high school, he had a concave chest and could "palm the basketball" with his shoulders. He called himself a "classic geek" who couldn't get a girlfriend and felt terrible about himself. Yet this is the same man whom L.A. Dodger manager Tommy Lasorda would later give the nickname "Bulldog" because he was such a fierce competitor. What made the difference between his being a loser and being a winner? Orel said it was because he didn't quit. He just kept trying. He told me if he had failed at baseball, he believes he would have made it in some other sport because he has always been a hard worker, a "tryer," a doer.[11]

That same attitude could turn your discouraged teenager into a champion. There is something he can do adequately. Find out what it is, perhaps with the help of a coach or trainer, and urge him to go for it. He may not grow up to be an MVP of the World Series like Orel Hershiser, but then again, maybe he will.

My son is a middle child in a three-boy family, and he seems to be more "lost" than the other two. Is there anything to that position in the family?

Not every middle child has trouble finding himself, but some of them do. Your son may be one of them. The discomfort results from the fact that he neither enjoys the status of the eldest nor the attention given to the baby. When he reached the toddler years or shortly thereafter, his territory was invaded by a cute little newborn who stole Mama from him. Is it any wonder that the middle child often asks, "Who am I and what's my place in life?"

I would recommend that you take steps to insure the identity of all of your children, but especially the one in the middle. Here are a couple of suggestions that may help. First, give your attention to each of your kids every few weeks, one at a time. You can play miniature golf or go bowling, play basketball, eat tacos or pizza, or visit a skating rink. It doesn't matter what you do together as long as it is something that particular child enjoys and it involves just the two of you. The choice should be made by the child whose turn has arrived. Second, ask each kid to design his own flag, which can then be sewn into canvas or cloth. That flag is then flown in the front yard on the child's "special" days, including birthdays, or after he has received an A in school. There are other ways to accomplish the same purpose.

The objective, again, is to plan activities that emphasize each boy's individuality apart from his identity within the group. The one most in need of that distinction is often the kid in the middle. Yours may be one of them.

MEN R FOOLS

CHAPTER 12

WE HAVE INDICATED that the weakening of the family and the absence of caring fathers are the primary reasons boys are in trouble today. We'll consider now two other powerful forces that arrived in the late sixties and took the world by storm. They are the sexual revolution and radical feminism, which have contributed mightily to masculine confusion today. That was a period when Western nations seemed to wobble on the brink of insanity. *Time* called it "a knife blade that severed past from the future."[1]

This era brought a new way of thinking and behaving that is still with us today. Never has a civilization so quickly jettisoned its dominant value system, yet that is what occurred within a single decade. Not only did traditional moral standards and beliefs begin to crumble, but the ancient code governing how men and women related to each other was turned upside down. It precipitated a war between the sexes that is still being waged these many years later. History teaches that the young and vulnerable suffer most from the ravages of war. In this case, the nation's boys have been wounded by the ricochet.

It is impossible to understand what is happening to our kids today, both male and female, without considering the influence of feminist ideology. Swirling out of it was an attack on the very essence of masculinity. Everything that had been associated with maleness was subjected to scorn. Men who clung to traditional roles and conservative attitudes were said to be too "macho." If they foolishly tried to open doors for ladies or gave them their seats on subways, as their fathers had done, they were called "male chauvinist pigs." Women presented themselves as victims who were "not gonna take it anymore," and men were said to be heartless oppressors who had abused and exploited womankind for centuries. Divorce skyrocketed as a surprising number of women simply packed up and left their husbands and children. *Anger* was the watchword on TV talk shows and sitcoms. Although it is almost embarrassing to write about now, I recall a televised interview with ex-Beatle John Lennon and his odd little wife, Yoko Ono, during which they sang their new song, "Woman Is the Nigger of the World."[2] The lyrics expressed the outrageous notion that women were nothing more than slaves for their male masters.

The war against men actually began with a speech by Kate Millet entitled "Sexual Politics." It was delivered to a "women's liberation" meeting at Cornell University, and it, for the first time, characterized men and women as political enemies.[3] From there, passions were set on fire. On June 3, 1968, pop artist Andy Warhol was shot in the stomach by Valeria Solanis, the founder of SCUM (Society for Cutting Up Men). The reason? He was a prominent male.[4] At a Miss America Pageant in 1968, feminist protesters threw "all the symbols of women's oppression," including their bras, into a trash can.[5] (It has never been quite clear why men were blamed for whatever it was that women disliked about their underwear.) Then the leaders linked all the Marxist causes together by proclaiming, "We want to destroy the three pillars of class and [a] caste society—the family, private property, and the state ."[6] Alas, the revolution was roaring down the runway.

Although these early feminists called attention to some valid concerns that needed to be addressed, such as equal pay for equal work and discrimination in the workplace, they went far beyond legitimate grievances and began to rip and tear at the fabric of the family. By the time the storm had blown itself out, the institution of marriage had been shaken to its foundation, and masculinity itself was thrown back on its heels. It has never fully recovered.

Well, the "bra burners" are gone now, and much of their rhetoric has been discredited. Nevertheless, disciples of those early feminists and their liberal allies in the media, universities, and entertainment industry continue to shape our attitudes and mores. The most radical among them still seek to discredit masculinity and destroy what they believe to be the last vestiges of a patriarchal society. This war between the sexes is extremely important for parents to understand, because it influences the way they raise their children. Feminist Karla Mantilla summarized the philosophy behind it in an article entitled "Kids Need 'Fathers' Like Fish Need Bicycles." She wrote, "I submit that men tend to emphasize values such as discipline, power, control, stoicism, and independence. Sure, there can be some good from these things, but they are mostly damaging to kids (and other living things). They certainly made my son suffer an isolated and tortured existence until he began to see that there was a way out of the trap of masculinity."[7]

The trap of masculinity? That is the way many feminists view maleness. A centerpiece of this hostility is seen in an ongoing effort to convince us that "Men are fools." It claims that the majority of males are immature, impulsive, selfish, weak, and not very bright. Evidence of that campaign can still be observed in almost every dimension of the culture. It is interesting to note, for example, how disrespect for men pervades the entertainment industry, including many television commercials. The formula involves a beautiful woman (or a bevy of them) who is intelligent, sexy, admirable, and self-assured. She encounters a slob of a man, usually in a bar, who is a braggadocio, ignorant, balding, and overweight. The stupid guy, as I will call him, quickly disgraces himself on screen, at which point the woman sneers or walks away. There are hundreds of these ads on TV today. Watch for them on the tube. They are constantly changing, but this is the kind of stuff you will see:

1. The stupid guy loves driving his Lexus so much that he puts lipstick all over his mouth, musses up his hair, and twists his shirt. He is trying to make his wife think he's been with another woman, but when he gets home, she looks at him scornfully and says, "You've been out driving again, haven't you?" He sighs and looks down, like a little boy caught stealing candy.

2. The stupid guy is too scared to talk to a gorgeous woman in a bar, so a friend writes inane notes to prompt him. They suggest that he say, "Hi" and "How are you?" Ultimately, the girl leaves with the writer, and the stupid guy is left bewildered and alone at the bar.

3. The stupid guy is a flabby man in his forties who is standing alone in front of his bedroom mirror. He is not wearing a shirt. Then he tentatively tries on his wife's bra. At that moment, his wife comes through the door. The crossdresser is caught. She fails to notice the bra and asks him something about sports. Relief spreads across his face. The caption then reads, "Some questions are easier to answer than others."

4. The stupid guy is trying to impress a gorgeous girl with his knowledge of professional football, but she corrects his

facts at every turn. He then reminds her that he was a "guard" for the Pittsburgh Steelers. The girl says sarcastically, "Larry! You were a parking lot attendant!"

5. Three stupid guys are standing together at a cocktail party when they spot a gorgeous woman in red. One of the men identifies her to the others as "the chairman's wife, Mrs. Robinson." (The setting recalls a Mrs. Robinson in *The Graduate* who seduced actor Dustin Hoffman.) At that point, the woman slithers over to one of the men and says, "Have you ever seen something and you just knew you wanted it?" The stupid guy swallows hard and trembles. This is his big moment. Then Mrs. Robinson grabs his "Killian's Irish Red" beer and walks away.

6. The stupid guy approaches a gorgeous girl in a bar who is pouring a Heineken beer into a glass. (Guess what is about to happen?) She smiles seductively. He is so taken by her beauty that he overflows his own glass. The announcer then calls this "a premature pour." There is little doubt about the meaning of that one.

7. A gorgeous "Jane Goodall" type is hiding behind a tree in a forest, "studying" the behavior of several stupid guys whom she calls "primates" and "nomadic males." She takes notes as the men freak out about a sporting event on television, dancing around their Honda and acting like chimpanzees in the wild.

8. This is the absolute worst. The stupid guy is a trainer in a gym who is showing a gorgeous girl how to toughen the "glutes," meaning the muscles in the buttocks. He stands before her and begins to grunt and strain, bending slightly forward and grimacing. One wonders if there is something terrible happening in his pants. Then he reaches behind to retrieve a walnut that he has apparently cracked with his rear end. Somehow that disgusting ad was supposed to make the viewer want to rent a car from Budget. It didn't work for me, I assure you.

We have to wonder why there are so many of these "stupid guy" ads on television today. The reason must be because they are effective—that is, they increase sales of the products they advertise. Agencies conduct exhaustive market research before committing millions of corporate dollars to advertising programs such as these. So what is going on here? Is it possible that men, especially male beer drinkers and sports-car enthusiasts, actually like being depicted as dumb, horny, fat, nerdy, and ugly? Apparently they do. We also have to assume that guys are not offended when they are made the butt of a thousand jokes. But why? Women would not tolerate that kind of derision. You'll note that the polarity of the stupid guy ads is *never* reversed. Not in a million years would you see a corpulent, unattractive woman lusting after a good-looking man who shows disdain for her as she does something ridiculous. Men, however, don't seem to notice that the joke is on them. Perhaps they (we) have been desensitized by thirty-five years of male bashing.

The Internet has become a never-ending source of humor directed against men. Here is a recent example from an anonymous author, called *Dumb Men Jokes—Strange but True*. It isn't very funny, but it makes the point.

1. Don't imagine you can change a man—unless he's in diapers.
2. Never let your man's mind wander—it's too little to be out alone.
3. Definition of a bachelor: a man who has missed the opportunity to make some woman miserable.
4. Best way to get a man to do something: suggest he is too old for it.
5. If you want a committed man, look in a mental hospital.
6. Go for a younger man. You might as well—they never mature anyway.
7. What's the best way to force a man to do sit-ups? Put the remote control between his toes.

Really clever, huh?

Inspirational films from the past that dramatized moral strength and heroism, such as *Mutiny on the Bounty* or *Good-Bye Mr. Chips,* gave way in the seventies and eighties to the man-hating diatribes in *Thelma and Louise* and *Nine to Five*. Meanwhile, the ideal woman in movies has gone from lovely, feminine ladies such as Donna Reed in *It's a Wonderful Life* to aggressive and masculine women such as those depicted in *Charlie's Angels* or the latest remake of *Joan of Arc*. Her character revealed no religious conviction at all, which is curious given the Christian origin of her story. Instead, she was a tough female military strategist who led her male subordinates to war. Maleness in such movies is almost always depicted in subservient and weak roles.

Even when popular films are not specifically hostile to men, they often undermine respect for masculinity in one way or another. A classic example of this bias was seen in the top-grossing movie of 1997, *Titanic*. It retold the tragic story of the great ocean liner that sank on October 12, 1912. On that frigid night, 1,509 people either drowned or froze to death near the Arctic Circle.[8] The wreckage lay undisturbed until 1985, when it was located by explorer Robert Ballard[9] nearly thirteen thousand feet down.[10] The vessel itself was observed to be deteriorating rapidly from an accumulation of rust caused by a particular bacteria that actually eats metal. Thus, an ambitious effort was launched to retrieve artifacts and memorabilia from the bottom. To date, the explorers and oceanographers have brought back an impressive number of fascinating objects.

My wife, Shirley, and I were fortunate to visit an exhibit in Boston that displayed some of the articles that have been recovered and preserved. We walked silently and almost reverently among the former possessions of those who died so long ago. The possessions included bottles of perfume, clothing, jewelry, candleholders, the ship's china, eating utensils, and a pocket watch that stopped ticking the moment its owner slipped into the sea. Several photographs and letters also survived, having been kept in watertight suitcases or safes. It was a very emotional experience for my wife and me, as we tried to imagine what the unfortunate passengers had gone through and what their final minutes must have been like.

Then we came to the last room of the exhibit, where the names of those who died were inscribed in alphabetical order on glass plates. What struck us both was the scarcity of females on the list. Indeed, 1,339 men died on that tragic night but only 114 women and 56 boys and girls.[11] Why this disparity? Because, with very few exceptions, husbands and fathers gave their lives to save their wives and children. It was one of history's most stirring examples of sacrificial love. Those doomed men disappeared into the icy waters of the Atlantic in order that their loved ones might survive to see another day. That is why the *Titanic* is called the "Ship of Widows" to this day.

I was discussing this historic event recently with a young author, Ned Ryun, son of U.S. Congressman Jim Ryun. He sent me a written account of Rev. John Harper of Glasgow, Scotland, who was on the *Titanic* the night it sank. He is one of the men who cried out as the mad rush for the lifeboats began, "Let the women, children, and unsaved into the lifeboats." Then he kissed his only daughter, Nana, good-bye for the last time and placed her in the hands of one of the ship's officers aboard a lifeboat. Soon he was immersed in the chilly waters of the Atlantic. This is Ned's description of what happened next:

Concerned not with his life, but for the dying around him, Harper with his last breaths swam to the dying souls and cried out for them to be saved— "Believe on the Lord Jesus Christ and thou shalt be saved."

As his strength began to ebb, Harper called out to a man clinging onto a piece of timber, "Are you saved?"

"No," was the reply.

A few moments later, Harper and the man came into contact again. "Are you saved yet?"

"No," was again the reply.

"Believe on the Lord Jesus Christ, and thou shalt be saved," Harper cried out one last time and with that, slipped beneath the waves. The young man clinging to the board was rescued and was later to testify that he had indeed been saved that night, not only by a rescuing ship, but by the words of John Harper.

There were many such accounts of masculine heroism that occurred as the great ship was going down. Unfortunately, James Cameron, who directed *Titanic*, chose to ignore them. Instead, he depicted the doomed men as cowardly and panic-stricken. In his version, hundreds of male passengers were kept out of the lifeboats at gunpoint. One man was shown sneaking past women and children and grabbing one of the precious seats. History confirms that there were a few men who behaved dishonorably, but most did not. Only 325 men survived the sinking,[12] and some of them were stewards who were assigned to take charge of the small crafts. The beautiful young heroine of the movie, Rose, was a feisty girl who also chose to go down with the ship. Her fiancé, Cal, was a despicable character who tried to bribe a steward for access to a lifeboat. When rebuffed, he grabbed a child and jumped onboard. There can be no doubt that Cameron wanted us to think that most of the male passengers would have stormed past the women and children if given an opportunity. As such, he tarnished the memories of those who stayed behind voluntarily. Suzanne Fields wrote, "If the *Titanic* were to go down today there would be no 'women or children first.' A male coward wouldn't have to wear a dress to get into the lifeboats. Some of the women would help him aboard."[13]

Notwithstanding the quality of *Titanic* and its remarkable special effects, the way men were depicted in the movie was characteristic of today's film industry. Rarely is an opportunity missed to show males as self-serving, dishonest, misogynous, or to otherwise present them in a disrespectful manner. This is the way the game is played today.

Television sitcoms also blast away at traditional masculinity, much like a wrecking ball crashing into a building. After enough direct hits, the structure begins to crumble. There is not a single example, as I write, of a healthy family depicted on network programming that includes a masculine guy who loves his kids and is respected by his wife. None! Beginning in the 1970s with redneck Archie Bunker and his browbeaten wife, Edith, prime-time TV programming has evolved into today's fare, most of which features profane and sexually explicit cohabitants who meander through one outrageous episode after another. The lead characters are usually men with the giddy mentality of fourteen-year-old boys. The best (or worst) example of this nonsense was seen in a sitcom some years ago called "Men Behaving Badly." The title says it all.

Invariably, sitcoms today feature at least one gay or lesbian character, who is cast in a sympathetic role. It is a powerful force in the culture. One overriding goal of homosexual activists is to influence the next generation and to recruit children to their movement, if not to their lifestyle. The fallout, however, is devastating. How can impressionable boys and young men possibly discern what it means to be a heterosexual male, let alone a dedicated and disciplined husband and father, when this tripe is fed to them every night and when their own dads are nowhere to be found? Remember, too, that other popular male role models are often raunchy, such as professional athletes who sire (and then abandon) six or eight children with as many mothers and rock stars who pierce their bodies with baubles and pickle their brains with mind-altering drugs. What does that behavior convey to boys who are trying to emulate these lost and irresponsible men?

We also see examples of the "men are fools" idea expressed in contemporary greeting cards. Although it is politically incorrect to ridicule women, homosexuals, or minorities, white male bashing—at least the heterosexual variety—is fair game. Visit a Hallmark store or other retail outlet sometime and you'll notice it has become a very lucrative business. Women purchase these humiliating cards by the millions. It is interesting, however, that cards intended for sale to men do not carry the same tone. Their messages are typically gentle and loving toward wives or sweethearts. The difference between the romantic cards for men and the disrespectful cards for women is striking. Author Warren Farrel writes, "If a man belittles a woman, it could become a lawsuit. But if women belittle men, it's a Hallmark card."[14]

I could fill a book with other examples of man-bashing in today's culture. Chief among them is the curricula of university women's studies programs whose central theme is hatred and ridicule of men. Roger Scruton, author of "Modern Manhood," explained what is happening to perceptions of masculinity. "Feminists have sniffed out male pride wherever it has grown and ruthlessly uprooted it. Under their pressure, modern culture has downgraded or rejected such masculine virtues as courage, tenacity, and military prowess in favor of more gentle, more 'socially inclusive' habits."[15]

Corporate psychologist Dr. Tim Irwin has observed these same trends in business settings. They have resulted in what he calls "the feminization of the workplace." Irwin said the effort to end sexual harassment and discrimination, which has been a legitimate concern that needed to be addressed, has placed great political power in the hands of women. A man's career can be ruined by even the implication, valid or invalid, that he has treated a female employee disrespectfully. The possibility of being accused of harassment has intimidated men, even in circumstances when disciplinary action is needed or when disagreements occur between male supervisors and female subordinates. Many men in that situation are afraid to exercise necessary leadership if doing so would displease or anger a woman. It is safer to "wimp out."

The best managers and leaders in the past were "take-charge" men who were assertive and self-assured. Now, would-be leaders are uncertain about how to play the game, since it is politically incorrect to be "macho" or traditionally masculine. This causes some men to be tentative in the workplace. The strengths of women are networking, cooperating, facilitating, teaching, training, and caring. The strengths of men are entrepreneurial enterprise, independent thinking, building, risk-taking, planning, and leadership. Both sexes have their contribution to make, but something is lost when women understand what it means to be women while men are confused about the meaning of masculinity. When powerful legal remedies are provided to one sex in order to eliminate a social injustice, the other sex is left vulnerable and confused.

The bottom line is that many men have lost their compass. Not only do they not know who they are, they're not sure what the culture expects them to be. This namby-pamby behavior is apparently what motivated columnist Walter Williams to pen this column entitled "Men Should Stand Up."

> Quite frankly the behavior of some women has gotten out of hand, and it's because we men have become cowards and wimps. The more men take of double standards, ridiculous demands and just plain nonsense, the more these women are going to give. You say, "What do you have against the fairer sex, Williams?" I say nothing. While some of my best friends are women, I'm getting tired of all the sex-based nonsense. Let's look at it.

On [the] *Today* show last November, Katie Couric suddenly deviated from her perkiness and asked a jilted bride, in reference to the groom who jilted her, "Have you considered castration as an option?" There was no storm of protest, and perky Katie remains on NBC's payroll. Fred Hayward, a men's rights organizer, is quoted by *U.S. News & World Report* writer John Leo: "Imagine the reaction if Matt Lauer had asked a jilted groom, 'Wouldn't you just like to rip her uterus out?'"[16] Matt Lauer would have been handed his walking papers.

Leo reports that up until recently the 3M company put out Post-it notes with the printed message "Men have only two faults: everything they say and everything they do."[17] Hallmark went further with a greeting card that said, "Men are scum. . . . Excuse me. For a second there I was feeling generous." Then there was the American Greeting Cards card that said on the front: "Men are always whining about how we are suffocating them," with the inside punch line "Personally, I think if you can hear them whining, you're not pressing hard enough on the pillow."[18] What do you think would happen if a company had an ad that joked about killing women?

Young boys aren't spared from the feminist attack. At a Boston area elementary school, nobody objected when girls wore shirts emblazoned with "Girls Rule" or when they taunted boys with a chant that goes, "Boys go to Jupiter to get more stupider; girls go to college to get more knowledge." But when boys donned shirts emblazoned with "Boys Are Good," there was protest. One of the teachers protesting sported a button saying, "So many men, so little intelligence."[19]

Women can get away with saying just about anything demeaning, evil, and harassing to men, while men get into trouble for making the most innocent compliment. That happened to Seth Shaw, a counselor at an elementary school in Fort Worth, Texas. He said, "Hello, good-looking," to a new female employee, was charged with sexual harassment and wound up suffering a 20-day suspension without pay.

Leo's August 21, 2000, *U.S. News & World Report* article suggests that all of this can get worse if foreign feminist demands reach our shores. Young women in Sweden, Germany and Australia have launched a new cause: They want men to sit down while urinating. Part of their demand is related to the "splash factor," but more crucially, men standing up to urinate is deemed by these women as triumphing in their masculinity, "a nasty macho gesture" and, by extension, degrading to women. Feminists at Stockholm University are campaigning to ban campus urinals and one Swedish elementary school has already removed urinals.[20] I don't know about you, but if I don't tell women to stand up to urinate, they're not going to tell me to sit down to urinate. The bottom line is that we men had better stand up to these feminist wackos before our last resort will be well-deserved spankings.[21]

© 2001 Creators Syndicate, Inc.

Those are Walter Williams' words, not my own, but I agree with the sentiment. It is time that men acted like men—being respectful, thoughtful, and gentlemanly to women, but reacting with confidence, strength, and certainty in manner. Some have *wimped out,* acting like whipped puppies. Others have boldly *spoken out* against feminist influence, refusing to be intimidated by the advocates of political correctness. Some have *lashed out,* reacting with anger and frustration. Some have *flamed out,* resorting to alcohol, drugs, illicit sex, and other avenues of escape. Some have *copped out,* descending into mindless TV, professional sports, and obsessive recreational activities. Some have *sold out,* becoming advocates of the new identity. Some have simply *walked out,* leaving their families in a lurch. Many, however, seem placidly unaware that they have lost their places in the culture. The result is a changing view of manhood with far-reaching implications for the future of the family.

Now, I can hear some of my readers saying, "Come on! You're overreacting. What's the big deal with having a little innocent fun at the expense of men?" I would agree that they are old enough to take care of themselves. My greater concern is for vulnerable, impressionable boys and what is being done to them. They, like their dads, are the objects of societal scorn today.

Please let me give the greatest emphasis to this point: Not only do radical feminists and elitists tell us that men are fools but that boys are fools too. Journalist Megan Rosenfeld said that our sons are seen as "politically incorrect." "[They] are the universal scapegoats, the clumsy clods with smelly feet who care only about sports and mischief."[22] Harvard psychologist William Pollack said women consider boys to be creatures who might "infect girls with some kind of social cooties."[23]

Michael Thompson, coauthor of *Raising Cain,* said that many women are hoping against hope that their sons won't turn out like their husbands.[24] Columnist Kathleen Parker wrote, "Today's boys grow up in a bizarrely hostile environment. They're told to be tough, not to cry, to be a man—an ironic insult in a culture that devalues men and fathers. They're bullied by schools intolerant of boy behavior, told they're less special than girls and left by too-busy parents to the tutelage of peers, media, and superheroes who wreak havoc to settle scores."[25]

No discussion of boy-bias would be complete without addressing the discrimination against males now evident in American public education. William Pollack said succinctly, "It sounds terrible to say, but coeducational public schools have become the most boy-unfriendly places on earth. It may still be a man's world. But it certainly isn't a boy's world."[26]

Christina Hoff Sommers, the most passionate and effective defender of boys, echoed these concerns in her outstanding book *The War against Boys: How Misguided Feminism Is Harming Our Young Men.* She says this is a bad time to be a boy in America because of the bias against them in our educational institutions.[27] This hostility found its manifesto in an inaccurate and terribly biased report written and released in 1992 by the ultraliberal American Association of University Women (AAUW). It was titled *How Schools Shortchange Girls,* and it resulted in years of discrimination against boys. Indeed, if your child is attending a government school today, it is likely that this political statement is still influencing his or her classroom experience. Its impact on American education has been profound.

This report described the typical classroom as a hellhole for girls, claiming that they were disadvantaged in every way. It asserted that female students are invisible, ignored, disrespected, and denied their share of educational resources. The most widely disseminated finding was that teachers permit boys to speak or participate eight times more often than they do girls, but as with the rest of the conclusions, this turned out to be pure nonsense. Their data was based on an old 1981 study that actually said boys are reprimanded eight times more often than girls,[28] and that three-fourths of both girls and boys said they thought teachers compliment girls more often, think they are smarter, and would rather be around female students.[29] That level of distortion was evident throughout the AAUW report.

Although the report has been widely discredited now in the professional community for what it was—a blatant attempt to skew educational resources away from boys and to characterize girls as victims—the damage had been done. It resulted in an unfair distribution of available resources that continues to this day.

Despite its flaws, the AAUW report took the nation by storm. It swept through the U.S. Department of Education, the National Education Association, universities, and local school districts. The media (including *Oprah* and the morning news programs) presented its conclusions to the public as gospel truth. *The New York Times* said the report created a period of "national soul searching" about the problems girls faced in public schools.[30] Then the U.S. Congress got into the act. Heaven help us when Congress begins to establish educational policy. Under heavy lobbying in 1994 from the AAUW and the National Organization for Women, it passed a far-reaching bill called the Gender Equity in Education Act, which allocated hundreds of millions of dollars per year to programs designed to redress the bias against girls. Included in the package were schools exclusively for girls in Harlem and elsewhere and money to "reprogram" teachers who were "unconsciously sexist."[31] Those are the words used to refer to anyone who clings to the notion that boys are special too. The bill sailed through Congress because few politicians dared vote against "equality." It gave feminists the money, the power, and the access they needed to retool the nation's schools. Thereafter, discrimination against boys was enshrined in national policy.

Numerous federal programs favoring girls began flowing from the flawed AAUW report. For example, the National Science Foundation developed a $9 million program to interest girls in science.[32] It was a good idea that continues today. Unfortunately, no comparable initiative has been developed to help boys "catch up" in reading and writing skills. Another federal program is called Girl Power! championed by then-Secretary of Health and Human Resources Donna Shalala.[33] She said, "We hope to reach girls at this key transitional age when they are forming their values and attitudes."[34] Again, that is a fine objective. But where are the comparable programs for boys? They don't exist!

The result of this de-emphasis on boys has now had its predictable effect. Girls are closing the gap on boys, and indeed, more of them are attending math and science classes than boys.[35] Those were the last bastions of masculine strength academically because of the way male brains are designed. Not even that physiological advantage can overcome the "stacked deck" in public education.[36]

This bias against males has many corollaries. Even the most influential privately funded organization, Boy Scouts of America, has been subjected to a withering attack from homosexual activists. As we mentioned before, some United Way chapters have refused to fund them,[37] and the New York City School District told school personnel that they were no longer permitted to sponsor Scout troops.[38] What on outrage! The Boy Scouts of America has provided wonderful training and role modeling for inner-city kids, those from single-parent families, and millions of other boys. There has been no more respected and effective organization for males than the Scouts, yet it has been vilified unmercifully because its leaders choose not to include self-professed homosexuals in their program. Girl Scout staffers estimate that one in three of the Girl Scouts' paid professional staff is lesbian.[39] Male homosexuals want to infiltrate the Boy Scouts to the same degree.

Boys are losing on almost every front because the system is stacked against them! Is it any wonder why they are in such disarray today?

How about private initiatives such as the much-vaunted Take Our Daughters to Work Day? Tell me why boys should not be introduced to the workplace too. Can you think of any good reason for leaving boys at home each year on April 22 while their sisters are being shepherded around the office or factory? Wouldn't it be reasonable, and much fairer, to suggest that parents take both their boys *and* girls to work occasionally? But who is out there promoting such an egalitarian idea? Boys have few advocates in government, media, or public education to articulate their needs. It is wrongheaded and discriminatory. Basing rights and privileges on gender is a zerosum game. When one sex is favored dramatically in the culture, the other is destined to lose. Guess who gets the leftovers?

British schools, by contrast to American public education, recognized several years ago that their boys were falling behind academically and warned of the possibility of "an underclass of permanently unemployed, unskilled men." According to Professor Sommers, "The British government reacted with a highly successful back-to-basics program in the primary schools, whose explicit purpose is to help boys catch up with girls. The British are also experimenting with all-male classes in coed public schools. They are again allowing 'gender stereotypes' in their educational materials: They found that boys enjoy and will read adventures with male heroes. War poetry is back. So is classroom competition. By contrast, our federal and state governments remain oblivious to boys' problems."[40] It is a national tragedy.

The bias against boys in the U.S. not only influences basic education curricula; it also manifests itself in hostility toward masculinity itself. As Michael Thompson wrote, "Energetic boys are likely to be disciplined for simply behaving normally."[41] Thomas Sowell, respected professor of economics at Stanford University, expressed this same concern about the ongoing effort to redesign boys. He wrote:

> Unknown to most parents, there are federally-financed programs to prevent boys from acting the way boys have

always acted before. The things done by those who have taken on the role of changing boys range from forbidding them from running and jumping during recess to having them wear dresses and pretend to be girls or women in the classroom. Whatever the particular mix of things done at a particular school, it is accompanied by a barrage of propaganda prepared by radical feminists for nationwide distribution with the blessing—and the money—of the U.S. Department of Education. The people who are doing this see their role as changing your children into the kinds of people they want them to be—not the kind of people you want them to be. Boys in elementary school, or even kindergarten, have been punished for being politically incorrect toward girls. Tragically, radical feminists are just one of the many reckless zealots who have turned our schools into ideological indoctrination centers, instead of places for children to get an education in basic skills. One of the reasons American children do so badly in international tests of academic skills is that our schools are preoccupied with politically correct social crusades.[42]

© 2001 Creators Syndicate, Inc.

What Dr. Sowell and others are telling us is best illustrated in the story of little Jonathan Prevette, a towheaded, bespectacled six-year-old boy from Southwestern Elementary School in Lexington, North Carolina. On the playground one day, he leaned over playfully and kissed a little girl on the cheek (gasp!). A teacher observed the shocking behavior and promptly reported it to the principal. Bewildered little Jonathan, who said the girl had asked him to kiss her, was charged with "sexual harassment" and summarily suspended from school. This lad, fresh out of *Romper Room*, had violated a tenet of liberal dogma and paid a dear price for it.

Jane Martin, district spokeswoman, said with conviction, "A six-year-old kissing another six-year-old is inappropriate behavior. Unwelcome is unwelcome at any age."[43]

This incident would be humorous if it weren't so ridiculous. It reveals just how far the federal government, the courts, and the radical feminists have taken us in recent years. Indeed, on May 24, 1999, the U.S. Supreme Court handed down an unfortunate decision declaring that local school districts can be held liable if educators fail to respond to student complaints of sexual harassment.[44] From that moment forward, the petty bantering and teasing between boys and girls that have occurred since the beginning of human existence have become legal matters to be adjudicated by the courts. A thoughtless joke or comment, if ignored by a teacher, could embroil a school in a lawsuit. Could the five justices who imposed this decision on us really have been serious? What a strange ethic we have created.

About the same time as Jonathan's indiscretion, the president of the United States was being accused of sexually assaulting several women, and one of them won a nearly one-million-dollar settlement.[45] Isn't it interesting that the American people, knowing of these and other sexually related charges, reelected Bill Clinton by a landslide because he was "doing a good job," but a first-grader who can't even pronounce the word *harassment* was suspended from school for displaying childish affection to a classmate?

According to columnist Linda Chavez, elementary schools have become the new frontier in the effort to reorder the way children, and especially boys, think and act. She wrote, "Jonathan Prevette may be off the hook temporarily, but not for long. If the feds and their feminist allies have their way, every little boy and girl in the nation will be taught that flirting is a crime, and even an admiring look, much less a kiss, can land you in court."[46]

What happened to little Jonathan Prevette, therefore, is merely a product of leftist ideology run amok in some of the nation's schools. For a six-year-old boy to show affection to someone he likes is as natural as catching toads or playing ball. Norman Rockwell made scenes such as these a regular theme of his many illustrations.

There have been many similar episodes that reflect the war between the sexes. Columnist John Leo wrote, "My favorite [example] is . . . the third-grade boy accused of touching a girl on the breasts, though it is perhaps fairer to say that during a game of tag, he tagged her on the very spot where her breasts would presumably appear in three or four years. This is like being accused of robbing a bank that hasn't been built yet."[47]

It should be clear now why I have devoted this chapter to a review of feminist ideology and the postmodern philosophy from which it has sprung. It is because the proponents of these misguided and harmful ideas have become social engineers who are determined to reorder the way children think and to browbeat boys for being who God made them to be. That agenda is spelled out in a single sentence within the AAUW report that reads, "School curricula should deal directly with issues of power, gender politics and violence against women."[48] What this means is that boys are perceived by liberals as dysfunctional little troublemakers who grow up to be abusive and selfish men. They need to be "fixed" while they are young by reordering the way they think. And government schools are the instruments designated to straighten them out.

Please understand that I have nothing but respect and admiration for girls and women. I have been happily married to the "love of my life" for more than forty years and have articulated the needs and concerns of women in several of my previous books. Nevertheless, I have to call it as I see it. And as I see it, boys are desperately in need of friends.

They are the victims of a long and costly battle between the sexes that has vilified the essence of masculinity and ripped into the world of children. And that is not good. Pitting boys and girls against each other as competitors and enemies cannot be healthy for anyone! As Kathleen Parker writes, "It is moronic to continue insisting that one sex is the victor while the other is the victim, which besides being untrue is dastardly in effect. Boys made to feel superfluous, if not inferior, can't help but resent girls."[49]

These are some of the social conditions that make the job of raising boys more difficult today. Your task as parents is to counterbalance these forces by the training and guidance you give your boys at home. Stay involved in their local schools. Read the textbooks. Ask a million questions. Attend school-board meetings. Get acquainted with teachers and ask about their classroom objectives. Encourage educators who are trying to teach the basics. Oppose those who are not. Communicate with other concerned parents. Join a Moms in Touch chapter and pray diligently for your children and their school. If your level of concern gets too high, transfer your boys and girls to Christian schools or do the job yourself at home. By all means, do not get distracted during your children's impressionable years of childhood. They will pass very quickly. There is little in life that outranks this parental responsibility in importance.

QUESTION AND ANSWER

Now that you mention it, I can see that men are being depicted as being more feminine and women are made to appear more like men. I saw a film the other day in which a beautiful woman became angry at a big, tough man. She knocked him out with one blow and broke his front tooth. I am an orthopedic surgeon, and I can tell you that the tiny bones in a young woman's hand would break long before she cracks the rugged jawbone of a man. It would also be almost impossible for her to knock him unconscious with one haymaker. Why do you think Hollywood is trying to create a myth here?

As we have seen, it is part of the feminist agenda to show women as powerful, courageous, and indomitable, while men are weak, emotional, and easily manipulated. The entertainment industry, which seems determined to unravel us, works hand in glove with feminists and homosexual activists to bring us into that brave new world. Its presentation of male and female role models is almost always perverted or warped in one way or another.

Let me illustrate the point by referring to the blockbuster movie *Runaway Bride*, which was released back in 1999. It was one of the most popular films of the year. If you would permit me, I'd like to describe the story line in detail because this film was classic feminist propaganda, but few viewers I have talked to even noticed what was being said. It provided for us a blatant dramatization of the "new emasculated man" and the "new masculinized woman." The story line was a ninety-minute celebration of sex-role reversals that contradicted convention at every turn. It opened with the female star, Julia Roberts, racing through the trees on horseback, her gorgeous hair flowing behind and her wedding dress billowing in the wind. She had just left her third fiancé standing bewildered at the altar. Most girls dream from early childhood about having a romantic wedding someday, whereas guys are usually the ones who have trouble committing. In this film, however, the men were patsies who panted after this elusive, boylike creature.

From the beginning, the episodes of sexual confusion came at the viewer in dizzying array. Julia was a sometime mechanic, a plumber, and an air-conditioning specialist who created clunky-looking lamps out of electrical junk. She was very aggressive and selfish, in a charming kind of way. She managed her family's hardware store, drove an old pickup truck, often wore combat boots, and easily carried a heavy backpack that her boyfriend had difficulty lifting. When frustrated, she pounded and kicked a punching bag with a vengeance, grimacing and sweating profusely. At one point, the sound track included snippets of the pop rendition, "She's a Man Eater." We got the connection.

Julia exhibited what has become known as "the new androgyny," having both stereotypical masculine and feminine characteristics. She had clean, delicate hands, manicured fingernails, creamy skin, and a beautiful body, yet she made her living doing greasy work and fighting like a man. She high-fived with the guys at ball games, bumping bodies like NFL players after touchdowns. Speaking of the NFL, she recalled the name of superstar Jerry Kramer from the fifties, whereas her boyfriend—a football coach—couldn't remember it. No opportunity was missed to tell us that Julia was a "man." And yet, she was a pretty and delicate little thing.

Now consider how the movie handled the image of manhood. The male lead, played by Richard Gere, was a winsome but rather wimpish and bumbling guy. He was between jobs, having been belittled and fired by his boss—who happened to have been his ex-wife. Everything he did ended in failure. When his car malfunctioned, Julia simply looked under the hood and recognized instantly that he had stupidly put leaded gas in an engine designed for unleaded fuel. One wonders how Gere managed to purchase the wrong gasoline since it is no longer sold legally. Even if he had located a place to buy the leaded stuff, he couldn't have gotten it pumped into his tank because by law it is dispensed through a nozzle that is too large to fit. Gere's ineptitude as a man was pathetic, whereas Julia excelled in all things masculine. After Gere's engine stalled, the two of them walked home through a grassy field, where she calmly told him there were many snakes underfoot. Terrified, Richard began hopscotching through the weeds like a barefooted kid on a hot sidewalk. Julia laughed and strolled along unconcerned. Yeah, she was one tough dude, no doubt about that.

Every other character illustrated the central theme that women are more masculine than men and men aren't good for much of anything. There was a telling scene addressed to boys and girls that appeared only momentarily on screen. When Richard arrived in Julia's town, we saw a bored little boy slumped on a wooden horse just as a beautiful little girl passed him on a real pony. She had her nose in the air. That quick scene, which was irrelevant to the story, exemplified what the director and writers were trying to say: Females of every age are confident and strong, whereas males are invariably weak and ineffectual. Even Julia's elderly grandmother got into the act. She lusted after young men, remarking that she particularly liked guys with "tight buns." On and on it went.

Clearly, *Runaway Bride* had a political agenda, as does almost every contemporary movie. This is the usual fare in today's movies. Male characters are often depicted as stereotypically weak, lost, confused, and rather feminine. Masculine virtues, such as moral character, self-control, integrity, and confidence, rarely show up in the dramatizations. With the exception of *The Patriot,* released in 2000, men are almost never seen as strong, loving fathers and husbands who are faithful to their wives and deeply committed to their children. Women, on the other hand, come off as hardnosed, physically powerful professionals, usually lawyers or surgeons, who are in control. Not all films follow this formula, of course, but it is very common today. Columnist Maureen Dowd described them this way: "The new heroines are aggressive and calculating. They have adapted all those traits they once scorned in men. They lie, they spy, they cheat, they plot revenge, they treat sex casually and [then] they slither away."[50]

One last comment: You mentioned the fistfight you had seen in another movie that pitted a beautiful woman against a tough-looking man. She coldcocked him with a single blow. This scene is occurring more frequently in Hollywood movies today. It has the potential, however, to be very counterproductive for women. One of the absolutes in culture is that

Boys in School

CHAPTER 13

WE HAVE TAKEN a hard look at the bias against boys in schools and how they are often discriminated against sexually. There are other concerns that we must consider now about how boys learn, why too many of them fail, and how their masculine makeup often works to their disadvantage.

Almost every authority on child development recognizes that schools are typically not set up to accommodate the unique needs of boys. Elementary classrooms, especially, are designed primarily by women to fit the temperament and learning styles of girls. Contrary to the blatant biases described in the previous chapter, however, this disadvantage for boys is largely unintentional. It is simply the way schools have always functioned. Harvard psychologist and author William S. Pollock said it this way: "Girls care more about school. They cope with it. Boys don't. Boys are taught at a tempo that doesn't fit them. They are taught in a way that makes them feel inadequate, and if they speak up, they are sent to the principal."[1]

Psychologist Michael Thompson, author of *Raising Cain: Protecting the Emotional Life of Boys,* has also expressed alarm about what is happening to very young boys in the classroom. He said, "Boys feel like school is a game rigged against them. The things at which they excel—gross motor skills, visual and spatial skills, their exuberance—do not find as good a reception in school."[2] Children are also being placed in formalized educational settings at younger ages, which is very hard on boys. They tend to be six months behind girls in development at six years of age, which makes it tough for many of them to sit quietly and work with pencils and paper and to cope with the social pressures suddenly thrown at them. Too many of them get off to a bad start and begin feeling "dumb" and inadequate.

A man in his twenties once said to me, "I remember sitting in my chair in first grade and thinking, *If they would just let me stand up. If only I could stand!* Millions of immature kids are like this. They have powerful afterburners but no rudder. They are in agony when required to endure long periods of relative inactivity, a prohibition on noise, and an environment where everything is nailed down tight. They long to run, jump, wrestle, laugh, and climb, which the system simply can't tolerate. Thompson said, "By fourth grade, [boys are] saying the teachers like girls better."[3] They are probably right.

Let's face it, school can be a rugged place for those who don't "fit in" with the typical classroom program. What do we do with these kids when they fall behind in the basics? We either anesthetize them with medication, or we require them to repeat a grade. That second alternative is becoming politically popular now. Retaining a very immature boy in first or second grade can be a good idea, because it gives him a chance to grow up without a major downside. But by the third grade or after, holding a child back can be disastrous. I can tell you from many years of experience that the only thing we accomplish by "failing" a kid after the primary grades is to humiliate and demoralize him. That leads either to apathy, rebellion, a broken spirit—or all three. Then he lumbers into puberty a year or two before his peers and causes havoc. Retaining those who fail is not the panacea today's hard-liners promise.

I've met thousands of little immature troublemakers through the years who drove teachers crazy. In fact, I used to be one of them. I remember not being able to keep my mouth shut when I was in the third grade. The teacher, Mrs. Hall, finally wrote my name on the board and warned that if I got two more "checks" for talking, there would be big trouble. I honestly tried to be quiet, but I couldn't keep my thoughts to myself. I leaned over and whispered something to someone sitting nearby. I was caught again by the long arm of the law. When this second check went on the board, Mrs. Hall was visibly ticked. She quietly walked over to her desk and began cutting something out of construction paper. I felt as though I was about to be executed. All the other children watched excitedly to see what the teacher was doing. I soon found out. She was making a sort of mask to fit over my mouth and around my neck. She pinned the paper in the back and left it in place until recess time. It was one of the most embarrassing moments of my life. In fact, I thought my life was over. The girls snickered and the guys pointed while I sat there draped in this ridiculous device. It was just awful.

I really don't blame Mrs. Hall for what she did. I was obviously getting on her nerves and she had had enough of it. But Mrs. Hall probably underestimated the humiliation this experience would cause me. Furthermore, she may not have understood that I was not being deliberately disrespectful. I was just an antsy kid who couldn't hold still and keep his mouth shut.

Variations on this theme happen every day at school. Writer Celeste Fremon described one of them in an article entitled "Are Our Schools Failing Our Boys?" She wrote:

> When my son first told me he had been punished for running on the playground of his Southern California elementary school, I figured he was exaggerating. What school would forbid running at recess? There had to be more to the story. But I learned that the school had recently instituted a no-running policy because, as the principal informed me in vaguely judgmental tones, "Kids could get hurt"—as if such an explanation should be unnecessary to the truly caring parent.
>
> The No-Running issue followed on the heels of another incident in which my son, whose name is Will, was nearly suspended from school for jumping over a bench. Apparently this was the second such infraction. "He knows that jumping over benches is against the rules, so this constitutes defiance," the principal said. I will be the first to agree that teachers must keep order, and Will has always been an active kid—a climber of trees, a hopper of benches, a wiggler. When he's sad, he is most likely to comfort himself by banging loudly on his drums or teaching himself a new trick on his skateboard.
>
> However, he's also a kind, extremely bright boy who doesn't get into fights, designs whiz-bang projects for the yearly science fair, and scores in the 97th percentile or above on those standardized tests schools give each spring. Yet throughout much of his academic career (Will is now an 8th grader), I've found myself called in for conferences by frowning teachers and administrators. His handwriting is messy, they say gravely. He fidgets during English, when he should be taking notes. And he put his cap on while still inside the classroom.
>
> In my darker moments, I wonder what's wrong with me as a mother that so many of the educators with whom Will comes in contact fail to perceive the exuberant future inven-

tor I believe him to be and see instead only an annoyingly rowdy boy. Worse, I fear that my smart kid is in danger of turning off to academics altogether—and I'm not sure what to do about it. However, I've learned my son is not alone in his experience.[4]

While I am sympathetic to this mother, I must, to be fair, point out that there is another side to this story, one with which I am very familiar. I taught seventh- and eighth-grade science and math when I was in my twenties. I also served as a high school counselor and administrator of psychological services. From this experience, I know very well how disrupting it can be to have a room full of giddy boys like Will who won't cooperate and think everything is hilariously funny. Furthermore, schools are too unstructured, if anything, rather than being too rigid. Discipline is what makes learning possible. Thus, I am not critical of schools for requiring order and deportment, but the fact remains that the way boys are constructed makes it harder for them to conform to school, especially when they are young. At least, we as parents should understand what is going on and try to help them fit in. Let's talk about some of those approaches.

First, I'll offer some ideas for the schooling of boys in various developmental stages and temperaments. We'll begin by considering two kinds of children that are seen commonly in every school classroom. Those in the first category are by nature rather organized individuals who care about details. They take their assignments very seriously. To do poorly on a test would depress them for several days. Parents of these children don't have to monitor their progress to keep them working. It is their way of life. Unfortunately, there just aren't enough of them to satisfy parents and teachers.

In the second category are the boys and girls who just don't adapt well to the structure of the classroom. They're sloppy, disorganized, and flighty. They have a natural aversion to work and their only great passion is play. Like bacteria that gradually become immune to antibiotics, these classic underachievers become impervious to adult pressure. They withstand a storm of parental protest when the report cards come out and then slip back into apathy when no one's looking. They don't even hear the assignments being given in school, and they seem not to be embarrassed in the least when they fail to complete them. If they graduate at all, it won't be cum laude; it will be "thank you, laudy."

God made a huge number of these kids, most of them boys. They drive their parents to distraction, and their unwillingness to work can turn their homes into World War III.

If you have one of these flighty kids, it is important to understand that they are not intrinsically inferior to their hardworking siblings. Yes, it would be wonderful if every student used his talent to best advantage, but each child is a unique individual who doesn't have to fit the same mold as everyone else. Besides, the low achiever sometimes outperforms the young superstar in the long run. That's what happened to Albert Einstein, Thomas Alva Edison, Eleanor Roosevelt, Winston Churchill, and many other highly successful people. So don't write off that disorganized and apparently lazy kid as a lifelong loser. He or she could surprise you. In the meantime, there are ways that you can help.

One thing is certain: Getting mad at this youngster will not solve the problem. You will never transform an underachieving youngster into a scholar by nagging, pushing, threatening, or punishing. It just isn't in him. If you try to squeeze him into something he's not, you'll only aggravate yourself and wound the child. His disorganization is a product of his laid-back temperament and elements of immaturity—not rebellion or deliberate disobedience. Testosterone is in there working on him too.

You should, on the other hand, stay as close as possible to this child's school. Your playboy isn't going to tell you what's going on in the classroom, so you will need to find out for yourself. Seek tutorial assistance, if possible, to help him keep up. Clearly, your child lacks the discipline to structure his life. If he's going to learn it, you will have to teach it to him. Finally, having done what you can to help, accept the best he can give. Go with the flow and begin searching for other areas of success.

The disorganized boy in elementary school is likely to remain flighty as he grows older unless he gets help. That characteristic of his temperament is deeply ingrained and becomes the primary source of his academic problems. It doesn't just "go away" quickly. What can parents do to help? Educational consultant Cheri Fuller suggests that moms and dads with junior high and high school students take a look at their notebooks. She says it is possible to tell whether a kid is a B student or a D student just by examining his school papers. An achieving student's notebook is organized with dividers and folders for handouts and assignments. A failing student's notebook is a mess of jumbled drawings, silly notes, folded airplanes, half-finished sentences, and written work that wasn't turned in. There might even be a teacher's note to Mrs. Smith or Mr. Johnson that never got home.[5]

Fuller says the missing organizational skills in these cases can be learned, and the sooner the better. A good tutor usually knows how to teach them. This early training must be completed before junior high school, where as many as five teachers each day will be distributing handouts, assignments, and projects drawn from different textbooks. It takes a high level of organization to keep them straight and accessible. How are children supposed to know how to handle this requirement if they have never been taught? Boys also need to learn how to complete long-term assignments little by little. The right supervision can help a flighty adolescent become more self-disciplined and self-propelled in time—even if he never performs quite like the natural scholar.

There is one other factor that must be given the greatest priority. If your son does not learn to read properly, everything else will be in jeopardy. He is also likely to struggle with a damaged self-concept. I worked with a high school boy who had decided to drop out at sixteen years of age after being retained a couple of years along the way. He was a tough, angry kid who seemed not to care about anything. When I asked him why he wanted to leave school, big tears filled his eyes. He told me that he had never learned to read. Then he said through clenched teeth, "You people have made me feel worthless all my life. But you've done that for the last time. I'm getting out!" I can't say I blamed him.

The tragedy is that this kid could have been taught to read. Almost every youngster can master this skill if approached properly and with methods that suit his learning style. As a place to start, I am among those who believe in teaching phonics, which are still not incorporated in many public-school reading programs. For whatever reasons, millions of kids are illiterate when they graduate from high school. Wonderful opportunities to make readers of them were squandered when they were in elementary school.

The National Assessment of Education Progress shows that two-thirds of fourth-grade children in the United States cannot read at a proficient level, three-fourths of them cannot write proficiently, and four-fifths of them are not proficient in math.[6] That is a national disgrace! There was a time in the 1800s when 98 percent of the population was literate, having been taught by their parents so they could read the Bible.[7] We'll talk in a moment about what has gone wrong in public schools, but our focus now is on your boy, who may be foundering. As a parent, I would turn heaven and earth to find someone who could teach my kid to read. There are gifted tutors in almost every community, and there are private organizations that guarantee they can teach your child to read. Even if you have to hock the house to pay for it, I urge you to solve this problem. It is the key to all academic objectives, and a world of adventure awaits those who learn to read.

Profamily leader Phyllis Schlafly taught all her grandchildren to read before kindergarten. She developed a program based on phonics that is available to parents. If you want more information, contact Focus on the Family in Colorado Springs at www.family.org and we will send you the details.

Once your son has learned the basics of reading, you need to motivate him to practice it. Children's author Sigmund Brouwer says that even "reluctant readers" can learn to love books if they are approached properly.[8] Here are some suggestions geared for boys provided in an article in the *Orlando Sun-Sentinel* entitled "Boys and Books Can Be a Great Mix."

- In general, boys want more action than girls, who prefer character development.
- Boys like their characters to be doing something. If the book doesn't move fast enough, a lot of boys will stop reading. Boys want facts and a fast plot.
- If you want boys to read fiction, let it be full of information.
- Snakes, spiders, and airplanes are also captivating to them.
- Boys don't like to read stuff they would call "ooey-gooey." They prefer sports and adventure.
- Boys tend to gravitate toward nonfiction—books about sports cars, UFOs, yo-yos, magic, mystery, and science fiction.
- Make reading a regular part of household activities. Let your son see you read.
- Give books as presents. When you give your son a soccer ball, for instance, include a book on the sport.
- Acknowledge that reading nonfiction and factual information—the sports page, for example—is just as legitimate as reading novels.
- Boys will jump on books that match their interests, but reading level must also be considered. If the book is too difficult, they won't finish. Too easy, and they'll get bored. Make it a challenge but not an impossible one.
- Take your son to the bookstore or library and let him explore reading options. The librarian can be urged to talk to him about his hobbies and interests and then listen carefully to his response. That will give the librarian a sense of what kind of books he might enjoy. The secret is involving him in the decision.
- Never give them just one book. Try five or six. If they don't like the first or second, they have a bigger choice.
- Another secret is repetition. Learning to read better is like playing any sport. Unless there is an eyesight problem or physiological problem, most reluctant readers can be turned around through nothing more than practice.[9]

I hope these suggestions have been helpful. Let's turn our attention now to the kind of school that your child should attend, assuming you have the resources and the commitment to consider some alternatives. No school structure is perfect, whether public, Christian, secular-private, charter school, or homeschool. Each has advantages and disadvantages, depending on the needs of an individual child and the quality of the programs available in a particular area. That is why I have never made a blanket recommendation to parents about where they should place their children. It depends on finances, family pressures, the quality of local schools, and other individual circumstances. Shirley and I chose Christian schools for our kids, from kindergarten all the way through college, except for a few short forays into public education. I am thankful to this day for the men and women who sacrificed mightily to teach in those Christian institutions. They hardly earned enough money to live on. They did it because they wanted to share their faith with students. God bless 'em.

Still, if we had to do it over again, Shirley and I would probably homeschool our children. I think we could have done the job very well. At the time they were young, however, homeschooling was not fashionable. I had never even heard of it. Given that lack of information, I unwittingly helped start the homeschool movement that is now spreading around the world. The year was 1979, and someone handed me a book by a man named Dr. Raymond Moore. It was called *Better Late Than Early*. He soon wrote a companion text entitled *School Can Wait*. Since Moore and I had both earned our Ph.D.s in child development at the University of Southern California, we had crossed paths a time or two. On that basis, I invited him to be a guest on my then-new radio program, *Focus on the Family*. I was totally unprepared for what would happen next.

Dr. Moore talked that day about the basic concept of homeschooling and why it is risky and unwise to place very young children, especially immature boys, in formalized educational settings. He explained how research had demonstrated conclusively that kids can be taught in very informal home settings with their parents until ages eight, nine, ten, or even older before being plugged in with their age-mates. They tend to catch up quickly and be leaders in their classes.[10] These ideas were new to me because I had been taught that early formal schooling was necessary for a child to reach his full potential. That was the rage when I was in graduate school. It has turned out to be wrong, and yet people like actor Rob Reiner and other zealots are still promoting the concept.[11] As I listened to Dr. Moore and read the related research, I began to see the folly of the early-schooling perspective.

No sooner had my radio interview with Dr. Moore hit the air than an avalanche of responses landed in our offices. I wasn't even aware at that time that I had so many listeners. We were buried for weeks by requests for Dr. Moore's book and additional information about how to start a home school. The rest is history. The concept skyrocketed and continues to expand. It is now the fastest-growing educational movement in the country, still growing at a rate of 15 percent per year.[12] Raymond and Dorothy Moore are still my friends, and I appreciate the enormous contribution they have made to children and families around the world.

Why is homeschooling growing so rapidly? Perhaps the following transcript of a recent *Focus on the Family* broadcast will help explain it. My guest was Dr. Bill Bennett, the former secretary of education under President Ronald Reagan and the drug czar under President George Bush. He has written and lectured for years about public schools and holds a Ph.D. from the University of Texas and a law degree from Harvard. If anyone has a clear-eyed "fix" on education, Dr. Bennett is that person. Here is a portion of his comments on that day, edited slightly for clarification:

> **James C. Dobson:** Bill, welcome back to *Focus on the Family.*
>
> **Bill Bennett:** Thank you so much. It's a pleasure to be here.
>
> **JCD:** Let's talk about public education today. Why don't you start by giving us a report card on today's schools? How are they doing compared to years past?
>
> **BB:** Well, let's look at the academics. I can do it in shorthand, Jim. There are lots of feel-good reports out there in the country. There are a lot of high grades. When parents are told how the children are doing, they're told they're doing fine. When you evaluate the test scores from the states, it looks pretty encouraging. Then you put our children in an international competition against children from other industrialized nations, and it's very bad.
>
> In the third grade, in math and science, our children score near the top compared to third graders in other industrialized nations. In the eighth grade, they score in the middle. In the twelfth grade, they score at the bottom. In short, the longer you stay in school in America, the dumber you get, relative to kids in other countries.
>
> **JCD:** What an indictment that is.
>
> **BB:** It's a dumbing-down process. But it's interesting

because our children do reasonably well in the third grade, which suggests it's not the children's fault; there is something wrong with the system. This has been studied and examined. This has happened now several times, and we see that the longer kids stay in school, the further they fall behind, relative to the children from other nations.

JCD: What is wrong with the system?

BB: It is a failure of competition. There is no competition in the system. There's very little accountability in the system. There are some wonderful teachers in our schools, but there are others who have no business being there. The last numbers I saw said that only 20 percent of our high school math teachers had majored in math in college. So the lack of preparation in subject matter is a very serious problem.

A study done at the University of California at Berkeley pointed out that one-half of elementary school math teachers could not divide one-and-three-quarters by one-half. All of the Chinese teachers from the People's Republic of China (I call it Communist China because that's what it is) who were tested could divide one-and-three-quarters by one-half. Now you need to be able to do that if you're going to teach math to my child or your child. I think this is what explains some of the numbers from the international comparison.

Up to the third-grade level, it's pretty basic stuff: decoding a text, doing addition, doing subtraction. Things really fall apart in the middle grades. More important, Jim, there is curricular confusion. There is chaos. There is a lack of agreement about what should be taught. You've got all sorts of theories coming from schools of education in universities. Once you get past the fourth and fifth grade, it's really anybody's guess about what a child might be getting in school.

JCD: Given these results, you would think professional educators would be saying, "My goodness. We've got to get busy here or somebody's going to blame us for failing our kids. They are not doing well academically. Too many of our kids are not making it. Let's see if we can fix the problem." Instead, one of the primary objectives of the National Education Association and the U.S. Department of Education is assuring that homosexual propaganda is taught to every kid in America—kindergarten to grade twelve. If they have their way, the gay and lesbian point of view will be integrated into every academic subject—math, science, language arts, and social studies. There's something crazy about that.

BB: Yeah, there *is* something crazy. It's the old story. When something goes wrong, change the subject. If the subject is math, change it to something else. If the subject is science, change it to something else. So here's yet one more cause to be promoted. We have larded onto the schools job after job, task after task, things that are not central to the educational mission. But the last thing the American people want is to have their schools preaching to their children about the need to accommodate homosexuality and to encourage the view that all lifestyles are equal.

Do you remember the curriculum called Heather Has Two Mommies? It was a program to promote a new definition of families involving gay or lesbian parents.

JCD: Yes, I do.

BB: I was with some of those brave folks in New York recently—those citizens who stood up and said, "No, we will not permit this." They were right to oppose it, but now we're seeing a resurgence of this effort to foist this stuff on the entire school system. These values, these ideas, are inimical to most parents. They won't stand for it.

JCD: You told me in my office a few minutes ago that if California and other schools move in this direction that millions of parents will flee. Homeschooling is one of the places that they will go.

BB: Jim, if the NEA wants to see a further exodus out of the schools and a further increase in the ranks of homeschoolers, and a further dissatisfaction with public education, it will proceed in this way. When parents read in the newspapers about the shooting at Santee and about the shooting in Granite Hills or the shooting near here in Littleton, Colorado, then they will begin to ask, "Why are we sending our children to public schools? There are risks of all sorts."

I don't mean to overdramatize this; we know that the incidence of school violence is actually lower than it's been for years before. But there are so many things that parents have to worry about now when it comes to sending their children to school. Why encumber the system with one more tangent? Why would the schools or the NEA irritate parents and cause them to look for alternatives? Look, you and I have talked about this a number of times. It is now known that the success of homeschoolers is virtually universal.

JCD: Kids are getting a great education there. That is undeniable.

BB: The kids in public schools score, appropriately enough, at the fiftieth percentile on tests of academic competence. In other words, their combined score is "average." Homeschoolers, however, are at the eighty-seventh percentile—for about one-sixth the cost. These homeschool kids are getting into the colleges that their parents want them to attend, and the program produces a high degree of parental and child satisfaction.

One other very interesting thing we've just found out about these wonderful kids is that they tend to be active in political affairs. They tend to be joiners. They tend to be people who are engaged in civic activities—just the opposite of what people have said. I have a theory about that, which I would defer to you. But I think these kids are so filled with mother love—you know, so much affection and devotion from their moms and dads (dads do occasionally play a role in homeschooling; let's get in a word for dads)—that they are just supremely confident.

JCD: Many homeschool kids come here to Focus on the Family on field trips. It is interesting to watch them. They are very confident, as you said. They look adults in the eye and respond to them respectfully. There is something different about homeschool boys and girls, and that difference is good. I believe in that movement. It's not for everybody, but it sure works when people are committed to it.

BB: Not all teachers are parents, but all good parents are teachers.

JCD: I was watching television and saw the finals of the national spelling bee. I'm telling you, that was a thrilling experience. The first-, second-, and third-place winners had each been homeschooled, which has also occurred in other competitive programs of that nature.

BB: That's right. That's exactly right.

JCD: The winner looked into the camera and thanked God that He had given him the ability to compete. His father was even more impressive. He said to the interviewer, "I'm proud of what my son has accomplished. He did a good job.

But I'm much more pleased about the development of his character than I am his intellectual accomplishments."

BB: That's right.

JCD: This is the value system that parents are able to instill at home, which their kids will not get in public schools, where it is prohibited by law.

BB: Do you remember the great Ronald Reagan story? It was written up in *Reader's Digest.* The president read about a little girl who found a purse and returned it to its owner. She told her counselor and then asked, "Did I do the right thing?" The counselor said, "Well, let's talk about it with the rest of the children." They all talked about it and the counselor said, "Now let's vote." The children voted in the majority that the girl had done the wrong thing, that she was stupid. She should have kept the money. So, of course, the child looked up plaintively to the counselor and he threw up his hands and said, "I'm just here to see what people think, just to facilitate discussion." There was a time when a counselor or teacher would have reinforced the rightness of what the child had done. Now the kids are asked to vote on what is correct morally.

JCD: When I was in the first grade, I found a dime on the school playground one day. A dime was a lot of money when I was six years old. I don't mean to imply that I was some kind of little saint, but I had been taught at home that I shouldn't keep something that didn't belong to me. Now children are asked to debate what is right or wrong, based not on an established standard of morality but on peer-group opinion. That is just incredible.

BB: Think of that poor lost child who looked to the adult for guidance, but the adult couldn't give an answer. He or she had been told not to favor one point of view over another in this kind of "values clarification"—and not to use language of right and wrong because there are no absolutes.

[Later in the interview]

JCD: I understand you now have a new on-line curriculum available for children in grades K-12 to assist homeschool parents and others wanting to teach children directly. Give us the basic idea.

BB: In many ways, this is a very simple idea. What I am doing with my colleagues is developing an educational program on the Web, for kindergarten through twelfth grade, in six subjects: math, English, history, science, art, and music. We are developing a lesson for every day for every year of those thirteen years. It will consist of books and materials and programs on the Internet.

We are offering it to parents, teachers, or whoever would be interested in it. We've looked at science programs in different states; we've looked at reading and writing programs everywhere. We have assembled what we think is the best educational program that a parent or a school can have. We are hoping that homeschoolers will be interested in the whole thing, or a piece of it, or a part of it. We're hoping that public-school systems will look at it too, and that parents will consider it.

JCD: How can parents get more information about the program?

BB: Just log on the Internet at <http://www.K12.com.>

JCD: Thanks for being our guest again, Bill. You are always welcome at these microphones.

BB: Thanks, Jim. I always enjoy talking with you.[13]

I hope our readers understand that despite the concerns expressed by Dr. Bennett and me about public schools, neither of us is "negative" about them. There are many deeply dedicated and conscientious teachers and administrators in public education today who are just as committed to children as those I described in Christian schools. I do have to admit, however, that if government schools continue to drift much further away from traditional morality and common sense, such as today's over-the-top sex education programs and the postmodern stuff being promoted now by the NEA and the U.S. Department of Education, I soon will be very decidedly opposed to them.

One of my most serious criticisms is with a philosophy that was expressed in 1973 by former first lady and now U.S. senator Hillary Rodham Clinton. Perhaps her words written so long ago have been forgotten. No matter. The philosophy she expressed is reflective of the direction taken by public educators in many locations and, certainly, among its union leaders. Here is a summary of Mrs. Clinton's viewpoints, written by columnist George F. Will:

If children are miniature adults, naturally endowed with most of the qualities necessary for participation in adult society; if they require scant shaping; if there is little need to restrain and redirect their natural impulses—well, then, "the legal status of infancy or minority should be abolished and the presumption of incompetency reversed" regarding motherhood, abortion, schooling and much else.[14]

This statement makes no sense to me. Children, said Mrs. Clinton, are not immature little people who need to be disciplined, shaped, trained, and directed. They are fully competent individuals who should be given the legal status of adults. Schools, therefore, should get out of the way and let nature take its course. Educators are not supposed to "teach" kids, which implies a superior status. They are "colearners" and "facilitators" who simply help children discover for themselves what is in their best interests. The continuation of this philosophy is why, as Dr. Bennett said, there is "chaos in the curriculum." Many educators profess not to know what they should teach—or even whether they have the right to teach it. No wonder our kids get whipped in international academic competition. They may know how to use condoms, but too many of them can't compute, read, or write.

This is why many parents have turned to homeschooling as a means of coping with a hostile culture. It allows them to transmit their values to the next generation. And as we have seen, it has also been demonstrated to be a highly effective learning environment. Students educated at home are now enrolled in some of the most prestigious colleges and universities in the nation, where they have distinguished themselves academically and personally. Homeschooling offers a highly successful approach for parents committed to it.

Those who have chosen to teach their own children are often warned that their "isolated" boys and girls will grow up to be misfits. This concern about "socialization," as it is called, is a dark cloud hanging over the heads of homeschooling parents. I believe it is a bum rap—for several reasons. First, to remove a child from the classroom is not necessarily to confine him to the house! Once beyond the schoolyard gate, the options are practically unlimited! Homeschool support groups are surfacing in community after community. Some are highly organized and offer field trips, teaching co-ops, tutoring services, social activities, and various forms of assistance and resources. There are even athletic leagues and orchestras in some areas. Furthermore, some public-school districts permit homeschooled students to participate in activities and programs.

Even if you're operating completely on your own, there are outings to museums and parks, visits to farms, factories, hospitals, and seats of local government, days with Dad at the office, trips to Grandma's house, extracurricular activities such as music, church youth groups, service organizations, and special-interest clubs. There are friends to be invited over and relatives to visit and parties to attend. The list is limitless. Even a trip with Mom to the market can provide younger students with invaluable exposure to the lives and daily tasks of adults in the real world. While there, a multitude of lessons can be learned about math (pricing, fractions, pints vs. gallons, addition, subtraction, etc.), reading labels, and other academic subjects. And without the strictures of schedules and formal curricula, it can all be considered part of the educational process. That's what I would call socialization at its best! To suggest that home-educated students are strange little people in solitary confinement is nonsense.

The great advantage of homeschooling, as we have described, is the protection it provides to vulnerable children from the wrong kind of socialization. I'm referring now not only to the cultural influences we have considered but to what children do to each other. When thrown together in large groups, the strongest and most aggressive kids quickly intimidate the weak and vulnerable. It is the immature and "different" boys and girls who suffer under these circumstances. When this occurs in nursery school or in kindergarten, they learn to fear their peers. There stands a knobby-legged kid who doesn't have a clue about life or how to cope with things that scare him. He has to sink or swim. It is easy to see why such children tend to become more peer dependent because of the jostling they get at too early an age. It stays with them well into adolescence. Research shows that if immature boys in particular can be kept at home for a few more years and shielded from the impact of social pressure, they tend to be more confident, more independent, and often emerge as leaders three or four years later.[15]

If acquainting children with ridicule, rejection, physical threats, and the rigors of the pecking order is necessary to socialize our children, I'd recommend that we keep them "unsocialized" for a little longer.

I know I have given an inordinate amount of attention in this chapter to one approach to education, that of homeschooling. There are many other alternatives, and I have not done them justice. Furthermore, there are many parents who are not cut out emotionally or temperamentally to make a go of home teaching. Others can't afford to live on one salary. Therefore, it is not for everybody. In that environment, I continue to be grateful for Christian teachers in both public and private education who are working every day for the betterment of children. There is also great promise in the charter-schools movement and what are called "magnet schools" that offer attractive alternatives. Without them, public schools would have a hammerlock on every child in America.

To the parents of immature boys who are not ready to sit in class hour after hour, I urge you to at least consider the other possibilities while your boys are small. Your sons can excel if given an opportunity.

QUESTIONS AND ANSWERS

What is your perspective on vouchers that allow parents to select the school of their choice and pay for schooling with government money?

Let me give you a roundabout answer. The enormous success of free enterprise and capitalism as economic systems is linked directly to the presence of competition. It is why America leads the world in productivity and efficiency. The absence of competition explains the dismal failure of communism and other socialistic forms of government. The simple fact is that competition improves human performance in almost every context. McDonald's, Wendy's, and Burger King dare not fall behind their competitors in the quality and quantity of the food and service they provide. It would be fatal to do so. That principle has endless applications. Take a look at how the Department of Motor Vehicles, the local Social Security office, the post office, and other federal agencies operate. Contact them and see if you get a prompt return call. I don't mean to disparage the fine people who are working in those and other government offices, but if you need something from them, you will recognize immediately that they don't need your business. They have a state-run monopoly for which there is no competition. People get sloppy when they don't have to hustle.

Do you remember when the Bell Telephone system held a virtual monopoly on America's long-distance service? A call out of the area cost approximately thirty cents per minute. After Ma Bell was broken up and competition from other companies was permitted, the rate dropped to six or seven cents. It is still falling. The relevance of this point to public education should be obvious. It will never provide the service parents want, or reach a high level of efficiency, until educators are forced to compete. That is why I support the concept of vouchers. Giving parents the right to choose their child's school will put power in their hands and motivate public schools to do a better job. The only thing blocking this proven idea is the powerful education lobby, which holds sway in Washington and in state governments.

The teacher of my son's third-grade class told me in a conference last week that my son was the "class clown." She said he would do anything for a laugh. He's not generally that way at home. What do you think is going on with him?

Your son is not alone. There is at least one class clown in every classroom. These skilled little disrupters are usually boys. They often have reading or other academic problems. They may be small in stature, although not always, and they'll do anything to draw attention to themselves. Their parents and teachers may not recognize that behind the boisterous behavior is often the pain of a poor self-concept. Humor is a classic response to feelings of inadequacy, and that's why many successful comedians have been hurting little boys or girls. Jonathan Winters's parents were divorced when he was seven years old. He said the other boys teased him about not having a dad. He said he acted like he didn't care, but when no one was watching, he would go behind a tree and cry. Winters said all of his humor has been a response to sorrow.[16] Comedienne Joan Rivers often joked about her unattractiveness as a girl. She said she was such a dog, her father had to throw a bone down the aisle in order to get her married.[17]

These comedians and most others got their training during childhood, using humor as a defense against childhood hurts. That is often the inspiration for the class clown. By making an enormous joke out of everything, he conceals the self-doubt that churns inside.

Knowing that should help you meet the needs of your son and help him find more acceptable ways of getting attention. Playing a musical instrument, participating in sports, or acting in a school play are good alternatives. Cracking down on his silly behavior would also be a good idea.

PREDATORS

CHAPTER 14

WE HAVE DISCUSSED several major social problems that account for much of the trouble facing boys and their parents today. This chapter will deal with yet another difficulty that we have referred to several times without defining it. It is called postmodernism, which helps explain further how families, and especially how boys, came to be in such a mess. This system of thought, also called moral relativism, teaches that truth is not only unknowable from God, whom postmodernism perceives as a myth, or from man, who has no right to speak for the rest of us. Rather, truth doesn't exist at all. *Nothing* is right or wrong, *nothing* is good or evil, *nothing* is positive or negative. Everything is relative. All that matters is "what's right for me and what's right for you." Those ideas evolve from person to person as they go along.

Incredibly, some professors contend today that not even the Nazi's extermination of 6 million "undesirables" in World War II was immoral, because the idea of morality itself is bogus.[1] To say that something is inherently wrong implies that a Great Judge sits somewhere in the heavens issuing ultimate values and commandments for the world. The postmodernist is convinced that no such authority exists. In the absence of a Supreme Being, tolerance becomes the "god" who endorses anything and everything except Christian beliefs. Public policies are determined by opinion polls or they are concocted from popular notions that simply seem appropriate to somebody at the moment.

The interesting thing about postmodernists is their ability to live comfortably with contradictions. Why? Because there are no troubling absolutes to be reckoned with. For example, moral relativists celebrate human dignity and racial harmony as precepts but then advocate killing (or helping to kill) the elderly, the unborn, and even full-term, healthy babies as they exit the birth canal. Human life is expendable if it is inconvenient. "Wait a minute!" you say. Those ideas can't coexist in the same mind. "Sure they can," says the postmodernist, explaining nothing.

It is this fractured philosophy that permitted U.S. Senator Barbara Boxer (D-CA) to insist during a Senate debate that we needed to preserve God's beautiful environment but then to assert on another occasion that babies are not human until parents actually take them home from the hospital. They can be murdered with impunity in those first hours or days.[2] What convoluted logic that was, and yet, conflicting ideas such as these don't have to make sense to postmodernists. There is no sense to a universe that sprang from nothingness and evolved into meaningless life forms without design or designer. That is the essence of postmodernism.

Bioethicist and professor at Princeton, Peter Singer is one of the world's foremost proponents of this valueless, immoral philosophy. He has said, "Killing a disabled infant is not morally equivalent to killing a person. The life of a newborn baby is of less value . . . than the life of a pig, a dog, or a chimpanzee."[3] This misguided man was recently granted tenure by Princeton, *after* he revealed his off-the-wall views on the worthlessness of human life. Of all things, the university has had the audacity to make Dr. Singer the chairman of their bioethics department.

Now what does this moral relativism have to do with raising boys? Just about everything, in fact. It has confused all the age-old distinctions between right and wrong, between proper and improper, between priceless and worthless, and between human and inhuman. It has also resulted in a moral free fall that has yet to hit bottom. Postmodernism has given credibility and free reign to every form of evil. Yes, I said *evil.* Boys, with their tendencies to push the limits and defy authority, are the ones most vulnerable to it. They are enticed into terribly destructive behavior that would have been stopped cold in its tracks by previous generations, who knew that some things are unquestionably wrong and that all ideas have consequences.

The notion of postmodernism teaches children, teens, and adults that they owe their existence to random chance in a chaotic universe with no design and no designer. We are accountable to no one and live for a meaningless moment in a dying cosmos that will end in total darkness. We have no inherent value as human beings and no significance beyond our short journey on the river of time. No wonder low self-esteem and disrespect for others are at an all-time high. It is a damnable worldview that assaults the family and warps its young.

Remember, too, that ideas determine behavior. The book of Proverbs says, "As [a man] thinks in his heart, so is he" (Proverbs 23:7 NKJV). Those who are told they resulted from nothing more than happenstance have fewer reasons to be moral, lawful, respectful, or thankful. And indeed, many of them are not.

When translated into a million destructive ideas and images, the postmodern system of thought assaults the family and warps its youngest and most impressionable members. It also shapes child-rearing practices today. I read an outrageous example of this freewheeling approach in a question-and-answer column published in the August 2000 issue of *Maryland Family Magazine*. A "concerned dad" had written to ask the columnists, Laura Davis and Janis Keyser, about his seven-year-old son, Brett, who was engaging in sex play with his best friend, Jacqueline. They had been hiding under the covers naked, examining each other's genitals, and "giggling a lot" for the past several years. Neither family had been concerned about the activity, which had apparently been going on since the kids were four or five years old. More recently, they had been shutting the door and spending more time naked together. When the father entered the room, they shouted indignantly and ordered him to stay out. When Dad asked what they were doing, Jacqueline said they wanted to see Brett's eggs and sperm. Dad wanted the columnists to tell him what guidelines should be set for the children.

Would you believe, the self-appointed "experts" who wrote the column thought it was perfectly normal and acceptable for kids to engage in this kind of sexual behavior? "Children," they said, "are curious about sexual intercourse and where babies come from." Remember, now, that Brett and Jacqueline were under five when this activity began. Davis and Keyser warned the father "not to jump in with too many ideas of [his] own," and that maintaining an open-door policy "might be tricky because children often demand privacy." Then the "experts" offered this: "If [your] children are spending more than a quarter of their time in body exploration and sex play, or if they seem 'fixated' on it, they may need your help answering some of their questions and finding other activities to enjoy together." And finally, "If children are enjoying the sensuality of the play, you could devise some other more structured ways to engage in tactile play. Back rubs and foot massages with lotion or oil are wonderful alternatives."[4] But that is only if the kids are spending more than 25 percent of their time under the covers!

Have we gone completely mad?! At times I'm convinced that we have done just that. Or at least postmodernists have.

Columnist Ellen Goodman, who to my knowledge does not claim to be a Christian, wrote an insightful editorial about this battle to protect children from the harmful influences of our day. Here is her perspective:

> At some point between Lamaze and PTA, it becomes clear that one of your main jobs as a parent is to counter the culture. What the media deliver to children by the masses, you are expected to rebut one at a time.
>
> But it occurs to me now that the call for "parental responsibility" is increasing in direct proportion to the irresponsibility of the marketplace. Parents are expected to protect their children from an increasingly hostile environment. Are the kids being sold junk food? Just say no. Is TV bad? Turn it off. Are there messages about sex, drugs, violence all around? Counter the culture.
>
> Mothers and fathers are expected to screen virtually every aspect of their children's lives. To check the ratings on the movies, to read the labels on the CDs, to find out if there's MTV in the house next door. All the while keeping in touch with school and, in their free time, earning a living.
>
> Barbara Dafoe Whitehead, a research associate at the Institute for American Values, found this out in interviews with middle-class parents. "A common complaint I heard from parents was their sense of being overwhelmed by the culture. They felt relatively more helpless than their parents."
>
> "Parents," she notes, "see themselves in a struggle for the hearts and minds of their own children." It isn't that they can't say no. It's that there's so much more to say no to.
>
> Without wallowing in false nostalgia, there has been a fundamental shift. Americans once expected parents to raise their children in accordance with the dominant cultural messages. Today they are expected to raise their children in opposition.
>
> Once the chorus of cultural values was full of ministers, teachers, neighbors, leaders. They demanded more conformity but offered more support. Now the messengers are Ninja Turtles, Madonna, rap groups, and celebrities pushing sneakers. Parents are considered "responsible" only if they are successful in their resistance.
>
> It's what makes child raising harder. It's why parents feel more isolated. It's not just that American families have less

time with their kids, it's that we have to spend more of this time doing battle with our own culture.

It's rather like trying to get your kids to eat their green beans after they've been told all day about the wonders of Milky Way. Come to think of it, it's exactly like that.[5]

© 2000, The Boston Globe Newspaper Co./Washington Post Writers Group. Reprinted with permission.

For Christian parents, the struggle to protect children from the culture goes far beyond junk food and celebrities pushing sneakers. Indeed, today's kids have been bombarded with more dangerous ideas than any generation in American history. It has become a daunting task for mothers and fathers to shield them from "safe-sex" instruction in school, from New Age gurus, from profane and filthy language in the neighborhood, and from enticements of every stripe. Dogging the young like hungry wolves are predators who would exploit them for financial gain, including drug pushers, unprincipled movie and television producers, sex abusers, abortion providers, heavy-metal freaks, and now, those who inhabit the Internet. As a case in point, Planned Parenthood has distributed thousands of tiny boxes to teens in the Minneapolis area, called "Prom Survival Kits." Each contains three condoms, two breath mints, a confetti party favor, and a discount coupon for a first visit to a Planned Parenthood clinic. These not-so-subtle enticements to sexual activity are characteristic of messages given to teens by adults who ought to know better. How sad that parents have to fight continually to preserve common sense and decency at home.

At times it feels as though there is nothing wholesome left for our children and teens to enjoy. For example, the most popular programs on cable television today feature the violent antics of the World Wrestling Federation (WWF). They are kid favorites, with their blood-and-guts brand of entertainment. Watching grown-ups behave in such violent and outrageous ways has to be deleterious to children. Remember the twelve-year-old boy in Florida, Lionel Tate, who body-slammed and beat a six-year-old girl to death, crushing her skull and lacerating her liver? He said he had been watching wrestlers on television and wanted to try their moves. The young killer was given a life sentence.[6] I have not heard a single commentator say that the WWF and their commercial sponsors bear major responsibility for this tragedy, but they do.

Over-the-top comedy shows on cable television also have an enormous impact on young minds. Executives of MTV, with their emphasis on sex and violence, admit attempting to shape each generation of adolescents. One of their corporate ads pictures the back of a teenager's head with

"MTV" shaved in his hair. The copy reads, "MTV is not a channel. It's a cultural force. People don't watch it, they love it. MTV has affected the way an entire generation thinks, talks, dresses, and buys."[7] The amazing thing about this ad is that MTV not only admits they are trying to manipulate the young and immature; they spend big bucks bragging about it.

If you still have any doubt that MTV is exploiting your kids, I suggest that you watch some of its popular broadcasts. They should chill your soul. Although producers are constantly changing to attract more viewers, they tend to get worse all the time. A current program called *Jackass* is downright awful. It "stars" an adolescent nut named Johnny Knoxville, who depicts himself in various disgusting settings. He was videotaped while being turned upside down and sloshed around in a portable toilet. He called it a "poo cocktail." He ate a live goldfish and then vomited it into the bowl. He dressed like a disabled person in a wheelchair and then crashed into a wall.[8] On one occasion, he put on a bulletproof vest and shot himself in the chest with a 38-caliber pistol, a scene that MTV, uncharacteristically, refused to air.[9] The name of the game with these and other shows is to do absolutely anything to garner ratings—most of it sensational, reckless, and immoral. As we speak, more than 2 million young viewers watch *Jackass* every week.[10] How many boys are immature and unstable enough to imitate the behavior they are watching? The majority of kids, at one time or another, I suspect.

By the time you read this book, something new will have been concocted for your impressionable children—something even worse. Author James Poniewozik says the result of these grossed-out offerings is what he calls the "Rude Boy" phenomenon.[11] Today's males, he said, have had to figure out how to alienate their parents, many of whom have "been there and done that." To outdo the rebellion of the past, their behavior has become even more extreme and audacious. But have you thought about this? Someday the children yet to be born to the Rude Boys and their kooky girlfriends will have to figure out how to shock *their* parents. It will not be easy. There aren't many crazy things left for them to do.

The rock-music industry takes the prize for producing the most outrageous and dangerous material for kids. I doubt if parents are fully aware of the filth and violence that is being marketed to their children. Let me share just one example, which is no worse than a thousand others, taken from a CD released a few years ago. It was recorded by a popular group called Korn and included these lyrics:

> *Your throat, I take grasp—can you feel the pain?*
> *Then your eyes roll back—can you feel the pain? . . .*

Your heart stops beating—can't you feel the pain?
Black orgasms—can't you feel the pain?
I kiss your lifeless skin—can't you feel the pain?
There you are my precious with your broken soul[12]

Incredibly, these terrible lyrics were titled "My Gift to You." The CD (produced and distributed by Sony Records) premiered at number one on the charts and sold two million copies. Most kids who bought this recording, some of whom had to be preteens, not only listened to the words but memorized them by playing the CD repeatedly. Given these echoes from the culture, we wonder why more Christian moms and dads aren't storming the gates of the companies and organizations such as Sony that are warping and twisting the values of their kids. Why, pray tell, is shock jock Howard Stern still permitted to have his own show on radio or television despite the unbelievable things he has said and done? A few days after twelve teenagers and one adult were murdered in cold blood at Columbine High School in Littleton, Colorado, Stern said, "A bunch of good-looking girls go to that school. There were, like, really good-looking girls running out of there with their hands over their heads. Did those kids try to have sex with any of those good-looking girls? They didn't even do that. At least if you're going to kill yourself and kill all the kids, why wouldn't you have some sex?"[13]

Where was the outrage that should have rained down on Stern's hairy head? Why were the sponsors of his program not besieged by angry parents? Where was the news media that expresses such indignation when political correctness is assaulted? Why was Stern not sacked and never heard from again? Good questions! A few days after his unforgivable remarks, however, it was business as usual. He never missed a beat. As of this moment, he has the third most popular talk show on the radio.

What goes on in universities these days is another sad story, where postmodernism is unopposed and where binge drinking is an every-weekend affair. Some campuses are even more extreme. An article that appeared in *The New York Times* on March 18, 2000, described what they called "The Naked Dorm" at Wesleyan University, a coed residence hall where clothing is optional. There is a "Naked Hour" when men and women get together to socialize. One student said, "It's the idea of not judging anyone, or respecting one another's beliefs. It does not have sexual overtones." Yeah, right! I'll spare you the other details except that the article claims that these parties at the dorm are among the most popular on campus. I'll bet. The question I would ask, again and again, is this: "Where are the parents who pay the bills for this kind of craziness?" One female student told her dad about the dorm and, "He just laughed."[14]

The Luntz Research organization conducted a poll that addressed the issue of morality. Surprisingly, they found that 80 percent of Americans believe immorality is our greatest problem as a nation.[15] Still, most of them are too busy or too demoralized to take on those who are exploiting their kids. That's how the manipulators manage to get away with murder.

There are still some moms and dads out there, thankfully, who are determined to protect their children. One of them, Michelle Malkin, is pretty burned up about weak-willed parents who tolerate such nonsense. She wrote:

Baby Boom Parents Are Asleep on the Job

"When pigs fly. When hell freezes over. When the cow jumps over the moon. N-O. No, no, no! End of discussion." This is what I'll tell my daughter when she asks me, many years from now, if she can attend a coed sleepover party. All across the country, believe it or not, adolescent boys and girls are romping around in their skivvies together under one roof with their parents' approval.

The Washington Post devoted 1,200 words to this booming teen fad. A newspaper database search turned up nearly 200 other stories on coed sleepovers. Popular teen shows such as the Warner Brother's network's *7th Heaven* have featured boy-girl slumber parties. A recent Abercrombie & Fitch Christmas catalog featured four preteen girls in bed under the covers with an older boy, lewdly waving his boxer shorts in the air.

"It's the newest thing," one 17-year-old boy named "J. D." explained to the *Post* reporter. The mixed overnight parties "are a variation on group dating," the *Post* reports, "where teenagers hang out together but often don't pair off. Some parents say the parties became more common a couple of years ago after school administrators in several districts asked hotels to stop providing rooms to students after big high school events." To win over his parents, J. D. argued that hosting a coed slumber party is "better than us lying about where we are and renting some sleazy motel room."

Many parents—and I use the term loosely—are buying into this bubblegum logic. "I just feel it's definitely better than going to hotels, and this way you know all the kids who are coming over, you know who they are with," said Edna Breit, a Maryland mom who allows her teen son to invite up to 20 girls and boys to sleep over, bathe in a hot tub, and stay up until dawn watching movies in the family basement.

Breit shared her furtive method of policing her young overnight guests: "You keep the serving bowls for snacks small. That way you have the pretext to go down there and refill." This is pathetic. How is it that we arrived at a point where a grown woman is proud of turning her home into a coed Comfort Inn, where parents must dream up sneaky ways to spy on their own children? When did "better than" judgments replace doing what's best for your children?

Pushover parents who think this is all harmless fun—that we should just chill out, lighten up, and relax—need to wake up. Teenage boys and girls do not belong in adult settings of intimacy. Coed sleepovers send the wrong message to teens too immature to handle sexually charged situations. It is only the latest sign of a culture that has given up on enforcing traditional roles of authority and on passing down moral sense and wisdom from one generation to the next.

Thanks largely to the radical egalitarian ethos embraced by the Baby Boomers, American notions of discipline have grown softer than the down filling in a teen's sleeping bag. Kay Hymowitz, author of *Ready or Not: Why Treating Children As Small Adults Endangers Their Future and Ours,* notes that nowadays "adults define themselves as children's allies, trainers, partners, friends, facilitators, colearners, and advocates. Their role is to empower children, advocate for them, boost their self-esteem, respect their rights, and provide them with information with which they can make their own decisions. But is this really what children need?"

My child needs her parents to be parents, not playmates. It is not easy to say no, and mean it, but we are prepared to say it again and again. Until then, I will cherish the fleeting days of innocence when a coed slumber party for our daughter means an afternoon nap in the crib with Mr. Wormy, Mr. Whoozit, and her dolly in pink pajamas.[16]

© 2001 Creators Syndicate, Inc.

Thanks, Mrs. Malkin. It is good to know that common sense can still be found among young families. The rest of us must join you in our determination to protect kids. Our first obligation is to heed the warning signs posted at railroad crossings. They tell drivers to Stop, Look, and Listen.

That is exactly what we need to do regarding the world in which our children live. We dare not get too busy to monitor their activities. That scrutiny is needed every single day because of the predators lurking near them in the tall grass, especially where young children are concerned.

Never forget that pedophiles (individuals who sexually abuse children) roam the landscape looking for victims. They do not have difficulty finding them. The average pedophile "captures" and exploits 150 children during his career.[17] Most do not get caught for many years, and even if they are, they may not be convicted. These men are highly skilled at their craft. They can enter a place where children hang out, such as a video-game room or a pizza parlor, and spot the most lonely and needy kids almost instantly. They look for boys and girls who are starved emotionally by disengaged parents. Within minutes, they can have those children under their control and begin abusing them. The average length of time that exploitation occurs in an individual is seven years![18] Why does the secret not leak out? Because kids are intimidated by threats and fear of parents.

Pedophiles also surf the Web looking for needy kids. That's why letting your children have unsupervised access to the Internet is like a greasy man showing up at your front door. He grins and says, "I know you are terribly busy and tired. How about letting me entertain your son or daughter for a while?" You let him in and he walks straight to the bedroom and closes the door. Who knows what goes on beyond your hearing? That is what you are doing when you place either a personal computer or a television set in your child's room. It is an invitation to disaster. But that is precisely what the majority of parents have done, and many of them have lived to regret that lack of supervision. I'll say more about that in a moment.

Another snake in the grass is the ready availability of pornography at every click of a mouse. It is not only *available* to kids, the pornographers usher them in. Children who regularly surf the Web will inevitably stumble onto hard-core stuff. If a boy clicks on the word *toys,* one of the options that may pop up is sex toys. If a girl clicks on a site called "love horses," she may see images of sex between a woman and a horse. In order to entice children and adults to a paying pornographic site, the purveyors of porn offer almost irresistible teasers. Concerned about this practice, the United States Congress passed a bill in 1996 that outlawed these obscene freebies. It became known as the Communications Decency Act. The Supreme Court in its wisdom struck down the law, claiming it was unconstitutional.[19] Can you imagine the founding fathers intending to protect such filth when they wrote the First Amendment?

The assault on young minds continues unabated. According to the Safe America Foundation, 53 percent of teenagers said they have come across

Web sites at some time containing pornographic, hate-based, or violent material. More than 91 percent said they had unintentionally stumbled onto this terrible stuff while studying for school or just surfing the Web.[20] Safe America said parents claim they monitor their children's explorations on the Internet, but the kids say that is not true. Most of them see whatever they choose.

Any kid can visit a local library and find the most awful stuff at his fingertips. Not only can he see the graphic sexual depictions on the Internet, but every other harmful image and idea is available to him—from how to make a bomb to instructions about committing suicide. When alarmed parents have demanded that filters and supervision be provided to protect their children from these Web sites, the American Library Association and the American Civil Liberties Union have fought like crazy to oppose them. Predictably, these libertarians claim with a straight face that the installation of filtering devices would violate the First Amendment rights of children.[21] They also say, "Libraries can't be parents." Get the implication here. It is a classic example of what we've been talking about. Parents are told, "You're on your own. It's not our problem." The provision of unsupervised computers represents the first time in history that government-sponsored machines have been set up to harm children, and yet this is exactly what is happening. Unsuspecting parents drop off their children at local libraries, assuming they will be safe in a learning environment. They have no idea what goes on inside. Does anyone still doubt that the culture is at war with families?

I hope you will read very carefully what I am about to write now, because it explains why this matter is so significant. Porn and smut pose an awesome threat to your boys. A single exposure to it by some thirteen- to fifteen-year-olds is all that is required to create an addiction that will hold them in bondage for a lifetime. It is more addictive than cocaine or heroine. That was one of the conclusions drawn during the Attorney General's Commission on Pornography, on which I served. It is known by those of us in the field of child development that the focal point of sexual interest is not very well established among young adolescents. It can be redirected by an early sexual experience (wanted or unwanted) or by exposure to pornography. A boy who would normally be stimulated by a "cheerleader" image of the opposite sex can learn through obscenity to find excitement in hurting someone, or in sex with animals, or in homosexual violence, or in having sex with younger children. Many men who have succumbed to these perverse sexual appetites have traced them to the dawn of their adolescence.

That is what happened to Ted Bundy, whom I interviewed just seventeen hours before he was executed for killing three girls, one of them little twelve-year-old Kimberly Leach.[22] Bundy confessed two days before his death to murdering at least twenty-eight women and girls; authorities say there may have been as many as one hundred. Bundy asked to talk to me because he wanted the world to know how pornography had led to (not caused) his murderous rampage. He was thirteen years of age when he discovered pornographic materials at a dump. Among them were detective magazines that showed scantily clad women who were being assaulted. Bundy found those images extremely exciting, and so began a tragic life that ended in a Florida electric chair.

I'm not suggesting that every adolescent who reads pornographic magazines or watches obscene videos will grow up to kill people. I am saying that a few of them will, and that many more—perhaps the majority—will develop full-blown addictions to smut. It is a huge cultural problem. More than 40 percent of *pastors* are afflicted by it![23] How did they get that way? By exposure to graphic materials that set them aflame. This pattern is responsible for untold numbers of divorces and dysfunctional marriages. I know this is true because I hear almost every day from women whose husbands are heavily involved with pornography. Availability of the Internet has increased the incidence of this tragedy immeasurably.

Let's return to the danger of putting personal computers and television sets in the bedrooms of your children. According to a recent survey, children ages two through eighteen spend on average five hours and twenty-nine minutes every day watching television, listening to music, or playing computer and video games. That total increases for children over eight, who spend nearly forty hours a week engaged in some sort of media-related activity. The survey also found that 53 percent of children have televisions in their bedrooms, which includes 32 percent of two- to seven-year-olds and 65 percent of eight- to eighteen-year-olds. Seventy percent of all children have radios in their rooms, and 16 percent have computers.[24]

What an ominous description this report provides of American children in the twenty-first century! The greasy man who knocked on the front door has taken up residence in the bedroom. It is all related, once again, to the frantic pace of living. We are too exhausted and harried to care for those we love most. We hardly know what they are doing at home, much less when we are away. What a shame! Yankelovich Partners Inc. said the image of families gathered around a single TV set in the family room is fading. Instead, many kids are off by themselves, where they can choose anything that they want to see. Ann Clurman, a partner at Yankelovich, said, "Almost everything children are seeing is essentially going into their minds in some sort of uncensored or unfiltered way."[25]

I strongly urge you to get those devices, whether they are television sets, computers, or VCRs, *out of the bedroom.* Locate them in the family room, where they can be monitored and where the amount of time spent on them is regulated. How can you do less for your children?

It is also our responsibility to watch various forms of entertainment *with* our boys and girls when they are young. What you see together can present teaching situations that will help them make the right choices for themselves when they are older. A member of our executive team shared a related incident with me that occurred while he was watching television with his thirteen-year-old daughter. In attempting to accommodate her, they selected a drama that was popular with teenagers. The dad was shocked by what he saw and heard, but he tried hard not to turn their time of "togetherness" into a parental lecture. Finally, he could take it no more.

"Honey," he said, "I just can't sit here and let this trash come into our home. This is awful. We're going to have to watch something else."

To his surprise, his daughter said, "I wondered when you would finally turn it off, Dad. That program is terrible."

Our children may resist our efforts to screen out the filth and violence that now permeates their world, but they know it's right to do so. They will respect us for saying, "God gave us this home, and we're not going to insult Him by polluting it with foul programming." However, in order to make this judgment, you have to be watching *with* your children to know what requires your attention. May I suggest that you then share this Scripture with your family, written 2,600 years ago by King David? "I will set no wicked thing before mine eyes" (Psalm 101:3, KJV). Also, read and discuss the following verse from the writings of the apostle Paul: "Finally, brethren, whatsoever things are true, whatsoever things are honest, whatsoever things are just, whatsoever things are pure, whatsoever things are lovely, whatsoever things are of good report; if there be any virtue, and if there be any praise, think on these things" (Philippians 4:8 KJV).

If the little box simply can't be subdued, you might try unplugging it, selling it, moving it into the garage, hacking it with an ax, or sticking a shoe in its flickering blue eye. If the personal computer becomes a problem, junk it! Then gather the family around and read a great book together!

Well, dear parents, I know that what I have shared in this chapter has been upsetting. It is no wonder that many of you feel caught in the backwash of a postmodern culture whose only god is self-gratification and whose only value is radical individualism. Nevertheless, you do need to know the truth and what you can do to protect those you love. In the following chapter I will offer what I consider to be the most effective way to deal with a postmodern culture. In the meantime, here are some things to consider:

First, let's give priority to our children. In days gone by, the culture acted to shield them from harmful images and exploitation. Now it's open season for even the youngest among us. Let's put the welfare of our boys ahead of our own convenience and teach them the difference between right and wrong. They need to hear that God is the author of their rights and liberties. Let's teach them that He loves them and holds them to a high level of moral accountability.

Second, let's do everything in our power to reverse the blight of violence and lust that has become so pervasive across this land. Let's demand that the entertainment moguls stop producing moral pollutants. Let's recapture from the courts that system of self-rule that traditionally allowed Americans to debate their deepest differences openly and reach workable solutions together. Radical individualism is destroying us! Postmodernism is a cancer that rots the soul of humanity. The creed that proclaims, "If it feels good, do it!" has filled too many hospitals with drug-overdosed teenagers, too many prison cells with fatherless youth, too many caskets with slain young people, and caused too many tears for bewildered parents.

Finally, let's vow together today to set for our children the highest standards of ethics and morality and to protect them, as much as possible, from evil and death. Our families can't be perfect, but they *can* be better—much better.

QUESTION AND ANSWER

I believe you said on your radio program one time that we are actually training children to kill. What did you mean by that?

That is the thesis of David Grossman, who, along with Governor Mike Huckaby of Arkansas, wrote *On Killing: The Psychological Cost of Learning to Kill in War and Society.* Professor Grossman was nominated for a Pulitzer Prize for exposing visual violence, which he called "[the most] toxic, addictive and destructive substance."[26] When he was asked to testify before a U.S. senatorial committee investigating youth violence, he explained in chilling detail what we are facing as a nation. Having spent twenty-four years in the air force, he is an authority on what is known as "killology." That term refers to "the study of killing," focusing on the training procedures used by the military to prepare men for the most violent combat assignments. Grossman's shocking conclusion is that the same methods and experiences used for this purpose are being employed to indoctrinate children. In short, children are being taught to kill without remorse.

Those techniques, which involve overexposure to disturbing behavior, have been understood for decades. They are very effective. It is an established fact that the human mind will accept even the most horrible and repugnant experiences if given time to adjust and if accompanied by a rationale that disarms the defenses. The best (or worst) example of this process was seen in the Nazi killing squads, called *Einsatzgruppen,* which moved across Eastern Europe during World War II. About four of these small groups of twelve to twenty men systematically murdered more than 1.4 million people in cold blood, sparing neither women, children, nor babies.[27] On numerous occasions, they killed as many as fifty thousand Jews, Gypsies, Poles, and political prisoners in a single day.[28] After the war, social scientists studying the murderous behavior of the participants assumed that they must have been deranged or else they wouldn't have been able to endure such horror day after day. Upon investigation, however, it was learned that they were primarily normal human beings—former businessmen, doctors, lawyers, and shopkeepers—who believed in the Nazi cause and quickly became immune to wanton murder. They evolved into "monsters" who actually enjoyed watching innocent people beg vainly for mercy. What happened is that overexposure to brutality had hardened the killers to the suffering of innocent people and even the cries of little children. The mental process by which human beings learn to accept what they have previously found repugnant is known as desensitization.

Again, overexposure is the mechanism by which this surprising accommodation is achieved. Nazi recruits were required to perform disturbing tasks repeatedly and systematically until they were no longer shocked or revolted by them. They gave these trainees beautiful German shepherd puppies as their own and allowed them to become attached emotionally. Then they forced the men to break the necks of the puppies with their bare hands. This was done to make them "tough." What the Nazi leaders were doing was desensitizing the recruits to cruelty. It is a short distance emotionally from killing cuddly dogs to murdering defenseless human beings.[29]

This desensitization procedure is used in far more productive ways today by the airline industry. It is the mechanism by which pilots are trained and tested. The fliers are placed in stationary devices known as simulators, which create virtual emergency situations, such as engine failure or landing-gear problems. The purpose is to develop skills to be used in the event of a real crisis but also to condition the pilots to stay calm during catastrophic circumstances. Later, when they have been through every possible emergency in training, they can presumably handle life-and-death situations without panicking. It works. Medical students are also desensitized to handle gory things in the emergency room or in surgery that were shocking to them in the beginning. Most of us have this capacity to adjust to disturbing experiences.

That, in effect, is what we are doing to millions of viewers—especially our children—by exposing them to rape and murder incessantly on television and in the movies. This is precisely what was found in a twenty-two-year investigation conducted at the University of Illinois at Chicago. According to psychologist Leonard Eron, 875 subjects from a semirural New York county were accepted for study when they were eight years old. By the time they were thirty, those who had watched the most television violence had been convicted of a significantly larger number of serious crimes.

Eron, who heads the American Psychological Association's Commission on Violence and Youth, concluded, "Television violence affects youngsters of all ages, of both genders, at all socioeconomic levels and all levels of intelligence, and the effect is not limited to children who are already disposed to being aggressive and is not restricted to this country."[30]

Consider now the violence to which today's children are exposed in everyday life, such as the video games now available. Mortal Kombat is a prime example. Very young children are learning not only how to kill but also how to remain unaffected when heads are blown off and blood is spattered everywhere. With a little practice, they learn to adjust to death and misery. Professor Grossman said it is inevitable that the desensitization our kids are experiencing can be directly transferred to school campuses.[31]

Referring again to Eric Harris and Dylan Klebold, the killers at Columbine High School, their favorite movie was *Basketball Diaries,* which depicted a scene very much like the massacre they would later perpetrate. They were also heavily influenced by the goth scene, which teaches death, violence, and sexual perversion. Given that "training," it should not be surprising that the young killers cheered, jeered, and even seemed to be having a "great time" while gunning down their schoolmates. How can any rational person deny this link between virtual violence and violence on the streets?

STAYING CLOSE

CHAPTER 15

IN THE PREVIOUS CHAPTER, I described a culture that is bearing down on families everywhere and threatening the welfare of their children. It has placed parents in a very difficult position. They must either close their eyes and ignore the harmful influences that are swirling around their kids, or they must figure out how to defend them. Let me put forward some ideas for those of you who intend to dig in and fight.

The focal point of this discussion sounds so obvious that it may appear to offer nothing new. I believe, however, that there is value in what I am about to write. The essence of my message is that you as parents must work harder than ever at building satisfying and affirming relationships with your kids. You must give them a desire to stay within the confines of the family and conform to its system of beliefs. If you fail in this task, you could lose the battle of wills later on. The law today favors rebellious teens. They are likely to prevail in any nose-to-nose confrontation between generations, perhaps even leading to legal emancipation at an early age. Here's what you can do to prevent it.

When I was a kid, parents didn't have to depend as much on communication and closeness to keep their children in line. They could control and protect them, more or less, by the imposition of rules and the isolation of their circumstances. Farmer John could take sassy little Johnny out to the back forty acres and get his mind straight. Just the threat of that happening was enough to keep most teens from going off the deep end.

215

My folks understood that system. They had a million rules. There were regulations and prohibitions for almost every imaginable situation. Coming from a minister's home in a very conservative church, I was not allowed to go to the movies (which were remarkably tame), or to dances, or even to use mild slang. I remember being reprimanded once for saying, "Hot Dog!" when I got excited about something. I'm still not sure what danger those words conveyed to my dad, but he warned me not to say them again. *Darn* was seen as a euphemism for *damn, geez* meant Jesus, *dad-gummit* (an old southern expression) was an obvious representation of God's name. I dared not utter anything that even vaguely resembled profanity, even if it were nonsensical. My cousin, who lived under the same general regime, invented a slang word called *gerrit* that he could use without being accused of saying something bad. "I'm sick of that gerrit school," he might say. The invention didn't work. *Gerrit* got banned too.

In those days, parental authority typically stood like a great shield against the evils in what was called "the world." Anything perceived as unwholesome or immoral was kept outside the white picket fence simply by willing it to stay put. Fortunately, the surrounding community was helpful to parents. It was organized to keep kids on the straight and narrow. Censorship kept the movies from going too far, schools maintained strict discipline, infractions were reported to the parents, truant officers prevented students from playing hooky, chaperones usually preserved virginity, alcohol was not sold to minors, and illicit drugs were unheard-of. Even adults outside the family saw it as their civic responsibility to help protect children from anything that could harm them, whether physically, emotionally, or spiritually. Most of these townsfolk were probably acquainted with the children's parents, so it was easier for them to intervene. This support system didn't always do the job, of course, but it was generally effective.

As we saw in the previous chapter, however, this commitment to the welfare of children has all but disappeared. Rather than assisting parents in their child-rearing responsibilities, the culture actually conspires against them. Alas, the white picket fence is gone. Harmful images and ideas come sliding under the front door or, as we discussed earlier, they slither directly into the bedrooms through electronic media. As the world has become more sexualized and more violent, there are just too many opportunities for kids to get in trouble. Further, innumerable "voices" are out there enticing them to do what is wrong.

Parental authority is also undermined at every turn. For example, when parents decide today not to allow their boys to see a bad movie, their order is likely to be countermanded. The kids might watch the flick at the home of friends or on video when parents are at work. And these days, grown-ups seem to work longer and longer hours. That introduces one of the greatest points of danger. It is almost impossible for moms and dads to screen out harmful aspects of the culture when they are rarely at home in the afternoon. An unsupervised kid can get into more mischief in a single day than his parents can straighten out in a year.

Considering how the world has changed, it is doubly important to build relationships with boys from their earliest childhood. You can no longer rely on rules to get them past the predators in the wider world. It still makes sense to prohibit harmful or immoral behavior, but those prohibitions must be supplemented by an emotional closeness that makes children want to do what is right. They must know that you love them unconditionally and that everything you require of them is for their own good. It is also helpful to explain why you want them to behave in certain ways. "Laying down the law" without this emotional linkage is likely to fail.

Author and speaker Josh McDowell expressed this principle in a single sentence. He said, "Rules without relationship lead to rebellion."[1] He is absolutely right. With all the temptations buzzing around our kids, simply saying no a thousand times creates a spirit of defiance. We have to build bridges to them from the ground up. The construction should begin early and include having fun as a family, laughing and joking, playing board games, throwing or kicking a ball, shooting baskets, playing Ping-Pong, running with the dog, talking at bedtime, and doing a thousand other things that tend to cement the generations together. The tricky part is to establish those friendships while maintaining parental authority and respect. It can be done. It must be done.

Building relationships with children does not require large amounts of money. A lifelong bond often emerges from traditions that give meaning to family time together. Children love daily routines and activities of the simplest kind. They want to hear the same story or the same joke until Mom and Dad are ready to climb the wall. And yet, these interactions are sometimes more appreciated by kids than are expensive toys or special events.

Beloved author and professor Dr. Howard Hendricks once asked his grown children what they remembered most fondly from their childhood. Was it the vacations they took or the trips to theme parks or the zoo? "No," they answered. It was when Dad got on the floor and wrestled with them. That's the way children think. It is especially the way boys think. The most meaningful activities in the family are often those simple interactions that build lasting connections between generations.

Let's describe what we mean by traditions. They refer to those repetitive activities that give identity and belonging to every member of the family. In the Broadway musical *Fiddler on the Roof,* remember that the fiddler was perched securely on top of the house because of tradition. It told every member of the Jewish community who he or she was and how to deal with the demands of life and even what to wear. There is comfort and security for children when they know what is expected and how they fit into the scheme of things.

Two friends, Greg Johnson and Mike Yorkey, offered some examples of how *not* to build good relationships with your kids in their book *Daddy's Home.* These suggestions were written with tongue in cheek, but I think they got their point across.

- Serve as their human quarter machine at the video arcade.
- Have the NBA game of the week on while you're playing Monopoly with them.
- Read the paper while helping them with their algebra assignments.
- Go to the local high school football field to practice your short-irons and have your kids collect the golf balls after you're done.
- Suggest they take a nap with you on a beautiful Sunday afternoon.
- Drive them to Cub Scouts and read a magazine in the car while the den mother instructs them on how to tie knots.
- Take them to your office on Saturday and have them color while you work.[2]

Clearly, there are many ways to fake it—appearing to care and "be involved" when you're actually just baby-sitting. I guarantee you, however, that your kids won't be fooled for long. They can see through adult pretenses with something akin to X-ray vision. And they will remember that you were or were not there for them when they were reaching for you. Someone said love is giving somebody your undivided attention. It is a great definition.

Here's another idea relevant to relationships that I think makes a lot of sense. It's called "the first five minutes" and is based on a book that was published many years ago. Its thesis was that the first five minutes occurring between people sets the tone for everything that is to follow. For example, a public speaker is given very few moments to convince his audience that he really does have something worthwhile to say. If he's boring or stilted in the beginning, his listeners will turn him off like a lightbulb and he'll never know why. And if he hopes to use humor during his speech, he'd better say something funny very quickly or they won't believe he can make them laugh. The opportunity of the moment is lost. Fortunately, whenever we begin a new interaction, we have a chance to reset the mood.

This simple principle relates to family members as well. The first five minutes of the morning also determine how a mother will interact with her children on that day. Snarls or complaints as the kids gather for breakfast will sour their relationship for hours. Greeting children after school with kind words and a tasty snack may be remembered for decades. And at the end of the day when a man arrives home from work, the way he greets his wife, or doesn't greet his wife, will influence their interaction throughout the evening. A single criticism such as, "Not tuna casserole again!" will put their relationship on edge from there to bedtime. Men who complain that their wives are not affectionate at bedtime should think back to the first moments when they came together in the evening. He could have messed up some great possibilities with his first snippy comments.

It all starts with the first five minutes.

To summarize, a close-knit family is what keeps boys grounded when the world is urging them to break loose. In this day, you dare not become disconnected during the time when everything is on the line.

While we are talking about relationships, there is another issue we should discuss. It concerns the sheer power of words. They are so easy to utter, often tumbling out without much reason or forethought. Those who hurl criticism or hostility at others may not even mean or believe what they have said. Their comments may reflect momentary jealousy, resentment, depression, fatigue, or revenge. Regardless of the intent, harsh words sting like killer bees. Almost all of us, including you and me, have lived through moments when a parent, a teacher, a friend, a colleague, a husband, or a wife said something that cut to the quick. That hurt is now sealed forever in the memory bank. That is an amazing property of the spoken word. Even though a person forgets most of his or her day-by-day experiences, a particularly painful comment may be remembered for decades. By contrast, the individual who did the damage may have no memory of the encounter a few days later.

Former first lady Hillary Rodham Clinton told a story about her father, who never affirmed her as a child. When she was in high school, she brought home a straight-A report card. She showed it to her dad, hoping for a word of commendation. Instead, he said, "Well, you must be attending an easy school." Thirty-five years later the remark still burns in Mrs. Clinton's mind. His thoughtless response may have represented nothing more than a casual quip, but it created a point of pain that has endured to this day.[3]

If you doubt the power of words, remember what John the disciple wrote under divine inspiration. He said, "In the beginning was the Word, and the Word was with God, and the Word was God" (John 1:1). John was describing Jesus, the Son of God, who was identified personally with words. That makes the case about as well as it will ever be demonstrated. Matthew, Mark, and Luke each record a related prophetic statement made by Jesus that confirms the eternal nature of His teachings. He said, "Heaven and earth will pass away, but my words will never pass away" (Matthew 24:35). We remember what He said to this hour, more than two thousand years later. Clearly, words matter.

There is additional wisdom about the impact of words written in the book of James. The passage reads,

> When we put bits into the mouths of horses to make them obey us, we can turn the whole animal. Or take ships as an example. Although they are so large and are driven by strong winds, they are steered by a very small rudder wherever the pilot wants to go. Likewise the tongue is a small part of the body, but it makes great boasts. Consider what a great forest is set on fire by a small spark. The tongue also is a fire, a world of evil among the parts of the body. It corrupts the whole person, sets the whole course of his life on fire, and is itself set on fire by hell.   JAMES 3:3-6

Have you ever set yourself on fire with sparks spraying from your tongue? More important, have you ever set a child's spirit on fire with anger? All of us have made that costly mistake. We knew we had blundered the moment the comment flew out of our mouths, but it was too late. If we tried for a hundred years, we couldn't take back a single remark. The first year Shirley and I were married, she became very angry with me about something that neither of us can recall. In the frustration of the moment she said, "If this is marriage, I don't want any part of it." She didn't mean it and regretted her words almost immediately. An hour later we had reconciled and forgiven each other, but Shirley's statement could not be taken back. We've laughed about it through the years and the issue is inconsequential today. Still, there is nothing either of us can do to erase the utterance of the moment.

Words are not only remembered for a lifetime, but if not forgiven, they endure beyond the chilly waters of death. We read in Matthew 12:36, "I tell you that men will have to give account on the day of judgment for every careless word they have spoken." Thank God, those of us who have a personal relationship with Jesus Christ are promised that our sins—and our harsh words—will be remembered against us no more and will be removed "as far as the east is from the west" (Psalm 103:12). Apart from that atonement, however, our words will follow us forever.

I didn't intend to preach a sermon here, because I am not a minister or a theologian. But I find great inspiration for all family relationships within the great wisdom of the Scriptures. And so it is with the impact of what we say. The scary thing for us parents is that we never know when the mental videotape is running during our interactions with children and teens. A comment that means little to us at the time may "stick" and be repeated long after we are dead and gone. By contrast, the warm and affirming things we say about our sons may be a source of satisfaction for decades. Again, it is all in the power of words.

Here's something else to remember. The circumstances that precipitate a hurtful comment for a child or teen are irrelevant to their impact. Let me explain. Even though a child pushes you to the limit, frustrating and angering you to the point of exasperation, you will nevertheless pay a price for overreacting. Let's suppose you lose your poise and shout, "I can't stand you! I wish you belonged to someone else." Or, "I can't believe you failed another test. How could a son of mine be so stupid!" Even if every normal parent would also have been agitated in the same situation, your child will not focus on his misbehavior in the future. He is likely to forget what he did to cause your outburst. But he will recall the day that you said you didn't want him or that he was stupid. It isn't fair, but neither is life.

I know I'm stirring a measure of guilt into the mix with these comments. (My words are powerful too, aren't they?) My purpose, however, is not to hurt you but to make you mindful that everything you say has lasting meaning for a child. He may forgive you later for "setting the fire," but how much better it would have been to have stayed cool. You can learn to do that with prayer and practice.

It will help to understand that we are most likely to say something hurtful when we are viscerally angry. The reason is because of a powerful biochemical reaction going on inside. The human body is equipped with an automatic defense system called the "fight or flight" mechanism, which prepares the entire organism for action. When we're upset or frightened, adrenaline is pumped into the bloodstream, setting off a series of physiological responses within the body. In a matter of seconds, the individual is transformed from a quiet condition to an "alarm reaction" state. The result is a red-faced father or mother who shouts things he or she had no intention of saying.

These biochemical changes are involuntary, operating quite apart from conscious choice. What *is* voluntary, however, is our reaction to them. We can learn to take a step back in a moment of excitement. We can choose to hold our tongue and remove ourselves from a provoking situation. As you have heard, it is wise to count to ten (or five hundred) before responding. It is extremely important to do this when we're dealing with children who anger us. We can control the impulse to lash out verbally or physically, doing what we will certainly regret when the passion has cooled.

What should we do when we have lost control and said something that has deeply wounded a child? The answer is, we should repair the damage as quickly as possible. I have many fanatic golfing friends who have tried vainly to teach me their crazy game. They never give up even though it is a lost cause. One of them told me that I should immediately replace the divot after digging yet another a hole with my club. He said that the quicker I could get that tuft of grass back in place, the faster its roots would reconnect. My friend was talking about golf, but I was thinking about people. When you have hurt someone, whether a child, a spouse, or a colleague, you must dress the wound before infection sets in. Apologize, if appropriate. Talk it out. Seek to reconcile. The longer the "divot" bakes in the sun, the smaller will be its chances for recovery. Isn't that a wonderful thought? Of course, the apostle Paul beat us to it. He wrote more than two thousand years ago, "Do not let the sun go down while you are still angry" (Ephesians 4:26). That Scripture has often been applied to husbands and wives, but I think it is just as valid with children.

Before I leave the subject of words, I want to address the issue of profanity. I find it very distressing to witness the way filth and sacrilege have infiltrated our speech in Western nations. Cursing and swearing are so common today that even some of our preschoolers talk like the sailors of yesterday. It has not always been the case. During my teaching days in a public junior high school, bad language was not permitted. I'm sure it happened when kids were alone but not often within the hearing of the faculty. One day, one of my better students used God's name in a sacrilegious way. I was very disappointed in her. Believe it or not, having taught several hundred kids per year, that was the only time I remember hearing a boy or girl talk like that. I pointed out to her that one of the Ten Commandments instructed us not to use the Lord's name in vain and that we should be careful how we talked. I think she believed me. That occurred in 1963.

How radically things have changed since then! Now almost every student, it seems, uses profanity—disgusting references to bodily functions and sexual behavior. Girls curse as much as boys. Since President Bill Clinton's escapade with Monica Lewinsky in the White House, even elementary school kids have talked openly about oral sex, as though it were no big deal.[4] More of them are trying it than ever before. As a matter of fact, sexually transmitted diseases of the mouth and throat are reaching epidemic proportions among junior- and senior-high school students. We have become a profane and immoral people, both young and old. Nevertheless, the ancient commandments haven't changed. This is what the Scriptures tell us particularly about the casual use of God's name:

> I will make known my holy name among my people Israel. I will no longer let my holy name be profaned, and the nations will know that I the Lord am the Holy One in Israel.
> EZEKIEL 39:7

> They are to teach my people the difference between the holy and the common and show them how to distinguish between the unclean and the clean. EZEKIEL 44:23

> Simply let your "Yes" be "Yes," and your "No," "No"; anything beyond this comes from the evil one. MATTHEW 5:37

If we are to believe the validity of these and other passages in the Bible, our profanity is an offense to God. It is a terrible thing to drag the names of God, Jesus, and the Holy Spirit through the gutter, using them as curse words or to punctuate sentences in everyday conversation. Even Christians often say, "God" in casual situations. At times when I hear what is very sacred being defiled and mocked, I utter a silent prayer, asking our heavenly Father to forgive our disrespect and heal our land. It is time we stand up for what we believe and teach those eternal truths to our children.

I am recommending herewith that you give major emphasis to your children's language. No, we shouldn't be as legalistic as my father was. The phrase "Hot dog!" is probably not a biggie. But there is still a place for clean, wholesome, respectful speech. Especially, you should not permit your children to mock the name of God. The primary reason I have provided the Scriptures above is to help you teach these biblical concepts in your home. Read and discuss "the Word" to establish this vital principle. By teaching a reverence for things that are holy, you are demonstrating that our beliefs are to be taken seriously and that we are accountable to the Lord for the way we behave. It is also a way of teaching principles of civility that should be a central objective of your leadership at home.

I've strayed a bit from my theme of relationships, but I think the discussion of words was important. Returning to the issue at hand, the day is coming when those of you with young children will need to draw on the foundation of love and caring that you have built. If resentment and rejection characterized the early years, the adolescent experience might be a nightmare. The best way to avoid this teenage time bomb is to defuse it in childhood. That is done with a healthy balance of authority and love at home. Begin now to build a relationship that will see you through the storms of adolescence.

QUESTIONS AND ANSWERS

I am one of the discouraged fathers you have talked about. My wife and I tried so hard to be good parents, but now our sixteen-year-old son is dour, disrespectful, and defiant. He's in serious trouble with the law and we have no idea where we went wrong.

Before you take the blame for everything that has happened, I urge you to stop and think about what has occurred. All of us who work with kids have observed that a teen's rebellious behavior sometimes results not from parental mistakes or failures but from bad choices made on his own initiative. Your child may be one of these teens.

Two things are clear from this understanding. First, parents have been quick to take the credit or blame for the way their children turn out. Moms and dads who are raising bright young superstars are inclined to stick out their chests and say, "Look at what we accomplished." Those with irresponsible kids wonder, "Where did we go wrong?" It is very possible that neither assessment is accurate. Even though parents are enormously influential in the lives of their children, they are only one component from which children are assembled.

Behavioral scientists have been far too simplistic in their explanation of human behavior. Despite their theories to the contrary, we are more than the quality of our nutrition. We are more than our genetic heritage. We are more than our biochemistry. And certainly, we are more than the aggregate of parental influences. God has created us as unique individuals, capable of independent and rational thought that is not attributable to any source. That is what makes child rearing so challenging and rewarding. Just when you think you have your kids figured out, you had better brace yourself! Something new is coming your way.

What role does heredity play in influencing the behavior of a kid like mine?

Child development experts have argued for more than a century about the relative influence of heredity and environment, or what has been called the "nature-nurture" controversy. Now, at last, it may have been settled. Researchers at the University of Minnesota have spent many years identifying and studying one hundred sets of identical twins who were separated near the time of birth. They were raised in varying cultures, religions, and locations, and for a variety of reasons. Because each set of twins shared the same genetic structure, it was possible for the researchers to examine the impact of inheritance by comparing their similarities and their differences on many variables. From these and other studies, it became clear that much of personality, perhaps 70 percent or more, is inherited. Our genes influence such qualities as creativity, wisdom, loving-kindness, vigor, longevity, intelligence, and even the joy of living.[5]

Consider the brothers known as the "Gem twins," who were separated until they were thirty-nine years old. Their similarities were astonishing. Both were married to women named Linda. Both had dogs named Toy. Both suffered from migraine headaches. Both chain-smoked. Both liked beer. Both drove Chevys, and both served as sheriff's deputies. They even shared a weird sense of humor. For example, both enjoyed faking sneezes in elevators to see how strangers would react.[6] This degree of similarity in the personalities of identical twins raised separately speaks to the remarkable influence of inherited characteristics.

A person's genetic structure is thought to even influence the stability of his or her marriage. If an identical twin gets a divorce, the risk of the other also divorcing is 45 percent.[7] However, if a fraternal twin divorces, sharing only half as many genes, the risk to the other is only 30 percent.[8]

What do these findings mean? Are we mere puppets on a string, playing out a predetermined course without free will or personal choices? Of course not. Unlike birds and mammals that act according to instinct, humans are capable of rational thought and independent action. We don't act on every sexual urge, for example, despite our genetic underpinnings. What is clear is that heredity provides a nudge in a particular direction—a definite impulse or inclination—but one that can be brought under the control of our rational processes.

Obviously, these findings are of enormous significance to our understanding of children. Before you take the full credit or blame for the behavior of your sons, remember that you played an important part in the formative years—but by no means the only one.

As for your rebellious sixteen-year-old, I suggest you give him some time. He will probably settle down in his early twenties. The prayer is that he won't do something with long-term implications before he comes through adolescence.

Disciplining Boys

CHAPTER 16

My wife and I made a quick trip to the supermarket several days ago to pick up a few items. When we arrived, we noticed that a woman shopper and her five-year-old boy were engaged in a clash of wills. He demanded that she buy something and then threw a classic temper tantrum when she refused. The conflict was still brewing when they reached the checkout counter where we were standing in line. Unmindful of my listening ear, Mama leaned down and spoke very quietly to her son.

"I was going to give you what you asked for," she said, "but there's no way I can do it now. We don't reward that kind of behavior."

But the lad wasn't going to back off. He continued to snort and complain. That prompted his mom to say matter-of-factly, "Do you know what is going to happen when we get home?"

"Yes," he said.

"What?" asked his mom.

"A swat."

"Yep," she said. "And if you keep acting like this, it will be two."

With that, the battle was over. Junior settled down and behaved like a little gentleman. I rarely inject myself into these kinds of parental episodes, but this was an exception. The woman deserved a word of praise.

"You're a good mother," I commented.

"Well, it isn't easy," she said with a smile.

The last time I saw them, this woman and her son were headed for the door. She had unwittingly given us a demonstration of firm but loving discipline under rather difficult circumstances. The boy had challenged his mother's authority in front of strangers, where she was at a disadvantage. Despite the embarrassment caused by that situation, she remained calm and in control. She didn't scream or overreact. Instead, she made it clear that the rules prevailing at home would also be applied, literally, in the marketplace. It was that kind of confident and loving discipline that my wise and godly mother applied when I was a child and that I tried to describe in my first book for parents and teachers, entitled *Dare to Discipline*.

I will not attempt to summarize the "how to" elements of that book or the others I have written on the subject of discipline. It might be helpful, however, to offer some additional suggestions of relevance to boys. Let's begin by examining the role of authority, which is pivotal to the proper training of boys and girls—but especially boys. The key for parents is to avoid the extremes on either side. Over the course of the past 150 years, parental attitudes have swung radically—from oppressiveness and rigidity at one end of the continuum to permissiveness and wimpiness at the other. Both are damaging to kids. During the Victorian era, children were expected to be seen but not heard. Father was often a repressive and fearsome character who punished his kids harshly for their mistakes and shortcomings. Nurturance was sometimes provided by the mother, but she could be a pretty tough lady too. These overbearing and punitive techniques reflected the belief that children were miniature adults who needed to be whipped into shape, beginning shortly after birth and continuing well into young adulthood.

That rigidity eventually pushed the pendulum to the other end of the universe. By the late fifties and early sixties, parents had become decidedly permissive. What was called the "child-centered" approach tended to undermine authority and create some little terrors at home. Indeed, the baby boomers who were raised during that era came roaring through adolescence just in time to turn society on its ear.

Although the revolutionary spirit they generated has now subsided, today's families are still influenced by it. Many representatives of the sixties and seventies generation eventually raised their children by the same permissive techniques they had witnessed at home. They had no idea why it was important to teach respect and responsibility to their sons and daughters, because they had never experienced it personally. Now, a third generation has arrived on the scene that is even more unfamiliar with traditional principles of child rearing. I'm speaking in general terms, of course, and there are many exceptions. Still, it is my opinion that parents today are more confused than ever about effective and loving discipline. It has become a lost art, a forgotten skill. Well-meaning moms and dads have been misled by the liberal tenets of a postmodern culture, especially when it concerns naughty or rebellious behavior. Just watch the interactions between parents and their kids in public. You will see frustrated mothers screaming at their sassy, disrespectful, out-of-control kids. Even the uninformed observer can recognize that something is wrong here. It was from that perspective that I told the woman in the supermarket that I thought she was a good mother.

These trends are not simply my own observations of the changing social landscape. They are validated by research. A recent study conducted by the National Opinion Research Center at the University of Chicago confirmed that today's parents are more lax and permissive than a decade ago. The perfect child in the opinion of the participants is an "independent thinker" who is a "hard worker." Adherence to rules, standards, and prescribed behavior is of lesser priority. Center Director Tom W. Smith summarized the findings this way: "People have become less traditional over time with a shift from emphasizing obedience and parent-centered families to valuing autonomy for children. Parents now expect their children to be *self*-disciplined."[1]

For those moms and dads out there who expect their boys to discipline themselves, I can only say, "Lotsa luck." Self-discipline is a worthwhile goal, but it rarely develops on its own initiative. It must be taught. Shaping and molding young minds is a product of careful and diligent parental leadership. You can be sure, it requires great effort and patience. As for some parents' wish for independent thinkers and hard workers, that's another pipe dream. The adults who were surveyed apparently hoped for kids who would do magnificent things without much parental involvement. That is like saying to a child, "You can do it yourself, kid. Don't bother me." If it were that easy, dedicated mothers and fathers wouldn't be laboring at night to help their children finish their homework or teach them principles of character and values. The notion of effortless parenting by busy moms and dads is destined to fail—especially with tough-minded males who dearly love fun and games. Any way you slice it, parents are on the hook.

Smithsonian Magazine once featured a master stone carver from England named Simon Verrity, who honed his craft by restoring thirteenth-century cathedrals in Great Britain. As the authors watched him work, they noticed something very interesting. They wrote, "Verrity listens closely to hear the song of the stone under his careful blows. A solid strike and all is well. A higher-pitched *ping* and it could mean trouble. A chunk of rock could break off. He constantly adjusts the angle of the chisel and the force of the mallet to the pitch, pausing frequently to run his hand over the freshly carved surface."[2]

Verrity understood well the importance of his task. He knew that one wrong move could be devastating, causing irreparable damage to his work of art. His success was rooted in his ability to read the signals being sung by his stones. In a similar way, parents need to listen to the "music" of their children, especially during times of confrontation and correction. It takes a great deal of patience and sensitivity to discern how the child is responding. If you listen carefully, your boys and girls will tell you what they're thinking and feeling. By honing your craft, you too can become a master carver who creates a beautiful work of art. But remember this: The stone can't carve itself.

Let me say again what I have written twice before in this book: Boys need structure, they need supervision, and they need to be civilized. When raised in a laissez-faire environment that is devoid of leadership, they often begin to challenge social conventions and common sense. Many often crash and burn during the adolescent years. Some never fully recover. Here's another metaphor that may be helpful: A stream without banks becomes a swamp. It is your job as parents to build the channel in which the steam will run. And another: A child will be ruled by either the rudder or the rock. Authority, when balanced by love, is the rudder that steers your boys around the jagged boulders that could rip the bottom out of their fragile boats. Without you, disaster is inevitable. Self-discipline, indeed!

We received a letter at Focus on the Family this week from a mother who has observed the same trends that concern me. She wrote, "What has become of the backbone of parents today? My husband and I have been amazed again and again by the fearfulness of parents to take a stand—even with their small children. They don't seem to grasp the idea that God has put them in charge for a very good reason, and it is He who will hold them accountable. If parents were to instill the concept of proper, God-honoring authority in their children from the start, it would be far easier to enforce when the preteen years arrive."

This mom is absolutely right. Parents are obligated to take charge of their young sons and teach them respectful and responsible behavior. When they fail in that mission, trouble stalks both generations.

You're probably aware by now that I am a lover of animals and draw many of my illustrations from them. Here's a relevant example that focuses on horses. Specifically, we can learn something about disciplining children by studying how mares handle their foals. I learned about this from Monty Roberts, who is the author of the best-selling book *The Man Who Listens to Horses*. I recently visited Monty at his ranch in Solvang, California, to witness for myself his celebrated methods of training horses. Monty began by telling me how he grew up around horses and used to ride them in shows and rodeos when he was only four years of age. A little later, he appeared in dozens of western movies as a double for child actors who couldn't ride. When Monty was thirteen years of age, he loved to observe wild horses in the deserts of Nevada. He would get up early in the morning and spend the day watching a herd with binoculars from quite a distance away. Gradually, he learned to decipher a language that is "spoken" by all horses. They communicate together with their ears and various gestures and movements.

The oldest mare, Monty told me, is the boss of the herd. She determines where they will eat, drink, and move. The stallion thinks he's in charge, but his only role is to protect the mares and to reproduce. When a foal, usually a colt, is misbehaving by biting and kicking his neighbors, the mare runs straight toward him. She will knock him down if he doesn't move in a hurry. Then she chases him about a half-mile away. The mare returns to the herd and squares her body to the foal while staring directly at him. She is telling the colt not to come back, which is very threatening and unsettling to him. Horses are herd animals, and they feel frightened when they are alone in the wild. A mountain lion or other predators could kill them unless the rest of the herd is there to provide protection.

Soon the nervous colt begins making a big circle around the other horses. All the while, the mare is moving in a small circle to keep her body squared to his and her eyes focused in his direction. Finally, the young horse becomes tired and begins to signal that he is ready "to negotiate." He does that by lowering his head, moving his lips, and grinding his teeth. He also aims one erect ear toward the mare while the other scans the landscape behind him for predators. After a while, the mare signals that she is willing to talk. She does that by turning her body slightly away from the colt and looking elsewhere. Gradually, he inches back to the herd until he actually nuzzles the old lady. At that point, he is accepted into her good graces again. It is not uncommon for the mare to have to discipline the colt by running him off several times before he decides to play by the rules. In the end, however, he acknowledges that she is the boss and he is subservient to her.

Monty uses this knowledge of horse language to break the magnificent animals to the saddle (although he calls it "starting" rather than breaking). By isolating and then staring at a horse as a mare would do, he can actually be riding a wild horse in thirty to forty-five minutes. You should see the process in action. It is something to behold.

Okay, so the horse illustration is not directly applicable to children, but there are some useful similarities. Mom and Dad are the authority figures, who must not tolerate rebellious or disrespectful behavior. When the child insists on breaking the rules, he is disciplined just enough to make him uncomfortable. No, the parents don't chase the youngster away, but they should make it clear that they are unhappy with the way he has behaved. This may be accomplished by a reasonable (but not severe) spanking in instances when the misbehavior has been defiant and disrespectful. Or they could administer a time-out period or other lesser punishment. Whatever the approach, the child must find it unpleasant and aversive. After the discomfort of that confrontation, there will come a moment when the child will ask, symbolically if not in words, "Can I come back again?" At that point, the parents should welcome him with open arms. That is the time to explain why he got in trouble and how he can avoid the conflict next time. Never during this process should parents resort to screaming or other indications that they are frustrated and out of control. Instead, the parent should demonstrate mastery of the situation—like the mare who stares intently at the wayward colt. A few quiet words spoken with conviction by a mother or father can often convey this confidence and authority better than a barrage of empty threats and wild gestures.

Although this understanding of discipline is fairly simple to comprehend, some parents have trouble getting it. If they are afraid to make their child uncomfortable or unhappy when misbehavior has occurred, or if they fear that permanent emotional damage is being done when they have to punish, they will not have the determination to win the inevitable confrontations that arise. The child will sense their tentativeness and push them farther. The end result will be frustrated, irritated, and ineffectual parents and rebellious, selfish, and willful children.

To elaborate on this approach to child rearing, I'll introduce you to a friend of mine, Rev. Ren Broekhuizen, who has an intuitive knowledge of kids. He has thirty-five grandchildren of his own who love him like a patron saint. Ren heard I was writing a book on the subject of boys and shared the following ideas with me. Children, he said, need to learn that "love can frown." Many parents today are afraid to show displeasure to kids for fear of wounding or rejecting them. To the contrary, little people need to know who is in charge and that they are "safe" in that person's care. Reminding a child that you are a benevolent boss emphasizes that you expect to be obeyed. There are times when a mom or dad needs to get down on one knee, look a little boy or girl straight in the eye (remember the mare?), and say confidently but without anger, "I don't want you to misbehave again. Is that clear?" Without screaming or threatening, your tone of voice says, "Take seriously what I'm saying."

Rev. Broekhuizen illustrated this point by relating an occasion when he took his grandson to a toy store. Before they entered the building he said, "Don't touch anything unless I say it's okay." The boy nodded. Grandpa's expectations had been clarified and the lad conformed to them perfectly. Conflict was averted.

To use another analogy, establishing unambiguous boundaries of this nature is not unlike state-highway officials setting up signs that warn, "Speed Monitored by Radar." They remind drivers that there are specific laws governing how fast a person can go and that there will be unpleasant consequences for those who exceed the limit. That's the way the adult world works. The IRS says to American citizens, "Pay your taxes by April 15 or face a 6 percent penalty." The night before the deadline, people line up for a city block to comply with the rule. Or to cite another example, your company says, "If you want to be reimbursed for your travel expenses, you must submit your receipts when you return from an authorized trip." There's no anger in those understandings. It's just the way it is. Many parents appear to believe, however, that a similar approach when applied to children is either harmful or unfair. I think they are wrong. Setting up the rules in advance and then enforcing them firmly is far healthier for children than chastising and threatening them after misbehavior has occurred.

Another point made by Rev. Broekhuizen reflected his observation that parents pose too many questions to their kids. "Do you want to go to bed now? Would you like to put away your Legos? Don't you think it is time to eat?" Moms and dads who offer these tentative proposals, followed by question marks, are actually trying to avoid saying, "Do this—because it is best and because I say so." There are appropriate times to say exactly that. Parents have been given the authority by God to direct and shape their kids' behavior. They should use it!

After writing the above recollections of my conversation with Ren, I sent this manuscript to him to be sure he was quoted accurately. He responded with a letter taking the ideas a step further. I think what he wrote will be valuable to parents, and I have included it here:

Dear Jim:

Thanks for your kind words. It is a privilege to be associated with you and your work.

I feel one of the big questions your readers have to settle is, "Do I really believe that I have the authority to be in charge around here?" I think that is one of the reasons there are so many question marks at the end of their parenting statements. They just aren't sure if this is all right or not. One harried mother of four said to me once, "How did you manage to raise five children? It must have been a continuous zoo." I said, "The main thing is that the kids have to know right from the start who's in charge." "Oh," she said, "but that sounds so authori-tative." I think she speaks for an entire generation that missed the authority growing up and don't know about the divine plan that parents are called to train up their children in the way they should go (Proverbs 22:6). The apostle Paul said, "If the trumpet makes an uncertain sound, who will prepare himself for battle?" (1 Corinthians 14:8, NKJV). What children hear is an uncertain sound. How many of your readers just flat-out believe that they know better than the children God has entrusted into their care? I'm reminded of the mother of a four-year-old son who refuses to go to bed before eleven. She has the authority to tell him what to do but is afraid to use it.

The chances of parents knowing more than their children operates on a sliding scale. From the time the kids are tiny and up to about five years of age, Mom or Dad knows 100 percent more than they do. Then it begins to change—slowly. By the time they are eight and then eighteen or twenty-eight, the probabilities continue to shift in their direction. In some areas, my sons and daughters know a lot more than I do now. But when they were small, I knew I had been put in charge by God's plan. He held me responsible for what I did with that authority.

You have me going now so I'll continue.

Another aspect of that uncertainty about who really is in charge is what I call "the moveable goal line." I watched a kid running across the park toward the street one day. His father said, "Keith, stop right there. Keith! Keith! I said stop right there. You heard me." But Keith had been "trained" not to listen and he kept running. He reached the car and swung on the door handle. His father shouted, "Hold on to that door handle." It was a total abdication of his authority. I see that same drama played out at the supermarket. Managers put the candy on those racks by the checkout counter so the kids sitting in the shop-ping carts can reach it. The kid says, "I want candy." His mother says, "No, it is too early." He raises his voice and says, "Candy." She shouts, "No." He reaches over and takes a roll of Life Savers. She says, "Don't eat them until you get to the car." Another total wipeout.

"Counting" to get kids to obey sounds deceptively like the parent is in charge but it is also a moveable goal line. "Bill, come here. I'm counting. One. Two. Thr— That's a good boy, Bill. Thank you for obeying Mommy." But something was lost in the process. Counting just moves the line of your authority back three more paces. What's next? Four? Five? Six? Your response should convey the message with-out screaming or threatening, "Take seriously what I'm saying!"

I'll say one more thing, this time about grandparents, and then I promise to quit. We smile benignly and think it's cute when we spoil our grandchildren. It is a big mistake. When something is spoiled I throw it away. My job as a grandfather is to set an example for both the parents and the grandchildren by being a loving leader. Grandmothers like to roll their eyes and say their grandchildren are just "active." "Active" when applied to a kid is a code word for "out of control." I feel responsible to help train my grandchildren to be polite and respectful of people and their property when we are together. I back off whenever the parents are around, however, because I don't want to undermine their authority.

Rev. Broekhuizen is right on target with this advice. But what about those parents who believe they should be eternally positive with their children and that anything interpreted as negative by them must be avoided? There are millions of moms and dads who seem to feel that way. Well, I disagree with them, not only with regard to kids, but with regard to life itself.

Admittedly, positive thinking can be a good thing. People who are naturally upbeat are more pleasant to be around and they seem to get so much more out of life. They are also more productive than those who are routinely "down" and discouraged. But negative thinking has its advantages too. It is negative thinking that leads me to buckle my seat belt when I get in a car. I might be hurt in a collision if I don't strap myself in. It's negative thinking that causes me to buy life insurance to protect my family. I could die suddenly and leave my loved ones in financial difficulty. It's negative thinking that encourages me to avoid behavior that could be addictive—such as using illicit drugs, alcohol, or pornography. There are millions of other examples of what might be called "beneficial negatives." The bottom line is that there is power in *any* kind of legitimate thinking. Indeed, if a person only allows himself to read or hear positive messages, he will have to skip over at least half of the Scriptures. Jesus said some of the most profoundly negative words that have ever been uttered, including the prospect of unregenerate people entering eternity without God. Yet His message to a lost and dying world is called the gospel, meaning "good news."

The interesting thing about positives and negatives is that they produce the greatest benefit when they work in concert. For example, if you place an electrical cable on the positive post of a car battery, nothing will happen. You can put it in your mouth if you wish, but there will be no power. If you take that cable off the positive post and put it on the negative, still there will be no charge. But what happens when you hook the cables to both the positive and the negative posts and then touch the contact points? Your hair will curl, if you have any left.

That principle, bringing positives and negatives together, is illustrated again and again in Scripture. Consider this passage from the book of Isaiah: "'Come now, let us reason together,' says the Lord. 'Though your sins are like scarlet, they shall be as white as snow; though they are red as crimson, they shall be like wool'" (Isaiah 1:18). What marvelous imagery this is of God's love and forgiveness. Yet four chapters later Isaiah wrote some terrifying words under divine inspiration: "Therefore the Lord's anger burns against his people; his hand is raised and he strikes them down. The mountains shake, and the dead bodies are like refuse in the streets. Yet for all this, his anger is not turned away, his hand is still upraised" (Isaiah 5:25).

This balance between compassion and judgment appears from Genesis to Revelation. It moves between Creation and the Fall, between condemnation and forgiveness, between the Crucifixion and the Resurrection, between heaven and hell. The greatest example is found in the book of Isaiah, where the wonderful prophecies of the coming Messiah appear intermingled with dire predictions of the destruction of Israel. Both proved accurate.

Learning to balance the intersection between these two forces is especially useful to the understanding of children. There's a time for affirmation, tenderness, and love. They nourish the spirit and seal the bond between generations. But there's also a time for discipline and punishment. Moms and dads who try to be eternally positive, ignoring irresponsibility or defiance in their children, fail to teach them that behavior has consequences. But beware! Parents who are continually punitive and accusatory can create serious behavioral and emotional problems. The apostle Paul recognized this danger and cautioned dads not to get carried away with discipline. He said, "Fathers, do not exasperate your children; instead, bring them up in the training and instruction of the Lord" (Ephesians 6:4). He mentioned the warning again in Colossians 3:21: "Fathers, do not embitter your children, or they will become discouraged." Remember that Paul also said emphatically to children, "Obey your parents in everything, for this pleases the Lord" (Colossians 3:20). What great wisdom there is in those convergent passages.

I have gone to some lengths here to address this issue of balance in discipline because it holds the key to the entire parent-child relationship. Frankly, remaining in the safety of the middle ground as moms and dads is difficult to achieve. None of us does it perfectly. But the best parents are those who steer a path between permissiveness and authoritarianism. Your boys, especially, will thrive under your leadership if you avoid the extremes and are careful to "season" your relationship with love.

The word *discipline* connotes not only the shaping of a child's behavior and attitudes but also giving him a measure of self-control and the ability to postpone gratification. Teaching a child to work is one of the primary mechanisms by which this self-discipline is acquired. But as we all know, most young boys have a great aversion to work. They can sit and stare at it for hours. It is such a struggle to get them to move that many parents give up. It appears much easier to do everything for them. "Life is hard enough," they say, "without making children do what is unpleasant for them." That is a serious mistake. Those who know how to work are usually better able to control their impulses, to stay on task until an assignment is completed, to overcome flightiness and immaturity, to recognize the connection between effort and opportunity, and to learn to manage money. It also serves as a preparation for life in the adult world to come. Unfortunately, one of the common complaints made by the business community is that too many kids won't work, or even if they will, they don't know *how* to work. That must be true, because a high percentage of teens seem to founder when placed on a job for the first time.

There is another factor to consider. It concerns the direct linkage between the self-concept and meaningful work. The Russian novelist Fyodor Dostoevsky once wrote, "If you want to utterly crush a man, just give him work that's of a completely senseless, irrational nature."[3] It is true.

In a concentration camp outside Hungary during World War II, Jewish prisoners were forced to move a mountain of dirt from one end of the compound to the other. The next day, they were told to move it back again. This went on for weeks until one day, an old man began sobbing uncontrollably. He was led away by his captors to be executed. Days later, another man who had survived three years in the camp suddenly darted away from the group and threw himself on an electrified fence. In the weeks to come, dozens of prisoners went mad, running from their work and eventually being shot by the guards. Only later was it learned that the wasteful activity had been ordered by a cruel commandant as an experiment in "mental health." He wanted to see what would happen when people were forced to do utterly meaningless tasks. The results illustrated the relationship between work and emotional stability within the tragic confines of a concentration camp.

That linkage is relevant to the rest of humanity too. Work gives significance and meaning to our existence. Those who are good at what they do usually feel good about who they are. They draw satisfaction in knowing that they have handled difficult assignments in a superior manner. Conversely, people who fail professionally often struggle in their families and in other areas of their lives. I remember one summer years ago when Shirley and I decided to take a two-week vacation to stay home and rest. We had been moving at a frantic pace and thought it would be fun to sleep late every day and just "dink around." What a disappointment. Both of us nearly went crazy. We had the "blahs" and walked around wondering what to do next. I even spent several dreary afternoons watching daytime television. That will drive anyone bonkers. I realized from that experience that work is integrally related to my sense of well-being and that doing nothing wasn't nearly as fun as I expected.

If work is something to be valued, how do parents teach their boys and girls how to perform it? I think they should begin requiring small tasks to be done when they are very young, such as picking up their blocks or bringing the dinner plates to the kitchen. Then at about four or five, every youngster should carry out simple household responsibilities, from helping to wash the dishes to taking out the trash. The amount of work required should be reasonable and age-appropriate, remembering that the primary activity of young children is play. The older they get, the more chores can be assigned for which they receive nothing in return but appreciation. Children are, after all, functioning members of the family and should help shoulder the load to keep it running.

Here's a related recommendation that is somewhat controversial. You might disagree with it. I believe children should be compensated when the amount of work they perform goes beyond the call of duty, such as spending all day Saturday helping Dad clean the garage, washing the car, or painting the fence. Many parents object strenuously to that idea. They call it bribery. I disagree. It is the way the world is set up. Most of us go to work each morning and receive a paycheck every two weeks. Paying a child when he is asked to invest "sweat equity" is not only fair, it acquaints him with the connection between effort and reward. It also makes work less miserable for the hard-core flake.

Another suggestion: Because children learn by imitation, hands-on instruction is helpful. Instead of saying, "Go make your bed," try completing the task with the child. Working with an adult is the most enriching form of play for a child, if it's handled right. Make it fun. Find things to laugh about. If you nag and criticize your child incessantly, he'll begin to develop bad attitudes toward work. Transform it into a game, which makes life easier for everyone.

Let me pass along yet another idea that was presented in the May 1992 issue of *Parenting* magazine. It suggested that children be introduced to work by helping them to become little entrepreneurs. The author told about a fourteen-year-old boy who actually assembled personal computers and sold them for upwards of one thousand dollars apiece.[4] Your child may not do anything that impressive, but there are definite benefits to letting him get some experience in the world of business. In fact, kids who make and manage money are much more likely to succeed as adults. Running a business enterprise can help them learn practical math applications, skills in relating to other people, and perhaps most important, the rewards of hard work. The options are many. Younger children can do extra chores around the house to earn money. By age nine or ten, most of them are ready to pick up odd jobs around the neighborhood. The possibilities include running a pet-sitting service, running errands for neighbors, collecting bottles and cans for recycling centers, baby-sitting, mowing lawns, and many more. It's important that jobs not consume too much time during childhood, when there is so much else to be accomplished.

You should also take your boy to work with you occasionally. Many kids have no idea how their parents earn a living. In fact, I've heard (although I haven't been able to substantiate this statistic) that only 6 percent of fathers ever take their sons to their places of employment. If that is true, it is unfortunate. A century ago, children not only knew what their parents did for a living, they typically worked alongside them—with boys learning their dads' occupations and girls identifying with their mothers. Now kids have no idea what happens each day at IBM, AT&T, or Ralph's Fine Eatery.

One more thought: Radio host and author Dennis Prager said that teaching boys to work is essential to preparing them for manhood. During one of his radio programs, he asked a number of women what characteristics came to mind when they thought about mature masculinity. Almost all of them mentioned "responsibility" in their replies. Prager agreed but said it wasn't enough. Some men hold good jobs but remain immature. Their willingness to work must be combined with a devotion to a cause, to something greater than themselves. Those two traits—the ability to live responsibly and have a sense of mission—help boys overcome their self-centeredness and begin to see themselves as men. As a parent, then, our job is not only to teach kids to work but to introduce them to the meaning that is associated with it. For boys, that comes right back to the idea of providing for and protecting their families, for which you are helping them prepare. It all fits together.

Your purpose in teaching your children to work is to give them a taste of the real world. By all means, do not let your boys sit in front of a television set or play mindless video games year after year. Get 'em going. Get 'em organized. Get 'em working.

QUESTIONS AND ANSWERS

My son is fourteen and he has absolutely no concept of money or how to use it wisely. He thinks it grows on trees. Do you have any suggestions for how I can get him ready to deal with the real world when he is older?

In keeping with our discussion of work, let me add that giving a child a job to do is the most effective way to teach him the meaning of money. When I was a teenager, I learned more about the value of a few bucks from digging a fifty-foot trench at $1.50 per hour than I ever did from my parents' lecturing. The $10 I earned took on great meaning for me. Digging that ditch put eight blisters on my hands and a bad sunburn on my face, but it was a very valuable lesson. I never forgot it.

Beyond learning to work, I suggest you teach your son a few simple principles of money management. There are some good books written on that subject, such as *Money Matters for Parents and Their Kids* by Ron Blue and *Surviving the Money Jungle* by Larry Burkett. Here are a few useful ideas that will give you a place to start.

1. God owns it all. Some people have the notion that the Lord is entitled to 10 percent of our income, which is called a "tithe," and that the other 90 percent belongs to us. Not true. I believe strongly in the concept of tithing, but not because God's portion is limited to a tenth. We are but stewards of all that He has entrusted to us. He is our possessor—and sometimes our dispossessor. Everything we have is but a loan from Him. When God took away his wealth, Job had the correct attitude, saying, "Naked I came from my mother's womb, and naked I will depart. The Lord gave and the Lord has taken away; may the name of the Lord be praised" (Job 1:21).

   If you understand this basic concept, it becomes clear that every spending decision is a spiritual decision. Waste, for example, is not a squandering of other resources; it is a poor use of His resources.

   Expenditures for worthwhile purposes, such as vacations, ice cream, bicycles, blue jeans, magazines, tennis rackets, cars, and hamburgers, are also purchased with His money. That's why in my family, we bow to thank the Lord before eating each meal. Everything, including our food, is a gift from His hand.

2. There is always a trade-off between time and effort and money and reward. You've heard the phrases "There's no such thing as a free lunch" and "You can't get something for nothing." These are very important things to understand. Money should always be thought of as linked to work and the sweat of our brow.

Here's how this second principle has meaning for us. Think for a moment of the most worthless, unnecessary purchase you have made in recent years. Perhaps it was an electric shaver that now sits in the garage, or an article of clothing that will never be worn. It is important to realize that this item was not purchased with your money; it was bought with your time, which you traded for money. In effect, you swapped a certain portion of your allotted days on earth for that piece of junk that now clutters your home.

When you understand that everything you buy is purchased with a portion of your life, it should make you more careful with the use of money.

3. There is no such thing as an independent financial decision. There will never be enough money for everything you'd like to buy or do. Even billionaires have some limitations on their purchasing power. Therefore, every expenditure has implications for other things you need or want. It's all linked together. What this means is that those who can't resist blowing their money for junk are limiting themselves in areas of greater need or interest.

And by the way, husbands and wives often fight over the use of their money. Why? Because their value systems differ, and they often disagree on what is wasteful. My mother and father were typical in this regard. If Dad spent five dollars for shotgun shells or for tennis balls, he justified the expenditure because it brought him pleasure. But if Mom bought a five-dollar potato peeler that wouldn't work, he considered that wasteful. Never mind the fact that she enjoyed shopping as much as he did hunting or playing tennis. Their perspectives were simply unique.

Again, this third principle involves a recognition that extravagance at one point will eventually lead to frustration at another point. Good business managers are able to keep the big picture in mind as they make their financial decisions.

4. Delayed gratification is the key to financial maturity. Since we have limited resources and unlimited choices, the only way to get ahead financially is to deny ourselves some of the things we want. If we don't have the discipline to do that, we will always be in debt. Remember, too, that unless you spend less than you earn, no amount of income will be enough. That's why some people receive salary increases and soon find themselves even deeper in debt.

Let me repeat that important concept: No amount of income will be sufficient if spending is not brought under control.[5]

Well, maybe these four principles will help your children build a foundation of financial stability without compromising their belief system. In short, the secret to successful living is to spend your life on something that will outlast it, or, as the writer of Hebrews said, "Keep your lives free from the love of money and be content with what you have" (Hebrews 13:5).

I think it is good to give your son a feel for what it takes to create and live on a budget. I knew a doctor with four daughters who gave each of his four kids an annual clothing allowance, starting at the age of twelve. They had to parcel out their money carefully throughout the year for everything they needed. The youngest girl was a little impulsive, and she celebrated her twelfth birthday by spending her yearly allowance on an expensive coat. By the following spring, she was down to shredded stockings and frayed dresses. It was very difficult for her parents to watch her go without. But they had the courage to stand back and let her learn a valuable lesson about money management. I remember a single mother who invited her fifteen-year-old son to help figure the family's income taxes. When the boy saw the hidden costs of running a household, things like paying mortgage interest and insurance premiums, he was shocked.

What your son must understand is that money is linked to work and that everything you buy with it is a trade-off. If you blow it for one thing, you won't have it for something that might be more important. Said another way, you must teach your son that there's no such thing in life as having it all. There is also no such thing as a free lunch—unless you provide it for him.

I wouldn't worry too much about your son not understanding these concepts at fourteen. I know very few youngsters that age who "get it." But it is time to begin the instructional process.

My teenager often complains that my husband and I don't trust him. He usually says that when he wants to do something that we object to. What should our response be?

Children are adept at throwing parents off balance when moments of confrontation occur. One of the most effective tools of adolescents is the one you are hearing. Mom and Dad typically begin backpedaling and explaining, "No, dear, it's not that we don't trust you being out so late, it's just that we . . . ," and then they run out of words. They're on the defensive and the initiative shifts to the other side.

Parents in that situation need to remind their kids that trust is divisible. In other words, their kids are trusted in some situations but not others. It's not an all-or-nothing proposition. Referring again to the business world, many of us are authorized to spend our company's money from a designated account but are not allowed access to the entire corporate treasury. Trust in that case is specifically limited. Likewise, we might be authorized to spend perhaps five thousand for supplies or equipment, but anything more than that amount requires the signature of a supervisor. It's not that the bosses fear that the company will be cheated. Rather, good business experience has taught that trust should be given for specific circumstances and purposes. It's called a "grant of authority." Applying that idea now to teenagers, they can expect to be granted permission to do some things but not others. As they handle privileges in a trustworthy manner, they will be given more latitude. The point is you as a parent shouldn't be sucker punched by your kids when they claim falsely that they are being mistreated. I suggest that you not take the bait.

My husband and I are doing far too much disciplining of our kids. Is there another way to encourage them to cooperate?

A child's continual misbehavior may reflect a need for attention. Some kids would rather be wanted for murder than not wanted at all. Try putting some fun and laughter into your relationship and see what happens. You might be surprised. Also, check the fundamentals. When a football or a basketball team is losing, the coach usually goes back to the basics. Get a good book on discipline and see if your mistakes can be identified.

We have a seven-year-old son who has been doing some pretty awful things to dogs and cats in the neighborhood. We've tried to stop him but not successfully. I wonder if there is anything to be more concerned about here.

Cruelty to animals can be a symptom of serious emotional problems in a child, and those who do such things repeatedly are not typically just going through a phase. It should definitely be seen as a warning sign that must be checked out. I don't want to alarm you or overstate the case, but early cruelty is correlated with violent behavior as an adult.[6] I would suggest that you take your son to a psychologist or psychiatrist for evaluation, and by all means, never tolerate any kind of unkindness to animals.

What should I do with my twenty-two-year-old son, who has moved back home after dropping out of school and making a mess out of his life? He doesn't have a job, won't carry his share of the load at home, and complains about the food he is given.

I would help him pack—this afternoon if not earlier. Some young people like yours have no intention of growing up, and why should they? The nest is just too comfortable at home. Food is prepared, clothes are laundered, bills are paid. There's just no incentive to face the cold, hard world of reality, and they are determined not to budge. They need a firm push. I know it is difficult to dislodge homebound sons. They're like furry little kittens that hang around the back door waiting for a saucer of warm milk. But to let them stay year after year, especially if they're not pursuing career goals, is to cultivate irresponsibility and dependency. And that's not love, even though it may very well feel like it.

The time has come for you to hand the reins over to your son, gently but forthrightly, and force him to stand on his own. If you don't do that, you will effectively paralyze him by taking away all incentive to get his life in order. Good luck!

THE ULTIMATE PRIORITY

CHAPTER 17

IT IS TIME NOW to put a ribbon on our work together. I hope you have enjoyed this meandering look at the wonderful challenge of raising boys. There is nothing to compare with the privilege of bringing precious children into the world and then guiding them step-by-step through their developmental years and on toward maturity. I wrote in the beginning of our discussion that our objective as moms and dads is to transform our sons from "immature and flighty youngsters into honest, caring men who will be respectful of women, loyal and faithful in marriage, keepers of commitments, strong and decisive leaders, good workers, and men who are secure in their masculinity." It's a tall order but one that can be achieved with wisdom and guidance from the Father. The primary mechanism by which these goals are realized is the application of confident leadership and discipline at home, tempered with love and compassion. It is an unbeatable combination.

Our focus has been on the ways boys differ from their sisters and the particular needs that are associated with masculinity. We have also considered the burgeoning crisis that confronts our boys in today's cultural context. Working against them, by way of summary, are the breakup of families, the absence or disengagement of dads, the consequent wounding of spirits, the feminist attack on masculinity, and the postmodern culture that is twisting and warping so many of our children. If there is a common theme that connects each of these sources of difficulty, it is the frantic pace of living that has left too little time or energy for the children who look to us for the fulfillment of every need.

Let me elaborate on that point. I hope it has been evident as this discussion has unfolded that the trouble we are having with our children is linked directly to what I call "routine panic" and the increasing isolation and detachment it produces. America's love affair with materialism has taken its toll on the things that matter most. Let's go back, as a case in point, to the epidemic of bullying and taunting that is occurring in our schools. All of us experienced similar difficult moments when we were young. So what is different now? It is the absence of parents, who have nothing left to give. Some of us as kids came home to intact and caring families that were able to "talk us down" from the precipice, to assure us of their love, and to help put things in perspective. Someone was there who clearly cared and who told us that the harsh judgment of our peers was not the end of the world. In the absence of that kind of wise counsel in times of crisis, such as my dad provided for me when I came home battered from school, today's kids have nowhere to go with their rage. Some resort to drugs or alcohol, some withdraw into isolation, and some, sadly, vent their anger in murderous assault. If only Mom and Dad had been there when the passions peaked. So many of the difficulties that confront our kids come down to that single characteristic of today's families: There is nobody home.

As we have seen repeatedly in these chapters, it is boys who typically suffer most from the absence of parental care. Why? Because they are more likely to get off course when they are not guided and supervised carefully. They are inherently more volatile and less stable emotionally. They founder in chaotic, unsupervised, and undisciplined circumstances. Boys are like fast-moving automobiles that need a driver at the steering wheel every moment of the journey, gently turning a half inch here and a quarter inch there. They will need this guidance for at least sixteen or eighteen years, or even longer. When left to their own devices, they tend to drift toward the center divider or into the ditch, toward misbehavior or danger. Yet 59 percent of today's kids come home to an empty house after school each day.[1] It is an invitation to disaster for rambunctious males, and the older they get, the more opportunities they have to get into trouble. Today, when the culture is in a tug-of-war with families for control of our children, we can't afford to be preoccupied with things of lesser consequence.

Your task as a mother or father is to build a man out of the raw materials available implicitly in your delightful little boy. Construct him stone upon stone and precept upon precept. Never assume for a moment that you can go off and "do your own thing" without serious consequences for him and his sister. It is my conviction that those who choose to bring a child into the world must give that boy or girl highest priority for a period of time. It will not always be required of moms and dads. Before they know it, that youngster will become a young man, who will pack his bags and take his first halting steps into the adult world. Then it will be their turn. By all expectations, you as a parent should have decades of health and vigor left to invest in whatever God calls you to do. But for now, there is a higher calling. I feel obligated to tell you this, whether my words are popular or not. Raising children who have been loaned to us for a brief moment outranks every other responsibility. Besides, living by that priority when kids are small will produce the greatest rewards at maturity.

I am convinced that most contemporary mothers care more about their husbands and their children than about any other aspect of their lives, and they would like nothing better than to devote their primary energies to them. But they are trapped in a chaotic and demanding world that threatens constantly to overwhelm them. Many of these young women also grew up in busy, dysfunctional, career-oriented households, and they want something better for their kids. Yet, the financial pressures and the expectations of others keep them on a treadmill that leaves them exhausted and harried. I have never written this before, and I will be criticized for saying so now, but I believe the two-career family *during the child-rearing years* creates a level of stress that is tearing people apart. And it often deprives children of something that they will search for for the rest of their lives.

My prayer is that a scale-back from a lifestyle of routine panic will someday occur. If it ever becomes a movement, it will portend wonderfully for the family. It should result in fewer divorces and more domestic harmony. Children will regain the status they deserve and their welfare will be enhanced on a thousand fronts. We haven't begun to approach these goals yet, but we can only hope that a significant segment of the population will awaken someday from the nightmare of overcommitment and say, "This is a crazy way to live. There has to be a better way than this to raise our kids. We will make the financial sacrifices necessary to slow the pace of living."

It is not enough simply to be at home and available to our children, however. We must use the opportunities of these few short years to teach them our values and beliefs. Millions of young people who have grown up in the relative opulence of North America have not had that training. They are terribly confused about transcendent values. We have given them more material blessings than any generation in history. They have had opportunities never dreamed of by their ancestors. Most have never heard the pounding of artillery shells or the explosion of grenades. More money has been spent on their education, medical care, entertainment, and travel than any who have gone before. Yet we have failed them in the most important of all parental responsibilities: We have not taught them who they are as children of God or what they have been placed here to do.

The late philosopher and author Dr. Francis Schaeffer wrote, "The dilemma of modern man is simple: He does not know why man has any meaning. . . . This is the damnation of our generation, the heart of modern man's problem."[2]

Although Dr. Schaeffer's penetrating statement was written almost three decades ago, it is even more relevant to today's teenagers and young adults. Its validity became apparent when I was writing my book for young people called *Life on the Edge*. To assist me in that project, Word Publishers assembled focus groups in various cities to determine the stress points and needs of the younger generation. True to our thesis, the most common concern to emerge was the absence of meaning in life. These kids, most of whom professed to be Christians, were confused about the substance and purpose in living.

Let me share a brief section of the above-mentioned book. I believe it applies not only to those for whom it was written (ages sixteen to twenty-six) but to all of us in this materialistic society that emphasizes the false values of money, power, position, and other empty symbols of significance. This is what I wrote:

> It is so important to pause and think through some basic issues while you are young, before the pressures of job and family become distracting. There are several eternal questions everyone must deal with eventually. You will benefit, I think, from doing that work now. Whether you are an atheist, a Muslim, a Buddhist, a Jew, an agnostic, or a Christian, the questions confronting the human family are the same. Only the answers will differ. They are:
>
> Who am I as a person?
> How did I get here?
> Is there a right or wrong way to believe and act?
> Is there a God, and if so, what does He expect of me?
> Is there life after death?
> How do I achieve eternal life, if it exists?
> Will I someday be held accountable for the way I have lived on earth?
> What is the meaning of life and death?[3]

The sad observation from our study is that most of the young people with whom we talked found it difficult to answer questions such as these.

They had only a vague notion of what we might call "first truths." No wonder they lacked a sense of meaning and purpose. Life loses its significance for a person who has no understanding of his origin or destination.

Human beings tend to struggle with troubling questions they can't answer. Just as nature abhors a vacuum, so the intellect acts to fill the void. Or to state it differently, it seeks to repair a hole in its system of beliefs. That is why so many young people today chase after twisted and alien "theologies," such as New Age nonsense, the pursuit of pleasure, substance abuse, and illicit sex. They are searching vainly for something that will satisfy their "soul hunger." They are unlikely to find it. Not even great achievement and superior education will put the pieces together. Meaning in life comes only by answering the eternal questions listed above, and they are adequately addressed only in the Christian faith. No other religion can tell us who we are, how we got here, and where we are going after death. And no other belief system teaches that we are known and loved individually by the God of the universe and by His only Son, Jesus Christ.

That brings us back to the subject of boys and what they and their sisters need from parents during the developmental years. At the top of the list is an understanding of who God is and what He expects them to do. This teaching must begin very early in childhood. Even at three years of age, a child is capable of learning that the flowers, the sky, the birds, and even the rainbow are gifts from God's hand. He made these wonderful things, just as He created each one of us. The first Scripture our children should learn is, "God is love" (1 John 4:8). They should be taught to thank Him before eating their food and to ask for His help when they are hurt or scared.

Moses takes that responsibility a step further in Deuteronomy 6. He tells parents to talk about spiritual matters continually. Reciting the children's poem "Now I Lay Me down to Sleep" at bedtime is not going to get it done. Scripture tells us: "These commandments that I give you today are to be upon your hearts. Impress them on your children. Talk about them when you sit at home and when you walk along the road, when you lie down and when you get up. Tie them as symbols on your hands and bind them on your foreheads. Write them on the doorframes of your houses and on your gates" (Deuteronomy 6:6-9).

If this passage means anything, it is that we are to give the greatest emphasis to the spiritual development of our children. Nothing even comes close to it in significance. The only way you can be with your precious children in the next life is to introduce them to Jesus Christ and His teachings, hopefully when they are young and impressionable. This is Task Number One in child-rearing.

For those of my readers who need a little help in clarifying those objectives, let me ask you to project yourself momentarily to the end of your days, perhaps many years from now. What will give you the greatest satisfaction as you lie there on your sickbed, thinking about the experiences of a lifetime? Will your heart thrill to the memory of honors, degrees, and professional accolades? Will fame be most highly prized, even if you manage to achieve it? Will you swell with pride over the money you've made, the books you have written, or the buildings and businesses that bear your name? I think not. Temporal successes and accomplishments will not be very gratifying in that moment of destiny. I believe the greatest sense of fulfillment as you prepare to close the final chapter will be in knowing that you lived by a consistent standard of holiness before God and that you invested yourself unselfishly in the lives of your family members and friends. Most important, knowing that you led your children to the Lord and will be with them in eternity will outrank every other achievement. All else will fade into insignificance. If that is a true representation of how you will feel when your days are growing short, why not determine to live according to that value system now, while you still have the opportunity to influence the impressionable kids who look up to you? This may be the most important question you as a mother or father will ever be asked to answer!

Not only is spiritual development of relevance to eternity, it is also critical to the way your children will live out their days on this earth. Specifically, boys need to be well established in their faith in order to understand the meaning of good and evil. They are growing up in a postmodern world in which all ideas are considered equally valid and nothing is really wrong. Wickedness is bad only in the minds of those who think it is bad. People who live by this godless outlook on life are headed for great pain and misery. The Christian worldview, by contrast, teaches that good and evil are determined by the God of the universe and that He has given us an unchanging moral standard by which to live. He also offers forgiveness from sins, which boys (and girls) have good reason to need. Only with this understanding is a child being prepared to face the challenges that lie ahead. Yet most American children receive no spiritual training whatsoever! They are left to make it up as they go along, which leads to the meaningless existence we have discussed.

The most effective teaching tool, as we have seen, is in the modeling provided by parents at home. Children are amazingly perceptive of the things they witness in their parents' unguarded moments. This was illustrated for Shirley and me when our son and daughter were eleven and sixteen. We had gone together to Mammoth, California, for a ski retreat with another family. Unfortunately, our arrival coincided with a huge blizzard on that Thursday, confining us to the lodge and frustrating the kids beyond description. Each of us would take turns walking to the window every few minutes in hopes of seeing a clearing that would set us free, but none came. Friday we were also socked in, and Saturday's storm absolutely buried our cars in snow. By that time, the two families had big-time "cabin fever," and even our dog was getting antsy.

With the dawn on Sunday morning, wouldn't you know, the sun came streaming into our condo and the sky was a brilliant blue. The snow on the trees was gorgeous and all the ski lifts were up and running. But what were we to do? We had made it a lifelong policy to go to church on Sunday and had chosen not to ski or attend professional athletic events on what we called "the Lord's day." I know many Christian people would disagree with that perspective, and I have no problem with those who see it differently. This was simply the standard for our family and we had lived by it throughout our married life. We have always taken literally the Scripture that says, "Remember the Sabbath day by keeping it holy. Six days you shall labor and do all your work, but the seventh day is a Sabbath to the Lord your God. On it you shall not do any work, neither you, nor your son or daughter, nor your manservant or maidservant, nor your animals, nor the alien within your gates. For in six days the Lord made the heavens and the earth, the sea, and all that is in them, but he rested on the seventh day. Therefore the Lord blessed the Sabbath day and made it holy" (Exodus 20:8-11).

Admittedly, skiing on Sunday is not tantamount to work, as prohibited in this Scripture, but it is a day set aside for another purpose. Furthermore, if we skied that morning, we would be requiring ski-company employees to be on the job. Right or wrong, this is what we have believed. But what was I to do in the present situation? Everyone wanted to hit the slopes, and to be honest, so did I. Shirley and I were going bonkers cooped up with all those bored kids. Therefore, I gathered our family with our guests and said, "You know, we don't want to be legalistic about this thing [smile]. I think the Lord would forgive an exception in this case. It's such a beautiful day outside. We can have our devotions tonight when we get home from skiing, and I think it would be okay to go."

Everyone was jubilant, or so I thought, and we proceeded to dress for the outing. I finished first and was upstairs fixing a do-it-yourself breakfast when Shirley came and whispered to me, "You had better go talk to your son." He was always *my* son when there was a problem. I went to Ryan's bedroom and found him crying. "Goodness, Ryan, what's wrong?" I asked. I will never forget his answer.

"Dad," he said, "I have never seen you compromise before. You have told us it is not right to ski and do things like that on Sunday, but now you're saying it's okay." Tears were still streaming down his cheeks as he talked. "If this was wrong in the past, then it is still wrong today."

Ryan's words hit me like a blow from a hammer. I had disappointed this kid who looked to me for moral guidance. I had violated my own standard of behavior, and Ryan knew it. I felt like the world's biggest hypocrite. After I had regained my composure, I said, "You're right, Ryan. There's no way I can justify the decision I made."

At my request, the two families gathered in the living room again and I related what had happened. Then I said, "I want you all [our guests] to go ahead and ski today. We certainly understand. But our family is going to attend a little church in the village this morning. This is how we spend our Sundays, and today should not be an exception for us."

Members of the other family, both children and adults, said almost in unison, "We don't want to ski today either. We will go to church with you." And so they did. That afternoon, I got to thinking about what had happened. The next morning, I called my office to say that we would not be returning until Tuesday. Our friends were able to change their schedule too. So we all went skiing on Monday and had one of the finest days together we have ever had. And my conscience was quiet at last.

I had no idea that Ryan had been watching me on that Sunday morning, but I should have anticipated it. Children get their values and beliefs from what they see modeled at home. It is one reason why moms and dads must live a morally consistent life in front of their kids. If they hope to win them for Christ, they can't afford to be casual or whimsical about the things they believe. If you as a parent act as though there is no absolute truth, and if you are too busy to pray and attend church services together, and if your kids are allowed to play soccer or Little League during Sunday school, and if you cheat on your income tax or lie to the bill collector or fight endlessly with your neighbors, your children will get the message. "Mom and Dad talk a good game, but they don't really believe it." If you serve them this weak soup throughout childhood, they will spew it out when given the opportunity. Any ethical weak spot of this nature—any lack of clarity on matters of right and wrong—will be noted and magnified by the next generation. If you think that faith and belief are routinely absorbed by children, just look at the sons of the great patriarchs of the Bible, from Isaac to Samuel to David to Hezekiah. All of them saw their offspring fall away from the faith of their fathers as the years unfolded.

Again, timing is critical. Researcher George Barna confirmed what we have known—that it becomes progressively more difficult to influence children spiritually as they grow older. Here are his disturbing findings:

The data show that if a person does not accept Jesus Christ as Savior before the age of fourteen, the likelihood of ever doing so is slim.

Based on a nationwide representative sampling of more than 4,200 young people and adults, the survey data show that people from ages five through thirteen have a 32 percent probability of accepting Christ as their Savior. Young people from the ages of fourteen through eighteen have just a 4 percent likelihood of doing so, while adults (ages nineteen through death) have only a 6 percent probability of making that choice. The years prior to age twelve are when a majority of children make their decision as to whether or not they will follow Christ.[4] (Note: These statistics reflect polling done with all parents, regardless of their faith. The results would undoubtedly be different with a sample of committed Christian parents.)

"The earlier the better" when it comes to introducing our children to the Lord. Furthermore, everything we do during those foundational child-rearing years should be bathed in prayer. There is not enough knowledge in the books—not in this one or any other—to secure the outcome of our parenting responsibility without divine help. It is arrogant to think that we can shepherd our kids safely through the minefields of an increasingly sinful society. That awesome realization hit me when our daughter, Danae, was only three years old. I recognized that having a Ph.D. in child development was not going to be enough to meet the challenges of parenthood. That is why Shirley and I began fasting and praying for Danae, and later for Ryan, almost every week from the time they were young. At least one of us bore that responsibility throughout their childhoods. In fact, Shirley continues that practice to this day. Our petition was the same through the early years: "Lord, give us the wisdom to raise the precious children whom you have loaned to us, and above all else, help us bring them to the feet of Jesus. This is more important to us than our health or our work or our finances. What we ask most fervently is that the circle be unbroken when we meet in heaven."

Again, prayer is the key to everything. I'm reminded of a story told by a rookie playing for the Chicago Bulls in the National Basketball Association. One night, the incomparable Michael Jordan scored sixty-six points, and the rookie was sent in for the last couple of minutes of the game. When the young man was interviewed by a reporter afterwards, he said, "Yeah, it was a great night. Michael Jordan and I scored sixty-eight points."[5] That's the way I feel about parenting and prayer. We do all we can to score a few points, but the greater contribution is made by the creator of children.

Parents need assistance from other members of the family too, if it is available. I was blessed to have a grandmother and a great-grandmother who helped my mom and dad lay a spiritual foundation that remains with me to this day. These two godly women talked regularly about the Lord and His goodness to us. My great-grandmother, whom we called Nanny, could pray the heavens down to Earth. One of my earliest memories, believe it or not, is of her bending over me when I was in a crib of some type. I couldn't have been more than fifteen months of age. She was wearing an old-fashioned knitted cap that had strings with furry balls hanging at the end. I recall playing with those fuzzy things while Nanny laughed and cuddled me. When this woman, whom I deeply loved, began telling me about Jesus in the ensuing years, I believed her. Her husband, my great-grandfather, prayed every day between 11 A.M. and noon, specifically for the spiritual welfare of his children and for the three generations of his family yet to be born. He died the year before my birth, and yet his prayers continue to echo through the corridors of time. I look forward to meeting him someday and to having the opportunity to thank him for the heritage of faith he and my other forebears handed down to my generation.

My grandmother on the other side of the family was called Little Mother, because she weighed only ninety pounds. She was the delight of my life. She talked often about how wonderful heaven was going to be, which made me want to go there. My father told me how when he was a boy, Little Mother would gather her six kids around her for Bible reading and prayer. Then she would talk about the importance of knowing and obeying Jesus. Many times she said, "If I lose a single one of you to the faith, it would have been better that I were never born." That was the priority she gave to the spiritual development of her kids. She and the others effectively passed this commitment on to me.

Let me specifically address the grandparents and great-grandparents among my readers. You have been given a wonderful opportunity to deliver a spiritual heritage to your progeny. It is a God-given responsibility that in some ways is more effective than what busy moms and dads are able to accomplish. I hope you will not squander it. Pray for your sons and daughters, who are raising their children in a very difficult time. It is not easy to be moms or dads today. Help them teach their children about Jesus, about heaven and hell, and about the principles of right and wrong. I can't tell you how many Christians have told me they accepted Christ as adults because of the early training given to them by their grandparents.

Geoffrey Canada is an African-American man who grew up on the streets of the Bronx. He is the author of the book *Reaching Up for Manhood: Transforming the Lives of Boys in America*. In it, he shares some of his personal experiences and tells how he overcame many adverse circumstances. Canada gives great credit to his grandmother, who eventually turned him around and gave him a moral compass. He relates a story about her final days while dying of cancer. It was during a terribly difficult period in his own life. Both his brother and his infant son had recently died. This is what he wrote:

> I might have been able to accept one of these deaths, but not all three. Why had God taken my infant son, my brother whom I worshipped, and now [was going to take] my grandmother whom I cherished? The answer to me was that there simply was no God. Not only did I doubt the existence of God, but my own life lost meaning. Why was I working so hard in college, away from my family and friends, sacrificing so much, when death could come at any instant, making all of my hard work folly?
>
> When I went home to see my grandmother she was bedridden. The cancer had robbed her of her strength and would soon take her life. Right before I went back to school I went into her room and I asked her the question that was tearing me apart. I know it was selfish of me to ask her this while she lay dying, but I had to know.
>
> "Grandma, do you still believe in God?"
>
> "Of course I do. Why do you ask me that?"
>
> "Because you're sick. You have cancer."
>
> "Being sick doesn't have anything to do with faith."
>
> "But how can you have faith when God has done this to you? Made you suffer. And for what? What did you do to offend God so much that you have to be in pain like this?"
>
> "Geoffrey, listen to me. I know you've been through so much with the loss of your son and your brother. But don't lose faith in God or yourself. God has a plan and you're part of it, so you can't give up. Faith is not something you believe in until things don't go your way. It's not like rooting for a football team, and then when they start losing, changing sides and rooting for another team. Faith means you believe no matter what.
>
> "Do you hear me? It's easy to have faith when you have a million dollars and you're in perfect health. Do you think

that proves anything to God? Your problem is that you think if you study your books hard enough you will find all the answers. All the answers aren't in books. They never will be. [Remember Karen Cheng's comment about meaning?] So do I believe in God? Yes. More now than ever before."

I reluctantly went back to Bowdoin [where he was attending college] after spending a week with my grandmother, not knowing that this was to be the last time I would ever talk to or see her. She died within weeks of my leaving. I spent the rest of my sophomore year in a daze, the combined losses too much for me to comprehend. But I knew I had to keep trying, not lose my faith, because that's what my grandmother wanted. And when I became suddenly frightened or depressed, and found that my faith was weak and couldn't sustain me, I felt that I could borrow my grandmother's faith. Even though she was no longer alive, her faith was real and tangible to me. Many a night I leaned on her faith when I felt my own couldn't support my doubts.

Every child needs a grandmother like mine in their lives—a person who is older, and wiser, and is willing to fight for as long as it takes for that child's soul. A person who is willing to hold his or her life up as an example of faith. A person who both forgives and teaches forgiveness. A person whose abundance of faith will be there in sufficient supply when children need it. Because sooner or later children need more faith than they possess. That's where we come in.[6]

With that, we will hasten to a closing thought. Once your children have reached the latter years of adolescence, it will be important not to push them too hard spiritually. You can still have reasonable expectations for them as long as they are under your roof, but you can't demand that they believe what they have been taught. The door must be opened fully to the world outside. This can be the most frightening time of parenthood. The tendency is to retain control in order to keep your kids from making mistakes. However, teenagers and young adults are more likely to make the proper choices when they aren't forced to rebel in order to escape. The simple truth is that love demands freedom. They go hand in hand.

No matter how much you prepare, letting go is never easy. The late Erma Bombeck likened the parenting responsibility to flying a kite.[7] You start by trying to get the little craft off the ground, and sometimes you wonder if it's going to make it. You're running down the road as fast as you can with this awkward kite flapping in the wind behind you. Sometimes it crashes to the ground, so you tie on a longer tail and try it again. Suddenly it catches a little gust of wind and flies dangerously close to the power lines. Your heart is pounding as you survey the risk. But then without warning, the kite begins to tug on the string as it ascends into the sky. You release your grip little by little, and sooner than you expected, you come to the end of the twine. You stand on tiptoe holding the last inch between your thumb and forefinger. Then reluctantly, you let go, permitting the kite to soar unfettered and independent in God's blue heaven.

It's an exhilarating and a terrifying moment, and one that was ordained from the day of your child's birth. With this final release, your task as a parent is finished. The kite is free, and so, for the first time in twenty years, are you.

My prayers will be with you as you discharge your God-given responsibility. Cherish every moment of it. And hug your kids while you can. I hope something I have written on these pages has been helpful to you and yours. Thanks for reading along with me.

IT'S TOUGH ON A DOG
By Jean W. Sawtell

It's tough on a dog when his boy grows up,
When he no longer romps and frolics like a pup.
It's tough on a dog when his boy gets old,
When they no longer cuddle on his bed when it's cold.
It's tough on a dog when his boy gets tall,
When he's off with the boys playing soccer and baseball.
They no longer paddle through the mud in the bog,
Hoping to find a stray turtle or frog.
They no longer run through the grass up to their knees,
Or roll in the piles of fresh fallen leaves.
It's tough on a dog when his boy gets tall,
When's he's off to school, looking at girls in the hall.
It's tough on a dog when he has work to do,
When he forgets to play as he used to.
It's tough on a dog when instead of the woods or field
*   or pond,*
His boy becomes a man—and the man is gone.[8]

ENDNOTES

CHAPTER 1: The Wonderful World of Boys

1. John Rosemond, as quoted in Paula Gray Hunker, "What Are Boys Made Of?" *Washington Times,* 28 September 1999, 1(E).
2. Ibid.
3. Plato, *Laws,* 1953 edition 1, p. 164.
4. Kitty Harmon, *Up to No Good: The Rascally Things Boys Do* (San Francisco: Chronicle Books, 2000). From *Up to No Good: The Rascally Things Boys Do,* edited by Kitty Harmon. © 2000 by Tributary Books. Reprinted by permission of Chronicle Books, San Francisco.
5. Ira Dreyfuss, "Boys and Girls See Risk Differently, Study Says," Associated Press, 16 February 1997.
6. Ibid.
7. "That Little Boy of Mine." Words and music by Benny Meroff, Wayne King, and Walter Hirsch. Published by Forster Music Publisher, Inc. (Chicago, 1932).

CHAPTER 2: Vive la Différence

1. See for example: Mary Brown Parlee, "The Sexes under Scrutiny: From Old Biases to New Theories," *Psychology Today* (November 1978): 62–69; Jane O'Reilly, "Doing Away with Sex Stereotypes," *Time,* 23 October 1980, 1.
2. Marlo Thomas et al., *Free to Be You and Me* (Philadelphia: Running Press, 1974).
3. Germaine Greer, *The Female Eunuch* (London: MacGibbon and Kee, 1970).
4. "No Safe Place: Violence against Women: An Interview with Gloria Steinem," KUED-TV, Salt Lake City. See <http://www.media.utah.edu/prdction/interv/steinem.html>.
5. Ibid.
6. Elisabeth Bumiller, "Gloria Steinem: The Everyday Rebel; Two Decades of Feminism, and the Fire Burns as Bright," *Washington Post,* 12 October 1983, 1(B).
7. Ibid.
8. Greer, *The Female Eunuch.*
9. "Lawyer Wages War on Sexism in Toys," Associated Press, 9 December 1979.
10. Tracy Thomas, "A Gloria Allred Scorecard," *Los Angeles Times,* 29 October 1987, Metro, 2.

11. Joy Dickinson, "Child Advocates Decry Gender Stereotyping in Toys "R" Us Store Redesign," *Bradenton Herald*, 19 February 2000.
12. Christina Hoff Sommers, "The War Against Boys," *C-Span 2*, 16 July 2000.
13. Gina Kolata, "Man's World, Woman's World? Brain Studies Point to Differences," *New York Times*, 28 February 1995, 1(C).
14. Mary Brown Parlee, "The Sexes under Scrutiny: From Old Biases to New Theories," *Psychology Today* (November 1978): 62–69.
15. Dale O'Leary, "Gender: The Deconstruction of Women: Analysis of the Gender Perspective in Preparation for the Fourth World Conference on Women in Beijing, China," 6.
16. Dr. Stella Chess and Dr. Alexander Thomas, *Know Your Child: An Authoritative Guide for Today's Parents* (New York: Basic Books, 1987).

CHAPTER 3: So What *Is* the Difference?

1. Robert Sapolsky, "Testosterone Rules: It Takes More Than Just a Hormone to Make a Fellow's Trigger Finger Itch," *Discover*, March 1997, 44.
2. See <http://www.brainplace.com/bp/malefemaledf/default.asp>.
3. Bjork, Randall, M.D. (neurologist). Personal correspondence; Micheal D. Phillips et al., "Temporal Lobe Activation Demonstrates Sex-based Differences during Passive Listening," *Radiology*, July 2001, 202–207.
4. Sapolsky, "Testosterone Rules."
5. Andrew Sullivan, "The He Hormone," *New York Times Magazine*, 2 April 2000, 46. Copyright © 2000 by Andrew Sullivan. Originally published on April 2, 2000 in *The New York Times Magazine*.
6. Sapolsky, "Testosterone Rules."
7. Gregg Johnson, "The Biological Basis for Gender-Specific Behavior," chap. 16 in *Recovering Biblical Manhood and Womanhood: A Response to Evangelical Feminism*, ed. Wayne Grudem and John Piper (Wheaton, Ill: Crossway Books, 1991).
8. 2001 Fortune 500 CEO List. See <http://www.pathfinder.com/fortune/fortune500/ceolist.html>.
9. Congressional Handbook. 107th Congress.
10. Martina Navratilova, "Friends across the Net," *Newsweek*, 25 October 1999, 70.
11. John McEnroe, "Playing with Pure Passion," *Newsweek*, 25 October 1999, 70. From *Newsweek*, 25 October © 1999 Newsweek, Inc. All rights reserved. Reprinted by permission.
12. "Serotonin and Judgment," *Society for Neuroscience Brain Briefings* (April 1997). See <http://www.sfn.org/briefings/serotonin.html>.
13. Joseph LeDoux, "The New Brain." See <http://www.feedmag.com/brain/parts/ledoux.html>.
14. Joshua Freedman, "Hijacking of the Amygdala," *EQ Today*. See <http://www.eqtoday.com/hijack.html>.
15. Hunker, "What Are Boys Made Of?"
16. Claudia Wallis, "Life in Overdrive," *Time*, 18 July 1994, 42.
17. Ibid., 46.
18. Ibid., 48.
19. Ibid., 44.
20. George Will, "Boys Will Be Boys, or We Can Just Drug Them," *Washington Post*, 2 December 1999, sec. 39A.
21. James Dobson, *Solid Answers* (Wheaton, Ill.: Tyndale House Publishers, Inc., 1997).

CHAPTER 4: Wounded Spirits

1. Michael Gurian, *A Fine Young Man* (New York: Jeremy Tarcher/Putnam, 1998), 12–15.
2. Angela Phillips, *The Trouble with Boys* (New York: Basic Books, 1994), 21.
3. Amy M. Holmes, "Boys Today: Snakes, Snails and Guns," *USA Today*, 10 December 1999.
4. Phillips, *The Trouble with Boys*.

5. Carey Goldberg, "After Girls Get the Attention, Focus Shifts to Boys' Woes," *New York Times,* 23 April 1998.

6. Hunker, "What Are Boys Made Of?"

7. Michael Gurian, *The Wonder of Boys* (New York: Jeremy Tarcher/Putnam, 1996), 15.

8. "Newly Released Videotape Offering Insight into Mind of Teen Gunman Kip Kinkel," *NBC News Transcripts,* 22 January 2000.

9. Holmes, "Boys Today."

10. "A Devastating Cycle: Substance Abuse, Child Abuse Tragically Linked," *San Diego Union-Tribune,* 26 April 1999, 6(B).

11. Ronald Kotulak, "Why Some Kids Turn Violent: Abuse and Neglect Can Reset Brain's Chemistry," *Chicago Tribune,* 14 December 1993, 1.

12. Focus on the Family, "The Family at the End of the 20th Century," 8–9 June 1995.

13. Diane Frederick, "Therapist Discusses Roots of Violence," *Indianapolis Star,* 3 March 2000, 1(N).

14. Frank Peretti, *Wounded Spirits* (Nashville: Thomas Nelson/Word, 2000).

15. Erica Goode, "Study Finds TV Alters Fiji Girls' View of Body," *New York Times,* 20 May 1999, 17(A).

16. Karen Patterson, "Through Thick or Thin: Americans Lose Sense of Proportion in Struggling with Their Weight," *Dallas Morning News,* 29 August 1999, 1(J).

17. Joan Smith, "For 9-Year-Old Girls, the Big Fear Is Not the Bogeyman, but Getting Fat," *Chicago Tribune,* 12 November 1986, 30.

18. "Study: Elementary School Pupils Watch Their Wastelines," Associated Press, 2 May 1989.

19. "Children Aware of Dieting, Body Image," Reuters, 6 January 2000.

20. "Diana in a New Light," ABC News *20/20,* 6 October 2000.

21. Stephen S. Hall, "Bully in the Mirror," *New York Times Magazine,* 22 August 1999, 31.

22. Ibid.

23. "Boys as Bullies: Researchers Find Aggression Can Be a Road to Popularity," *Chicago Tribune,* 19 January 2000, 7.

24. "Psychologist Dorothy Espelage Discusses Report on Bullies in Schoolyard," *NBC News Transcripts,* 21 August 1999.

25. Phillips, *The Trouble with Boys.*

26. "Common Thread among School Shootings Is Bullied Teens Striking Back in Rage," *NBC News,* 9 March 2001.

27. Ibid.

28. Andrew Gumbel, "San Diego Killings: Nobody Believed the Scrawny Boy's Threat to Bring a Gun to School," *London Independent,* 7 March 2001, 5.

29. Ibid.

30. Adrian Nicole LeBlanc, "The Outsiders," *New York Times Magazine,* 22 August 1999, 36. Copyright © 1999 by the New York Times Co. Reprinted by permission.

31. Ibid.

32. Jules Crittenden, "High School Horror: United in Grief, 70,000 Mourners Open Their Hearts to Colorado Victims," *Boston Herald,* 26 April 1999, 1.

33. "Common Thread among School Shootings."

34. "Students' Review Makes Parents Want to Scream," *Plugged In,* 15 June 1997.

35. Rabbi Daniel Lapin, Family Research Council Washington Briefing, March 2000.

36. "Media Tied to Violence among Kids," Associated Press, 26 July 2000.

37. Steve Rubenstein, "Doctors Advise TV Blackout for Little Kids," *San Francisco Chronicle,* 4 August 1999, 1(A).

38. Archibald Hart, *Stress and Your Child* (Nashville: Thomas Nelson/Word, 1992).

39. Kathleen Parker, "Let's Give Our Boys A Gift: Self-Control," *USA Today,* 15 September 1999, 17(A).

40. American Academy of Pediatrics. Used by permission of the Family Research Council.

41. Harold M. Voth and Gabriel Nahas, *How to Save Your Kids from Drugs* (Middlebury, Vt: Paul S. Ericksson, 1987).

CHAPTER 5: The Essential Father

1. Warren Leary, "Gloomy Report on the Health of Teenagers," *New York Times,* 9 June 1990, 24.
2. Bureau of the Census, *Code Blue* (Washington, D.C.).
3. Kyle D. Pruett, *Fatherneed: Why Father Care Is As Essential As Mother Care for Your Child* (The Free Press, 1999).
4. U.S. Department of Health and Human Services, *Morehouse Report,* National Center for Children in Poverty, Bureau of the Census (Washington, D.C.).
5. "Back to School 1999—National Survey of American Attitudes on Substance Abuse V: Teens and Their Parents," *National Center on Addiction and Substance Abuse at Columbia University,* August 1999.
6. William Pollock, *Real Boys: Rescuing Our Sons from the Myths of Boyhood* (New York: Henry Holt and Company, 1998).
7. Barbara Kantrowitz and Claudia Kalb, "Boys Will Be Boys," *Newsweek,* 11 May 1998, 55.
8. Hannah Cleaverin Berlin, "Lads Night Out Can Save Your Marriage," *London Daily Express,* 25 April 2000.
9. John Attarian, "Let Boys Be Boys—Exploding Feminist Dogma, This Provocative Book Reveals How Educators Are Trying to Feminize Boys While Neglecting Their Academic and Moral Instruction," *The World and I,* 1 October 2000.
10. Don and Jeanne Elium, *Raising a Son* (Berkeley: Celestrial Arts, 1997), 21.
11. Phillips, *The Trouble with Boys,* 54-59.
12. Michael D. Lemonick, "Young, Single and Out of Control," *Time,* 13 October 1997.
13. Dave Simmons, *Dad, the Family Counselor* (Nashville: Thomas Nelson Publishers, 1992), 112.
14. Bureau of Justice, *Statistics of the Department of Justice.* See <http://www.ojp.usdoj.gov/bjs>.
15. Terri Tabor, "Keeping Kids Connected: Elgin High Program Puts At-Risk Students on Straighter Path," *Chicago Daily-Herald,* 17 September 1999, 1.
16. James Robison, *My Father's Face: A Portrait of the Perfect Father* (Sisters, OR: Multnomah Press, 1997).
17. Letter from Mrs. Karen S. Cotting. Used with permission.
18. Judith S. Wallerstein and Joan B. Kelly, *Surviving the Breakup* (New York: Basic Books, 1980), 33.
19. Karen S. Peterson, "Children of Divorce Struggle with Marriage," *Gannett News Service,* 25 October 2000.
20. D.M. Capaldi, "The Reliability of Retrospective Data for Timing First Sexual Intercourse for Adolescent Males," *Journal of Adolescent Research,* 11, (1996), 375-387.
21. Lawrence L. Wu, "Effects of Family Instability, Income, and Income Instability on the Risk of Premarital Birth," *American Sociological Review,* 61, (1996), 344-359.
22. Karla Mantilla, "Kids Need 'Fathers' Like Fish Need Bicycles," *Off Our Backs,* June 1998.
23. Carl Auerbach and Louise Silverstein, "Deconstructing the Essential Father," *American Psychologist,* 54, no. 6 (June 1999): 397–407.
24. Ibid.

CHAPTER 6: Fathers and Sons

1. Dale Turner, "'Dagwood' Image Hides the True Value of Fatherhood: It's No Minor Task to Mold Young Lives," *Seattle Times,* 19 June 1993, 8(C).
2. William E. Schmidt, "For Town and Team, Honor Is Its Own Reward," *New York Times,* 22 May 1987, 1.
3. Ibid.

4. David Blankenhorn, "Fatherless America: Life without Father," *USA Today Weekend*, 26 February 1995, 4.
5. Michael Gurian, *The Wonder of Boys* (New York: Jeremy Tarcher/Putnam, 1996).

CHAPTER 7: Mothers and Sons

1. Janet McConnaughey, "Romanian Orphans Show Importance of Touch," Associated Press, 27 October 1997.
2. "Parent's Love Affects Child's Health," Reuters, 10 March 1997.
3. Karen S. Peterson, "'Small but Significant' Finding: Kids Thrive on More Mom, Less Day Care," *USA Today*, 8 November 1999.
4. Sheryl Gay Stolberg, "Researchers Find a Link between Behavioral Problems and Time in Child Care," *New York Times*, 19 April 2001, 22(A).
5. Linda Seebach, "What Parents Want in Child Care," *Washington Times*, 19 September 2000, 20(A). See <http://www.publicagenda.org/issues/angles.cfm?issue_type=childcare>.
6. Deborah Mathis, "Growing Circle of Stay-at-Home Moms Can Click on Support," Gannett News Service, 5 September 2000.
7. Jean Lush, "Mothers and Sons," *Focus on the Family*, 5–6 March 1991.
8. Michael D. Resnick et al., "Protecting Adolescents from Harm: Findings from the National Longitudinal Study on Adolescent Health," *Journal of the American Medical Association*, 10 September 1999.
9. Marilyn Elias, "Family Dinners Nourish Ties with Teenagers," *USA Today*, 18 August 1997, 4(D).
10. Nancy Kellerher, "Literacy Begins at Home: Research Shows Conversation and Shared Reading Make the Difference; Family Dinner's the Winner," *Boston Herald*, 10 December 1996, 5; Andrew T. McLaughlin, "Family Dinners Provide Food for Thought As Well," *Boston Herald*, 14 March 1996, 1.
11. Tim Friend, "Heart Disease Awaits Today's Soft-Living Kids," *USA Today*, 15 November 1994, 1(D).
12. Louis Yablonsky, *Fathers and Sons* (New York: Simon and Schuster, 1982), 134. Used with permission.
13. Letter from Dr. C. H. McGowen. Used with permission.

CHAPTER 8: Chasing the Caterpillar

1. Zig Ziglar, "Following the Leader," September 20, 1999. See <http://www.crosswinds.net/infini/story043.html>.
2. James Davison Hunter, "Bowling with the Social Scientists: Robert Putnam Surveys America," *Weekly Standard*, 28 August 2000, 31.
3. "States with Lowest Voter Turnout," *USA Today*, 10 November 2000, 1(A).
4. Hunter, "Bowling with the Social Scientists."
5. Ibid.
6. "Survey: Overworked Americans Can't Use Up Limited Vacation, Raising Health Concerns," *Business Wire*, 21 February 2001.
7. George Barna, *Generation Next* (Ventura, Calif.: Regal Books, 1995), 55.
8. Armond Nicholi, psychiatrist at Harvard Medical School and Massachusetts General Hospital, speaking at White House Conference on the state of the American Family, 3 May 1983. Copies of this presentation are available in the *Congressional Record* (3 May 1983).
9. Ibid.
10. Deborah Mason, "The New Sanity: Mother's Lib," *Vogue*, May 1981.
11. Judy Dutton, "Meet the New Housewife Wanna-bes," *Cosmopolitan*, June 2000, 164–168.
12. "U.S. Couples Scaling Back Work to Care for Families," Reuters, 3 December 1999.
13. Maggie Maher, "A Change of Place," *Barrons*, 21 March 1994, 33–38.
14. Ibid.

15. Donna Partow, *Homemade Business* (Colorado Springs, CO: Focus on the Family, 1991).
16. E. Jeffrey Hill, "Put Family First—Work Will Be There When You Return," *Deseret News,* 25 November 1999, 8(C).

CHAPTER 9: The Origins of Homosexuality

1. Claudia Kalb, "What Boys Really Want," *Newsweek,* 10 July 2000, 52.
2. Joseph Nicolosi, *Preventing Homosexuality: A Parent's Guide,* Introduction. Used with permission.
3. Norman Podhoretz, "How the Gay-Rights Movement Won," *Commentary,* November 1996, 32.
4. William Bennett, "Clinton, Gays and the Truth," *Weekly Standard,* 24 November 1997, 13.
5. Larry Thompson, "Search for the Gay Gene," *Time,* 12 June 1995, 60.
6. Sharon Begley, "Does DNA Make Some Men Gay?" *Newsweek,* 26 July 1993, 59.
7. "Give Me a Break! Can Homosexuals Change and Become Straight?" ABC News *20/20,* 3 March 2001.
8. August Gribbin, "Public More Accepting of Gays, Survey Finds: Most Believe Orientation Is Genetic," *Washington Times,* 13 February 2000, 6(C).
9. Matthew Brelis, "The Fading 'Gay Gene,'" *Boston Globe,* 7 February 1999, 1(C).
10. Nicolosi, *Preventing Homosexuality.*
11. Malcolm Ritter, "Some Gays Can Go Straight, Study Suggests," Associated Press, 9 May 2001.
12. Nicolosi, *Preventing Homosexuality,* chap. 2.
13. Ibid.
14. Ibid.
15. Ibid., chap. 1.
16. Ralph Greenson, "Disidentifying the Mother: Its Special Importance for a Boy," *Journal of the American Psychoanalytical Association* 56 (1968): 293–302.
17. Nicolosi, *Preventing Homosexuality,* chap. 3.
18. Ibid., chap. 1.
19. I. Bieber et al., *Homosexuality: A Psychoanalytic Study of Male Homosexuals* (New York: Basic Books, 1982).
20. Ibid.
21. Nicolosi, *Preventing Homosexuality,* chap. 3.
22. Mary Eberstadt, "Pedophilia Chic Reconsidered," *Weekly Standard,* 1 January 2001, 18. Reprinted with the permission of *The Weekly Standard.* Original date of article, Jan. 18, 2001. Copyright © News America Incorporated.
23. Kathryn Jean Lopez, "The Cookie Crumbles: The Girl Scouts Go PC," *National Review,* 23 October 2000.
24. "Scout Leaders Relieved by Court Ruling on Gay Troop Leaders," Associated Press, 29 June 2000.
25. Jon Dougherty, "Scouts Still Face Funding Gauntlet," *WorldNetDaily.com.,* 20 February 2001.
26. Ibid.
27. Terence Neilan, "World Briefing," *New York Times,* 2 December 2000, 5(A).
28. "Context Affects Age of Consent," *Montreal Gazette,* 1 December 2000, 2(A).
29. Dan Izenberg, "Age of Consent for Homosexual Relations Lowered," *Jerusalem Post,* 2 November 2000, 3.
30. Michael Swift, "Goals of the Homosexual Movement," *Gay Community News,* 15–21 February 1987.
31. Suzanne Rostler and E. G. Mundell, "More Americans Having Gay Sex, Study Shows," Reuters, 14 March 2001.

CHAPTER 10: Single Parents and Grandparents

1. "Nuclear Family Fading," *Colorado Springs Gazette,* 15 May 2001, 1(A).
2. Don Feder, "Nuclear Family in Meltdown," *Boston Herald,* 23 May 2001, 33.

3. Ibid.
4. Barbara Kantrowitz and Pat Wingert, "Unmarried with Children," *Newsweek*, 28 May 2001.
5. "Nuclear Family Fading."
6. Kantrowitz and Wingert, "Unmarried with Children."
7. David Popenoe and Barbara Dafoe Whitehead, "The State of Our Unions," Rutgers University Marriage Project, 2000. See <http://marriage.rutgers.edu/state_of_our_unions>.
8. Ashley Estes, "More Women Are Raising Children on Their Own," *Salt Lake Tribune*, 18 May 2001, 6(A).
9. "Christians Are More Likely to Experience Divorce than Non-Christians," *Barna Research Online*, 21 December 1999.
10. Ibid.
11. "Breakdown on Family Breakdown," *Washington Times*, 25 March 2001, 2(B).
12. Don Feder, "Meltdown of Nuclear Family Threatens Society," *Human Events*, 4 June 2001, p. 9.
13. Barbara Dafoe Whitehead, "Dan Quayle Was Right," *Atlantic Monthly*, April 1993, 64.
14. Maggie Gallagher, "Fatherless Boys Grow Up into Dangerous Men," *Wall Street Journal*, 1 December 1998, 22(A).
15. Ibid.
16. Whitehead, "Dan Quayle Was Right."
17. Ibid.
18. Debra Gordon, "Mama's Boys," *The Virginian-Pilot*, 9 January 1994, 6. Copyright © 1994, *The Virginian-Pilot*. Excerpted with permission.
19. Eric Wiggen, *The Gift of Grandparenting* (Wheaton, Ill.: Tyndale House Publishers, 2001), 27–28.
20. Ibid., 29.
21. Ibid., 33–34.
22. Ibid., 69.
23. Ibid., 116.
24. Ibid., 162.
25. Tender Comrade, copyright 1943, RKO Radio Pictures. Used by permission of Turner Entertainment Co.
26. Cheri Fuller, "Motivating Your Child to Learn," *Focus on the Family*, 7 September, 1990.

CHAPTER 11: "Let's Go for It!"

1. NBC Olympic coverage from Sydney, Australia, September 2000.
2. H. Alexander Wise, Jr., "Lee: Why This Man, and His Era, Merit Our Consideration." See <http://www.civilwarhome/newslee.htm>.
3. Alfred Lansing, *Endurance* (Wheaton, Ill.: Tyndale House Publishers, 1999).
4. Lansing, *Endurance*.
5. Edward Wong, "New Rules for Soccer Parents: 1) No Yelling, 2) No Hitting Ref," *New York Times*, 6 May 2001, 1.
6. Rudyard Kipling, "If."
7. George Gilder, "Men and Marriage," *Focus on the Family*.
8. Mark Starr and Martha Brandt, " . . . and Thrilled Us All," *Newsweek*, 19 July 1999, 50.
9. Ibid., 54.
10. Raymond Lovett, "The Cut," *Focus on the Family*, October 1984. Used with permission.
11. Orel Hershiser, "A Visit with Orel Hershiser," *Focus on the Family*, 17 April 1989.

CHAPTER 12: Men R Fools

1. Lance Morrow, "1968: Like a Knife Blade, the Year Severed Past from Future," *Time*, 11 January 1988, 16.

2. "Woman Is the Nigger of the World," released 24 April, 1972.
3. Michelle Ingrassia, "NOW and Then: A Look at the Origins of Feminism," *Newsday,* 29 October 1991.
4. Gene Wyatt, "'Warhol' May Give Solanas Her Fifteen Minutes of Fame," *Tennessean,* 21 June 1996, 5(D).
5. David Jackson, "The Beat Goes On: 1968–1993: 25 Years Later, America Still Feels Era's Influence," *Dallas Morning News,* 26 December 1993, 1(J).
6. Peter Collier and David Horowitz, *Deconstructing the Left: From Vietnam to the Persian Gulf* (Lanham, Md.: Second Thoughts Books and Center for the Study of Popular Culture, 1991), 18.
7. Karla Mantilla, "Kids Need 'Fathers' Like Fish Need Bicycles," *Off Our Backs,* June 1998, 12–13.
8. "Demographics of Titanic Passengers: Deaths, Survivals and Lifeboat Occupancy." See <http://www.ithaca.edu/library/training/hotu.html>.
9. See <http://www.titanic-online.com/Discovery/discovery03.html>.
10. Encyclopedia Britannica Online. See <http://www.titanic.eb.com/01_01.html>.
11. "Demographics of Titanic Passengers."
12. Ibid.
13. Suzanne Fields, "Play, Boys: These Days It's All Women's Work," *Washington Times,* 18 October 1999, 19(A).
14. Cheryl Wetzstein, "Has Man-Bashing Become Hallmark of Greeting Cards?" *Washington Times,* 1 December 1999.
15. Roger Scruton, "Modern Manhood," *New York City Journal,* 19 January 2000.
16. John Leo, "Mars to Venus: Back Off," *U.S. News and World Report,* 7 May 1998, 16.
17. Ibid.
18. Ibid.
19. Ibid.
20. John Leo, "You Can't Make This Up," *U.S. News and World Report,* 21 August 2000.
21. Walter Williams, "Men Should Stand Up," *Washington Times,* 7 October 2000, 12(A). By permission of Walter Williams and Creators Syndicate, Inc.
22. Megan Rosenfeld, "Little Boys Blue: Reexamining the Plight of Young Males," *Washington Times,* 26 March 1998, 1(A).
23. Ibid.
24. Ibid.
25. Kathleen Parker, "Let's Give Our Boys Self-Control," *USA Today,* 15 September 1999.
26. Celeste Fremon, "Are Schools Failing Our Boys?" MSNBC, 5 October 1999. See <http://www.msnbc.com/news/310934.asp>.
27. Christina Hoff Sommers, "Is There a War against Boys?" CNN, 30 June 2000.
28. Christina Hoff Sommers, "Capitol Hill's Girl Trouble: The Flawed Study behind the Gender Equity Act," *Washington Post,* 17 July 1994, 1(C).
29. John Leo, "Gender Wars Redux," *U.S. News and World Report,* 22 February 1999.
30. Tamar Lewin, "All Girl Schools Questioned As a Way to Attain Equity," *New York Times,* 12 March 1998, 12(A).
31. Sommers, "Capitol Hill's Girl Trouble."
32. Fremon, "Are Schools Failing Our Boys?"
33. See <http://www.health.org/girlpower.html>.
34. "Secretary Shalala Launches Girl Power! at APHA Annual Meeting," *FDCH Federal Transcripts and Agency Documents,* 21 November 1996.
35. Jodi Wilgoren, "Girls Rule: Girls Outperform Boys in High School and in College Enrollment Rates," *New York Times Upfront,* 5 March 2001, p. 8.
36. Ibid
37. Laura Parker and Guillermo X. Garcia, "Boy Scout Troops Lose Funds, Meeting Places," *USA Today,* 9 October 2000.

38. Shaila K. Dewan, "Manhattan School District Withdraws Support for Scouts, Citing Bias," *New York Times,* 27 September 2000.
39. Kathryn Jean Lopez, "The Cookie Crumbles," *National Review,* 23 October 2000.
40. Christina Hoff Sommers, "What 'Girls Crisis'? Boys Get Short Shrift in Schools," *USA Today,* 17 July 2000, 17(A).
41. Daniel J. Kindlon and Michael Thompson, *Raising Cain* (New York: Ballantine Books, 1999).
42. Thomas Sowell, "Feminists Ensure Boys Can't Be Boys," *Denver Rocky Mountain News,* 21 June 2000. By permission of Thomas Sowell and © Creators Syndicate, Inc.
43. "Kiss Gets Youth in Trouble," Associated Press, 24 September 1996.
44. Joan Biskupic, "Schools Liable for Harassment: High Court Limits Ruling to Student Misconduct That Harms an Education," *Washington Post,* 25 May 1999, 1(A).
45. Brian Bloomquist and Vincent Morris, "Court OKs Bill's $850G Paula Settlement," *New York Post,* 3 December 1998, 4.
46. Linda Chavez, "Feminist Kiss Patrol Is on the March," *USA Today,* 2 October 1996, 15(A).
47. John Leo, "Expel Georgie Porgie Now!" *U.S. News and World Report,* 7 October 1996, 37.
48. Leo, "Gender Wars Redux."
49. Kathleen Parker, "Enough of Boys As Victors and Girls As Victims," *USA Today,* 24 February 1998, 15(A).
50. Maureen Dowd, "Liberties: Pretty Mean Women," *New York Times,* 1 August 1999, p. 15D.

CHAPTER 13: Boys in School

1. William Pollock, *Real Boys* (New York: Henry Holt and Company, 1998), 15.
2. Barbara Kantrowitz and Claudia Kalb, "Boys Will Be Boys," *Newsweek,* 11 May 1998, 55.
3. Ibid.
4. Celeste Fremon, "Are Schools Failing Our Boys?" MSNBC.com, Oct. 5 1999. Used with permission.
5. Cheri Fuller, "Preparing Children for Learning," *Focus on the Family,* 29–30 August 1991.
6. Morton Kondrake, "If Fourth Graders Can't Read, Congress is Failing to Lead," *Roll Call,* 23 April 2001.
7. William R. Mattox Jr., "The One-House Schoolroom: The Extraordinary Influence of Family Life on Student Learning," *Family Policy,* The Family Research Council, September 1995.
8. Mike Archer, "Boys and Books Can Be a Great Mix," *Orlando Sun-Sentinel,* 2 June 1999, 1.
9. Ibid.
10. Raymond and Dorothy Moore, "Home Grown Kids," *Focus on the Family,* 25–26 February 1982.
11. John K. Wiley, "Mona Locke, Melinda Gates, Rob Reiner Kick-Off Early Learning Campaign," Associated Press, 7 June 2000.
12. Linda Wetheimer and Robert Seigel, "Growing Popularity of Homeschooling," National Public Radio: *All Things Considered,* 28 February 2001.
13. William Bennett, "Merging Teaching and Technology," *Focus on the Family,* 16–17 May 2001.
14. George F. Will, "Are Children Little Adults?" *Newsweek,* 6 December 1999.
15. Raymond and Dorothy Moore, "Home Grown Kids."
16. Larry Kart, "Inside Jonathan Winters: The World is a Funhouse and Laughter is the Best Revenge," *Chicago Tribune,* 17 January 1998.
17. Nina Myskow, "I'm Like a War Victim with Food; I'd Fight My Dog for a Bone," *The Mirror,* 15 September 2000.

CHAPTER 14: Predators

1. John Leo, "No-Fault Holocaust," *U.S. News and World Report,* 21 July 1997, 14.
2. "Senator Barbara Boxer Clarifies Her Priorities," *Weekly Standard,* 12 February 2001.
3. John Leo, "Singer's Final Solution," *U.S. News and World Report,* 4 October 1999, 17.

4. Laura Davis and Janis Keyser, "7-Year Olds Exploring Each Other's Bodies," *Maryland Family Magazine,* August 2000, 28.

5. Ellen Goodman, "Battling Our Culture Is Parents' Task," *Chicago Tribune,* 18 August 1994.

6. Mike Clary, "Boy, 14, Gets Life Term in Wrestling Killing," *Los Angeles Times,* 10 March 2001, 1(A).

7. MTV 1993 Media Kit.

8. James Poniewozik, "Rude Boys," *Time,* 5 February 2001, 70.

9. Devin Gordon, "Laughing Until It Hurts," *Newsweek,* 2 October 2000, 70.

10. Poniewozik, "Rude Boys."

11. Ibid.

12. "My Gift to You" © 1997 by Korn. Published by WB Music Corp./Jolene Cherry Music/ Goathead? Music. From the CD *Follow the Leader* © 1998 Sony Music Entertainment.

13. Frank Ahrens, "A Stern Rebuke: Shock Jock's 'Joke' a Flop in Denver," *Washington Post,* 28 April 1999, 3(C).

14. Neil MacFarquhar, "Naked Dorm? That Wasn't in the Brochure," *New York Times,* 18 March 2000, 1(A).

15. Cheryl Wetzstein, "Polls Finding Growing Concern over 'Moral' Direction," *Washington Times,* 23 April 1997, 5(A).

16. Michelle Malkin, "Baby Boomer Parents Are Asleep on the Job," Creators Syndicate, 17 November 2000. By permission of Michelle Malkin and Creators Syndicate, Inc.

17. K. Freund and R. J. Watson, "The Proportions of Heterosexual and Homosexual Pedophiles among Sex Offenders against Children: An Exploratory Study," *Journal of Sex and Marital Therapy,* 18, no. 1 (spring 1992): 34–43.

18. Ibid.

19. John Schwartz, "Online Decency Fight Brews Anew after Ruling," *Washington Post,* 14 December 1998, 21(F).

20. "New Cyber-Safety Network Formed to Help Parents Connect with Teens to Openly Discuss Best Uses of the Internet." See <http://www.safeamerica.org/html/press/ press_093099_1.cfm>.

21. John Schwartz, "Internet Filters Used to Shield Minors Censor Speech, Critics Say," *New York Times,* 19 March 2001.

22. Bill Wood, "Urgent," *United Press International,* 24 January 1989.

23. Steven Butts, "Pornography: A Serious Cultural Disorder That Is Accelerating," *Lancaster (Pa.) Sunday News,* 9 March 1997, 4(P).

24. Ellen Edwards, "Plugged-In Generation: More than Ever, Kids Are at Home with Media," *Washington Post,* 18 November 1999, 1(A).

25. David Bauder, "Survey: It May Not Be Punishment to Send Children to Their Rooms," Associated Press, 26 June 1997.

26. Ginny McGibbon, "Columbine: Looking for Lessons; Visual Violence Triggers Dire Warning," *Denver Post,* 13 June 1999.

27. "The Einstatzgruppen—Mobile Killing Units." See <http://www.mtsu.edu/baustin/ einsatz.html>.

28. Ibid.

29. Eman, Diet. "Courageous Choices," *Focus on the Family,* 24 May 2001.

30. Patricia Brennan, "The Link between TV and Violence," *Washington Post,* 8 January 1995.

31. McGibbon, "Columbine."

CHAPTER 15: Staying Close

1. Josh McDowell, "Helping Your Kids to Say No," *Focus on the Family,* 16 October 1987.

2. Greg Johnson and Mike Yorkey, *Daddy's Home* (Wheaton, Ill.: Tyndale House Publishers, 1992), 56.

3. Martha Sherrill, "Mrs. Clinton's Two Weeks out of Time: The Vigil for Her Father, Taking a Toll Both Public and Private," *Washington Post,* 3 April 1993, 1(C).

4. Laura Sessions Stepp, "Parents Are Alarmed by an Unsettling New Fad in Middle Schools: Oral Sex," *Washington Post*, 8 July 1999, 1(A).
5. Thomas J. Bouchard et al., "Sources of Human Psychological Differences: The Minnesota Study of Twins Reared Apart," *Science*, 12 October 1990, 223.
6. "Twins Separated at Birth: The Story of Jim Lewis and Jim Springer," *Smithsonian Magazine*, October 1980.
7. Malcolm Ritter, "Study Suggests Genes Influence Risk of Divorce," *Associated Press*, 27 November 1992.
8. Ibid.

CHAPTER 16: Disciplining Boys

1. Tom W. Smith, "Ties That Bind: The Emerging 21st Century American Family," *Public Perspective*, 12:1, January 2001, 34.
2. Per Ola d'Aulaire and Emily d'Aulaire, "Now What Are They Doing at That Crazy St. John the Divine?" *Smithsonian Magazine*, 23:9, December 1992, 32.
3. Fyodor Dostoevsky, *The House of the Dead* (New York: Viking Press, 1860).
4. Parenting, May 1992, 45–46.
5. Ron and Judy Blue, *Money Matters for Parents and Their Kids* (Nashville: Thomas Nelson, 1988), 46.
6. Ray Reed, "Abusers Often Start with Animals," *Roanoke Times and World News*, 19 January 1995, 1(C).

CHAPTER 17: The Ultimate Priority

1. "Unsupervised Teens Do Poorly in School, Want Afterschool Activities, New Survey Finds," U.S. Newswire, 6 March 2001.
2. Francis A. Schaeffer, *He Is There and He Is Not Silent* (Carol Stream, Ill.: Tyndale House Publishers, 1972).
3. James Dobson, *Life on the Edge* (Nashville: Word Publishers, 1995), 41.
4. "Teens and Adults Have Little Chance of Accepting Christ As Their Savior," *Barna Research Online*, 15 November 1999.
5. Vice President Albert Gore, Jr. at Presidential Prayer Breakfast, 1995.
6. Geoffrey Canada, *Reaching Up for Manhood* (Boston: Beacon Press, 1998), 103–106. Copyright © 1998 by Geoffrey Canada. Reprinted by permission of Beacon Press, Boston.
7. Erma Bombeck, "Fragile Strings Join Parent, Child," *Arizona Republic*, 15 May 1977.
8. Jean W. Sawtell, "It's Tough on a Dog." Copyright © 2000 by Jean W. Sawtell. All rights reserved.

Whether you received *Bringing Up Boys* as a gift, borrowed it from a friend, or purchased it yourself, we're glad you read it. Dr. James Dobson, the author of this book, founded Focus on the Family in 1977 to address the many challenges and needs facing today's family.

If this book has been helpful and you would like to receive more information on child rearing or other family issues, Focus on the Family is here to assist you.

www.family.org
(800) A-FAMILY